FOLK CITY

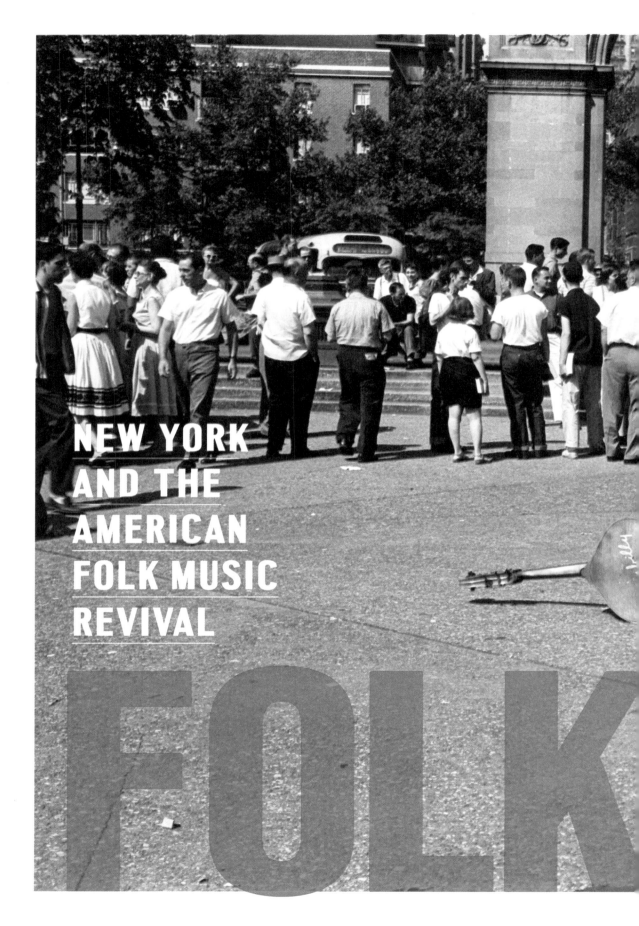

NEW YORK
AND THE
AMERICAN
FOLK MUSIC
REVIVAL

OXFORD
UNIVERSITY PRESS

Stephen Petrus
Ronald D. Cohen

CITY

Oxford University Press is a department of the University of Oxford.
It furthers the University's objective of excellence in research,
scholarship, and education by publishing worldwide.

Oxford   New York
Auckland   Cape Town   Dar es Salaam   Hong Kong
Karachi   Kuala Lumpur   Madrid   Melbourne   Mexico
City   Nairobi   New Delhi   Shanghai   Taipei   Toronto

With offices in
Argentina   Austria   Brazil   Chile   Czech Republic
France   Greece   Guatemala   Hungary   Italy   Japan
Poland   Portugal   Singapore   South Korea   Switzerland
Thailand   Turkey   Ukraine   Vietnam

Oxford is a registered trade mark of Oxford University Press in the
UK and certain other countries.

Published in the United States of America by
Oxford University Press
198 Madison Avenue, New York, NY 10016

Library of Congress Cataloging-in-Publication Data

Petrus, Stephen, author.
Folk city : New York and the American folk music revival /
Stephen Petrus and Ronald D. Cohen.
pages   cm
ISBN 978-0-19-023102-6 (hardback)
1. Folk music—New York (State)—New York—History and
criticism.   I. Cohen, Ronald D., 1940– author.   II. Title.
ML3551.8.N49P48 2015
781.62'1307471—dc23   2015000073

9 8 7 6 5 4 3 2

Printed in the United States of America on acid-free paper

FOLK CITY: NEW YORK AND THE AMERICAN FOLK MUSIC REVIVAL was published to accompany the exhibition of the same name presented at the Museum of the City of New York from June 17 – November 29, 2015.

EXHIBITION CO-CHAIRS
James E. Buckman
John R. Heller
Thomas M. Neff

EXHIBITION ADVISORY COMMITTEE
Chair: **Ronald D. Cohen**, Emeritus Professor of History at Indiana University Northwest, Gary

Ray Allen, Professor of Music,
Brooklyn College and the CUNY Graduate Center
Scott Barretta, Adjunct Instructor of
Sociology at the University of Mississippi
Michael Beckerman, Professor of Music,
New York University
David Hajdu, Professor of Journalism,
Columbia University Graduate School of
Journalism and *The Nation* Music Critic
Elijah Wald, Music Historian and
folk-blues guitarist
Sean Wilentz, Professor of History,
Princeton University
Steve Zeitlin, City Lore, Founding Director

The exhibition and companion book are made possible by

WYNDHAM WORLDWIDE
JOHN AND PATRICIA HELLER
THOMAS M. NEFF
MR. AND MRS. JAMES BUCKMAN
JAMES G. DINAN AND ELIZABETH R. MILLER

Additional support is provided by

ZEGAR FAMILY FOUNDATION
AN ANONYMOUS DONOR, IN HONOR OF JOHN HELLER
JILL AND JOHN CHALSTY
MARTIN GUITAR CHARITABLE FOUNDATION
MacLEAN-FOGG

The Museum is grateful to the Andrew W. Mellon Foundation, which supported the fellowship of **FOLK CITY** curator Dr. Stephen Petrus.

EXHIBITION TEAM
Curator: **Stephen Petrus**
Manager of Curatorial Affairs: **Autumn Nyiri**
Curatorial Associate: **Sara K. Spink**
Consultant: **Doug Yeager**
Registrar for Exhibitions and Loans: **Winona Packer**
Director of Exhibitions Installation: **Todd Ludlam**

The exhibition and the accompanying book were designed by Pure+Applied.

CONTENTS

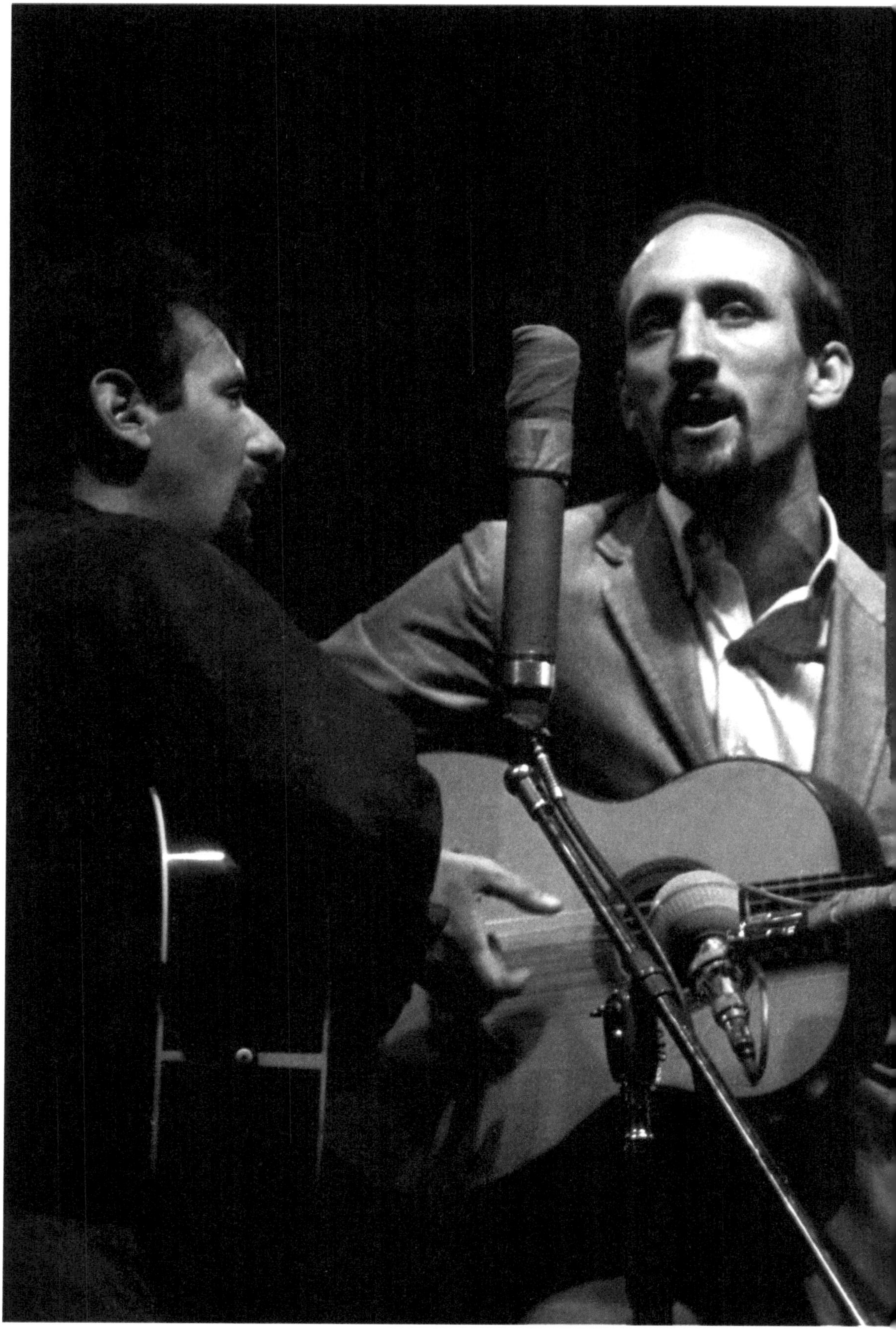

FOREWORD

PETER YARROW

Greenwich Village was, in many ways, the epicenter of the 1960s cultural revolution in America. Remarkable breakthroughs were made in painting, theater, design, photography, dance, film, etc., but none more so than in folk music. Folk songs reached people's hearts, inspiring them to challenge the established societal norms and break with antiquated traditions. Many of the values and mores that needed to be recast by a primarily youth-led movement were not only judged to be superficial, but were also seen as violating the basic tenets of freedom and equality that America was supposed to hold dear.

Listening to, or singing along with, traditional folk songs allowed us to enter a world that was not only a departure from the superficiality of the times, but also one that symbolized a break with what had been plaguing society: aberrations such as the artificiality of relationships between men and women with prescribed "proper" ways to converse and treat one another; prescribed ways for men to assert their dominance and for women to "keep their place"; prescribed ways of maintaining the stratified layering of who was important and who was superior to whom; prescribed ways that assured the continuing oppression of people of color, a remnant of slavery that flew in the face of the words of the Pledge of Allegiance, "with liberty and justice for all"—words that were supremely hypocritical given the rampant racism of the times.

Traditional folk music was, by its very nature, a call to the kind of humanity and equity that was in many ways absent from civil society. Singing folk music was as much an act of defiance towards these inequities as it was a way to share a people's art form that was beautiful, moving, and inspiring. Traditional songs were not written to become hits or big money makers. On the contrary, there was a humility and honesty in folk music. Folk music was not "selling" anything.

Singing the music of the people, particularly singing it together, was not merely a symbolic act. It was, literally, an act of liberation and an assertion of freedom. At the time, we did not know that our music would have a great and lasting effect and become regarded by future generations as the soundtrack of the awakening conscience of our nation. We were only dimly aware that our music was beginning to inspire people across the country who were soon to embrace a tectonic shift in societal perspective, with the awakening of legions of youth to the idea that their efforts were essential

previous: (From left) Peter, Paul and Mary perform at the Newport Folk Festival, Newport, Rhode Island, 1965. Photograph by Diana Davies.

above: Flier advertising the "Sing-In for Peace" concert held at Carnegie Hall on September 24, 1965.

to the betterment of this nation, and the world. Acceptance of the status quo was, to a large degree, over. Joining hearts and hands with the assurance that a new time was near was slowly becoming the new, accepted way. It was a golden era in our history and, though the prevalence of our way of thinking began to ebb by the end of the 1960s, the fact that this perspective once did exist, and did usher in amazing changes, remains a beacon for future generations.

Efforts to reach people's hearts crystallized not only when folks listened to the music, but when they sang together. This was true of audiences that fit into tiny coffeehouses or audiences as large as the Civil Rights March on Washington in 1963. When people sang together, they literally "owned" the message and the moment, knowing that each voice played a part in creating it.

Singing together created a strong bond, a community of togetherness, and a "pool of peace." We shared an empathy, a compassion, and a unity of spirit. In a word, this was the sound of "us" and this musical "us-ness" was transcendent. For many, it was love, though it needed no word or label. It did not matter if the song was "We Shall Overcome" or "The Water is Wide," a love song, but when shared in this unified way, it summoned the community saying, "We are one. We experience each other's heartaches and each other's hopes and dreams and, defiantly, we assert that the spirit of what we are determined to achieve will not be subdued or muted. It is unshakable!"

Did these moments achieve our objective? Though it certainly felt that way, they did not, of course. But when you share such conviction again, and again, and again, the feeling of not being alone in your quest becomes more tangible and more believable, and what starts out as a hope becomes a force that creates a collective strength to be reckoned with.

When a Southern mountain ballad of unrequited love was sung, or Woody's "This Land Is Your Land" that expressed a love of the heartland and hearts of "real people" in America, the feeling that we could care more about one another more than the

selfish, greedy, competitive version of who we had been, was extraordinary.

The Folk Renaissance of the 1960s was remarkable in many, many ways. We can only hope that the conjunction of people's music and the desire to create a better world will come to pass once more—not a reiteration of what was, but something that stands on the shoulders of those who have gone before yet addresses the ways of the new times, the net-based ways of communicating, as well as the intimate, acoustic ways of yesterday. Whatever it might be, however it might look or feel, I believe that it will find its way to joining the eternal struggle that we, in the '60s, were lucky enough to experience with great passion and, now, with ever greater gratitude.

When that happens, when folk music is once again in the ascendency, I believe that it will, once again, play a central role in igniting transformational change. Perhaps such a time is not far off. Perhaps this book and this exhibition will, by their very existence, hasten the time for a new Folk Renaissance that will carry us towards a better day. We can only hope so.

Peter Yarrow, 2015

above: Pete Seeger and Free Southern Theater guitarist Roger Johnson lead the singing of "We Shall Overcome" in the sanctuary of Mt. Zion Baptist Church, Hattiesburg, Mississippi, August 4, 1964. Photograph by Herbert Randall.

PREFACE

JOHN HELLER

In the summer of 1961, I attended a boys' summer camp in northern Wisconsin. One evening we took a field trip to the small town of Lac du Flambeau to go to a folk concert. When we arrived, the show was already underway, and the auditorium was filled to capacity. The campers, myself included, took seats on the stage. Excited and wide-eyed, I looked up and saw a guy named Bob Gibson, perched on a stool just inches from me, transforming the room with his tenor voice and orchestral sound. For the next hour, I was mesmerized as Bob performed, alternating between a 12-string guitar and a banjo and getting the crowd to sing along. Bob was at the top of his game, and it showed. I had never seen or heard anything like it. It changed my life.

When I returned to suburban Chicago at the end of the summer, I begged my parents for a guitar as a 12th birthday gift. I had saved up to buy some Bob Gibson LPs and taught myself nearly his entire catalog. I also discovered that Bob was part of a larger music scene that was taking shape. I immersed myself in the sounds of pioneers like Woody Guthrie, Pete Seeger, Josh White, Lead Belly, the Weavers, Theodore Bikel—and followed new artists like Bob Dylan, Peter, Paul and Mary, Joan Baez, Tom Paxton, and Ian & Sylvia.

I read everything I could about this exotic place called Greenwich Village, the eye of the folk storm where all of my new heroes were hanging out and performing. There were venues called The Bitter End, Cafe Wha? and Gerde's Folk City. And streets with names like Bleecker and MacDougal. And there was a park where artists shared ideas and songs. How could one neighborhood inspire so many? To a 13-year-old, all of this seemed a million miles away.

Forty years later, in 2001, I moved to New York City. I still love to wander the streets of the Village and think about this era and what it must have been like to be there in 1962. I was fortunate to make friends with some people who were there. I learned more and more about the folk scene and how it shaped our politics and culture. Feeling inspired, I brought the idea to the Museum of the City of New York to do a major exhibition on the subject. It's been a dream come true to be part of this project, both the exhibition and the book, from conception to completion.

Folk City by Stephen Petrus and Ronald Cohen provides a thoughtful and insightful look at the folk revival in New York. Through engaging stories and vivid images, Steve and Ron bring "Folk City" back to life and remind us of its lasting impact. So have a seat on the stage and enjoy the close up view of some iconic figures in American music and a few others maybe you hadn't heard of. And feel free to sing along.

opposite: Washington Square Park, ca. 1956. Photograph by Nat Norman.

New York sure is a funny place. ... The buildings
are so high the sun don't come out until 1:30 in
the afternoon, and then it's visible for seven
minutes between the Empire State Building and
the shoe sign over there.

Woody Guthrie, 1940[1]

SARAH M. HENRY

THE HEART OF FOLK CITY

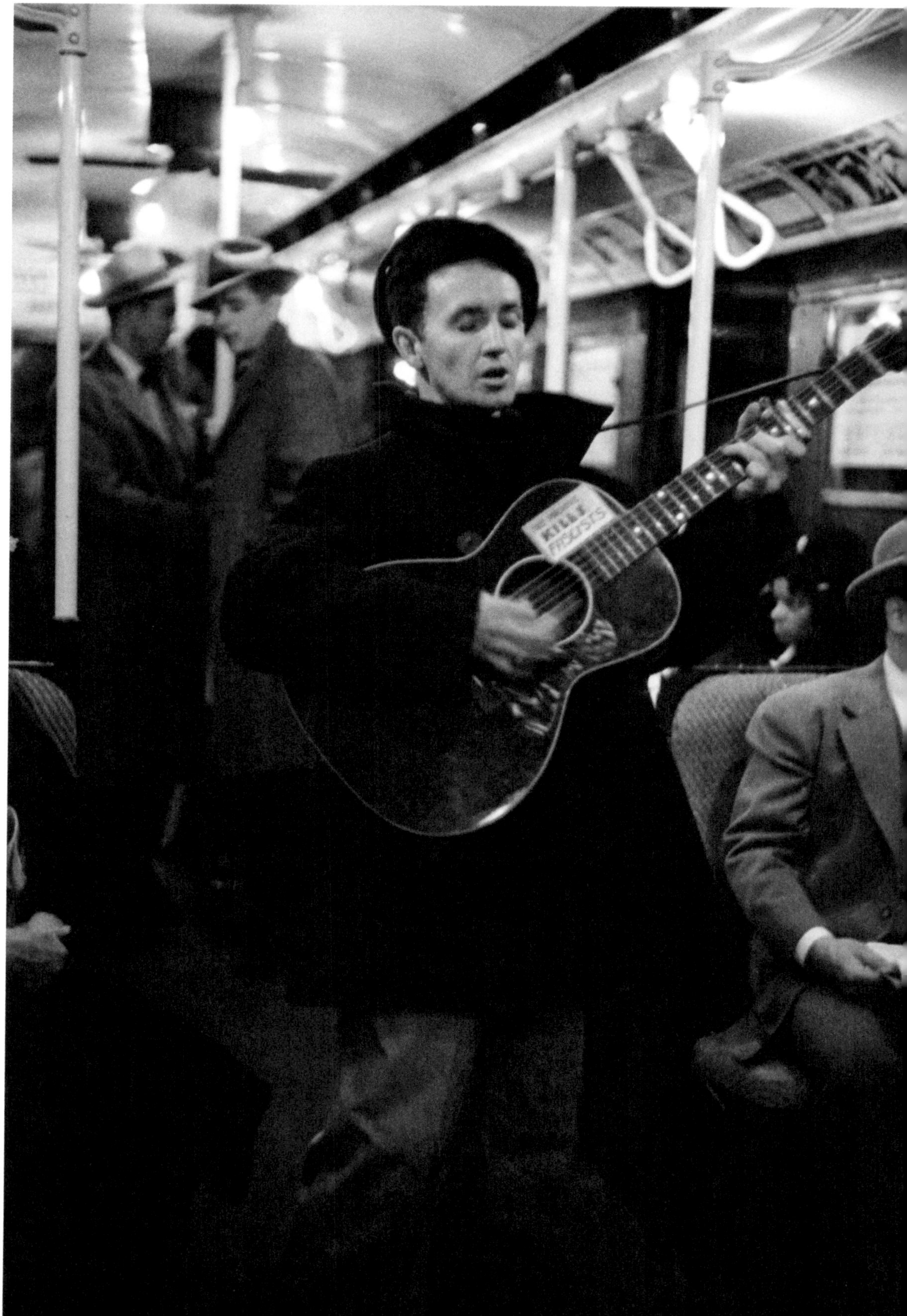
KILLS
FASCISTS

Folksinger Woody Guthrie sings aboard a subway train, December 31, 1942. Born in Okemah, Oklahoma, Guthrie left an indelible mark on New York City, where he lived for more than two decades.

When Dust Bowl troubadour Woody Guthrie arrived in New York in 1940, he found it to be a city of contradictions, both exhilarating and exasperating. On the one hand, while New Yorkers had suffered during the Depression, they had also leveraged the economic downturn to remake their city. Concrete symbols of the New Deal were everywhere: the recently completed Triborough Bridge, Lincoln Tunnel, and East River Drive were not only innovative works of infrastructure but also monuments to progress. New York's port was a hive of activity, annually handling thousands of ships and tens of millions of tons of cargo. And if Depression-weary New Yorkers still were anxious about the days ahead, they needed only to visit the World's Fair in Flushing Meadows, Queens, to catch a glimpse of the future, replete with exhibits on transportation, communications, housing, and food that promised a better tomorrow.[2]

But Guthrie found another New York as well. While he stayed at the Fifth Avenue home of his friends, husband-and-wife actors Will and Herta Geer, he spent much of his time roaming the Bowery, the city's skid row and a virtual synonym for penury and despair. Rates of homelessness and alcoholism were high. Lined with dilapidated flophouses and disreputable saloons, the Bowery left Guthrie disgusted with New York and moved him to write the song "I Don't Feel at Home on the Bowery No More." In it, Guthrie contrasted his hosts' Fifth Avenue apartment to the Bowery flophouses, alternating images of soft carpets in a penthouse dwelling with cramped spaces in fleabag hotels. At the bottom of the song sheet he wrote a double dedication: "to the Geer family and to the bum situation up and down every Skid Row and Bowery Street in this country."[3]

That same year, New York provided the backdrop for another Guthrie creation—a reply to the ubiquitous and, to his ear, grating anthem "God Bless America," the Irving Berlin song that was then flooding the airwaves in a recording by Kate Smith. The America that Berlin wrote about did not match the country that Guthrie had traveled—a land of migrants, the dispossessed, and the homeless. In a room in the ramshackle Hanover House on 43rd Street and Second Avenue, Guthrie penned a rebuttal to Berlin's anthem, beginning it "This land is your land, this land is my land/From California to the Staten Island" (although he quickly deleted "Staten" and inserted "New York"), and ending with the refrain "God blessed America for me." By the time he finally recorded it four years later, at Moe Asch's studio in midtown Manhattan, he had changed the last line of the refrain to the immortal "This land was made for you and me."[4]

If hardscrabble, down-to-earth, folksy Woody Guthrie seemed an unlikely candidate to compose and flourish in New York, he was not alone. His musical contemporaries included Pete Seeger, Lee Hays, Lead Belly, and Josh White, all of whom had made a home base in New York, soon to be followed by a new generation of talent including Phil Ochs, Tom Paxton, Len Chandler, and Eric Andersen. Indeed, a folk music revival had been taking root in the city before World War II, and it would continue to grow throughout the 1940s, finally

previous: Folksingers Woody Guthrie and Burl Ives read the *Hobo News* in this Columbia Broadcasting publicity shot taken in Central Park in 1940. Both artists were crucial in stimulating the folk music revival in New York.

below: Pete Seeger (on banjo, left) and Woody Guthrie (on fiddle) perform at the Music Inn, Lenox, Massachusetts, July 4th weekend, 1950. Photograph by Leonard Rosenberg.

above: Folklore Center owner Israel "Izzy" Young, seen here in August 1960, became a central figure in the New York folk scene in the late 1950s. His shop, centrally located in Greenwich Village at 110 MacDougal Street, not only sold books, records, and instruments, but also offered a place for folk singers to congregate, socialize, and perform informally. Photograph by David Gahr.

coming to full flower in the 1950s and 1960s. Inherent in this fact was an apparent paradox: while folk songs evoked tradition and were largely rural in origin, New York stood above all for progress, growth, and efficiency, with seemingly barely a moment for the nostalgia, sentimentality, and romance associated with folk music. That folk music burgeoned in this hyperactive environment is one of the striking cultural trends of the 20th century.[5]

Folk City tells the story of how this came to be, focusing on an array of cultural, artistic, and economic institutions in the city that nurtured folk music from the Great Depression to the tumultuous 1960s. Although the music associated with the revival stemmed mainly from songs of African slaves and Old World European peasants—transmuted by generations of cowboys, lumberjacks, coal miners, farmers, sailors, and chain gangs—its transmission to broader audiences in the 20th century had a strong urban base. The revival involved the efforts not only of musicians and their audiences, but also of a host of urban characters: record company producers and executives, club owners, concert promoters, festival organizers, political activists, musicologists, agents, managers, editors, folklorists, and journalists.

This book traces the roots of the urban postwar revival of folk music back to the 1920s, when New York City came to dominate network radio and the record company industry. Labels began to collect and promote various musical

Burl Ives performs in
Washington Square Park, 1947.
Photograph by Stanley Kubrick
for *LOOK* magazine.

styles—including "race" and "hillbilly" tracks gathered on recording trips to the South. Musicians flocked to the city as performance and recording opportunities grew, and in the economic downtown of the 1930s, the progressive political milieu continued to attract these artists. The left-liberal coalition that comprised the Popular Front embraced folk songs as a vehicle of political expression in support of workers' rights and against racism, albeit with limited success on the front lines. While World War II temporarily disrupted the burgeoning folk music scene, by war's end, many performers again were in New York, using songs to promote their political agendas.[6]

The story really takes off in the postwar period, as New York became an artistic center on an international scale. *Folk City* investigates the role played not only by artists, but also by key New York entrepreneurs, who drove the expansion of the folk music industry in the city during this period. New York record companies founded in the early 1950s fueled a national interest in the genre, as did the press, and new performance venues offered increased opportunities at the very moment when concert organizers turned their attention to establishing folk music programs. Folk became a pillar of the New York City music scene and it quickly found a home base in Greenwich Village—a neighborhood that was the center of artistic innovation of all kinds, where folk musicians, Beat poets, and an emerging counterculture could mingle and draw energy and audiences from each other. All seemed to offer a promise of "authenticity," in contrast to what many critics deemed a stale and conformist mass culture.[7]

At the hub of this story—at the heart of Greenwich Village—was Washington Square Park, which increasingly became a gathering place for folk music enthusiasts in the 1950s. The tradition of Sunday afternoon square singing became the focal point of cultural conflict, as folk singers and Village residents championed the importance of this public space and fought back against a ban on folk singing imposed in 1961. But what is best remembered is the triumph of folk music in the neighborhood, as a series of influential new venues and an influx of musicians, impresarios, and fans led to an increasingly energetic atmosphere.[8]

Fueling folk's popularity was its link to political activism, which gained visibility as it became inextricably intertwined with the politics of the civil rights movement. *Folk City* describes how music that was rooted in the African-American church became integral to the freedom struggle, in part through the efforts of New Yorkers. New York folk music activists traveled to the South, while other groups visited the city to participate in fundraisers for the cause. An informal network of publications, labels, singer-songwriters, and coffeehouses joined forces to promote the civil rights movement, and a similar coalition—including many of the same components—soon came to protest the political and economic policies

of America's military industrial complex at the dawn of the Vietnam War era.[9]

The final chapters of the book explore both the transformation and endurance of the folk revival. Nothing highlights this more than the mutable persona of Bob Dylan, who like so many others, reinvented himself in New York. As the authors show, Dylan's reinvention relied not only on his own ambition and talent, but on the opportunities and networks afforded by New York City—from fellow musicians, record producers, managers, critics, and fans. But even as Dylan eventually made his transition symbolically away from folk music, the folk roots that had been planted in New York City held on and led in new directions that can still be felt to this day.[10]

This publication was written to accompany an exhibition, *Folk City: New York and the American Folk Music Revival*, which opened at the Museum of the City of New York in June 2015. Both the exhibition and this publication were made possible by generous support from Wyndham Worldwide, John and Patricia Heller, Thomas M. Neff, Mr. and Mrs. James Buckman, James G. Dinan and Elizabeth R. Miller, Zegar Family Foundation, an anonymous donor in honor of John Heller, Jill and John Chalsty, Martin Guitar Charitable Foundation, MacLean-Fogg, and others. A benefit concert

Singer, guitarist, songwriter, actor, and civil rights activist, Josh White became a pop star and a sex symbol in New York in the 1940s. White, seen here in 1953, frequently performed in Greenwich Village's Cafe Society, the first integrated nightclub in the nation.

held in June 2013 raised additional funds and featured one of the last musical performances by the late Pete Seeger, who passed away just seven months later.

Many people contributed to the success of this book. First and foremost are the authors, distinguished folk music historian Ronald D. Cohen and Stephen Petrus, who took on this project as an Andrew W. Mellon Postdoctoral Fellow here at the City Museum. Our great gratitude goes out to them for their keen insights, masterful art synthesis, and hard work. Thanks are likewise due to John Heller and Doug Yeager for their advice and guidance, and to Ray Allen and Elijah Wald for their careful readings of the manuscript. From the City Museum, Autumn Nyiri, manager of curatorial affairs, and Sara K. Spink, curatorial associate, worked tirelessly to bring the project to fruition. We thank Natalie Shivers and William Strachan for their keen copyediting. Pure+Applied's Paul Carlos, along with Carrie Kawamura, created the wonderful design for this publication as well as for the exhibition. And we are immensely grateful to the individual collectors and photographers, particularly Joel Siegel and Bob Ward at the Estate of David Gahr, who provided us with the rich illustrations that accompany this book.

Finally, we honor the musicians, composers, songwriters, producers, and audiences who made New York a hub of folk music creativity in the years covered in this book. It is a pleasure to offer *Folk City* as a way of bringing the rich and multi-faceted tale of New York's folk music revival to life for new generations.

The extraordinary thing that cities do
throughout the world is to bring together
people who would not otherwise have met
each other. There was Woody from Oklahoma
meeting me from New England and Lee Hays
from Arkansas...and Millard Lampell...
from Paterson, New Jersey, and we all sang
together.

Pete Seeger, describing the Almanac Singers[1]

NEW YORK AND THE ORIGINS OF THE FOLK MUSIC REVIVAL

ON March 3, 1940, at the Forrest Theatre on West 49th Street, the Theatre Arts Committee, along with actor Will Geer and folklorist Alan Lomax, presented "A 'Grapes of Wrath' Evening for the Benefit of the John Steinbeck Committee for Agricultural Workers." It was a timely event, organized just after the opening of director John Ford's acclaimed film *Grapes of Wrath*, based on Steinbeck's novel published in 1939. Proceeds went to destitute farmers, many of them displaced by the Dust Bowl and struggling as migrant workers in California.[2]

The concert was a distinctively New York affair, an expression of the city's leftist sensibility, though, ironically, only one of the performers was actually born in New York. The organizers, Geer and Lomax, were themselves from Indiana and Texas, respectively. As they planned the fundraiser, Geer, a social activist and budding Hollywood actor, was playing the lead role in the Broadway production *Tobacco Road*, while Lomax, assistant in charge of the Library of Congress's Archive of American Folk Song, was hosting the radio series *American Folk Song* and *Wellsprings of Music* on CBS's nationally broadcast *American School of the Air* based in New York. The two found abundant musical talent in the city and assembled an ensemble of musicians and dancers, a mix of seasoned veterans and promising newcomers. Performers included Lead Belly from Louisiana, Woody Guthrie from Oklahoma, Aunt Molly Jackson from Kentucky, Burl Ives from Illinois, Josh White from South Carolina, Margot Mayo from Texas, and Richard Dyer-Bennet from England. Only the young Pete Seeger was born in New York City, and even he was more closely linked to New England, where he was primarily raised. Each artist had a rich personal biography and took a circuitous route to New York. Their reasons varied, but all shared the belief that New York's political, cultural, and economic resources offered the possibility of artistic transformation.

Pete Seeger performs at the Village Gate, May 1961. Photograph by David Gahr.

New York and the Origins of the Folk Music Revival

The "Grapes of Wrath" evening was a seminal event that forged numerous personal and artistic ties critical to the development of folk music. While several musicians gave memorable performances, Woody Guthrie stole the show, imparting Okie wisdom in fanciful and wry monologues between songs that evoked images of billows of dust and families in jalopies on lonely prairie nights. To remarkable effect, Guthrie cultivated his persona as the embodiment of the Dust Bowl, unpolished but sagacious, attached to the land. Few New Yorkers knew of his middle-class family background or his work as a broadcast performer on the Los Angeles commercial radio station KFVD. About the evening's star, Pete Seeger recollected, "Woody Guthrie just ambled out, offhand and casual ... a short fellow complete with a western hat, boots, blue jeans, and needing a shave, spinning out stories and singing songs that he'd made up." Seeger added, "Well, I just naturally wanted to know more about him. He was a big piece of my education." By contrast, Seeger, a Harvard dropout, floundered on the night of his public debut, fumbling nervously with his banjo on stage, singing the outlaw ballad "John Hardy." "I was a bust," he recalled. "I got a smattering of polite applause." But more than any individual performance, the import was the event as a whole—characterized by Geer as "the first hootenanny"—which created many lasting bonds among the artists, above all between Guthrie and Seeger. Alan Lomax, ebullient by the evening's end, recounted the significance with a smidgen of hyperbole: "Go back to that night when Pete first met Woody Guthrie. You can date the renaissance of American folk song from that night."[3]

Flier for the 1940 "Grapes of Wrath" benefit concert for agricultural workers held at the Forrest Theatre in New York City. Not only did the performance strengthen the connection between folk music and leftist politics, but it also marked the birth of a fruitful artistic relationship between Woody Guthrie and Pete Seeger.

FOLK MUSIC AS NEW YORK BUSINESS: THE 1920S

As Alan Lomax observed, the "Grapes of Wrath" concert in 1940 represented a turning point in the American folk music revival. In the years after World War I, the transformation of network radio and record company industry attracted a wave of musicians to the city.

The development of mass media, especially radio, in the 1920s expanded the possibilities for commercial sales of music of all genres, including folk. New York dominated radio broadcasting in the 1920s as the radio itself became a popular domestic consumer item: six million radios adorned American homes by 1927. New York's NBC and CBS radio networks, founded in 1926 and 1928, respectively, extended their reach nationwide. The stations promoted musicians in classical, jazz, opera, and popular musical genres.

Bill Tatnall plays guitar in Frederica, Georgia, June 1935. On a song-collecting expedition to the South and the Bahamas in 1935, Alan Lomax, who took this photograph, Zora Neale Hurston, and Mary Elizabeth Barnicle recorded Tatnall for the Archive of American Folk Song at the Library of Congress. Lomax, his father John, and other collaborators contributed more than 10,000 field recordings to the archive in the 1930s and 1940s, providing source material for the folk music revival.

At the same time, New York had become the national center of the recording industry. This supremacy stemmed from the city's ascendancy in the sheet music publishing business by 1900, thanks largely to the success of the firm T. B. Harms over competitors from Boston, Philadelphia, and Chicago. Building off the gains of music publishing companies, the city's budding recording industry blossomed. The trend, combined with the proliferation of phonograph records, signaled the decline of the piano and of sheet music publishing; in the middle of the decade, for the first time, record sales exceeded those of sheet music. During the 1920s, New York labels, including Columbia, Victor, Edison, and Brunswick, became prominent. In 1926 Columbia acquired Okeh Records and, in the 1930s, became part of the giant American Recording Company (ARC) under the CBS umbrella, along with Banner, Vocalion, and other labels.[4]

During the 1920s, the incipient record companies largely concentrated on local and regional markets. As they developed their catalogs, they collected various musical styles and began to play a major role in promoting and exploiting the emerging interest in traditionally inspired music. New York labels focused particularly on ethnic groups in immigrant

communities. Enriched by a massive influx of predominantly Jewish and Catholic immigrants from eastern and southern Europe from the 1880s to the early 1920s, the city's musical mosaic became increasingly complex. German, Swedish, and other ethnic groups formed choral societies to preserve their folk songs, while vaudeville incorporated many of the tunes into variety shows and other stage productions. Record companies such as Victor, Columbia, Brunswick, Gennett, and Okeh produced albums by Irish, Italian, Jewish, Greek, German, and Chinese musicians.[5]

At the same time, the New York labels began to send crews to the American South to record traditional folk songs by black and white musicians alike. The journeys grew out of broader cultural trends in the 1920s. Drawing on a transatlantic interest in reviving rural traditions and seeking more and more to distinguish their own culture from England and Europe, Americans searched for their heritage in folk art. Between 1923 and 1932, New York recording companies made approximately 100 field trips to the South, while at the same time at least 50 Southern performers trekked northward to record in the big city or at the Victor studio in Camden, New Jersey. Recordings by African-American blues singers were generally labeled as "race records," while those by white fiddlers, banjo players, and family singing groups were sold as "hillbilly" records, "old familiar tunes," or just "old time music." Talent scout and record producer Ralph Peer from Okeh Records spearheaded these field trips, focusing initially on recording African Americans and subsequently on rural whites. Peer's competitors at Columbia, Paramount, and Victor followed suit and issued their own "race" and "hillbilly" records.[6]

The output of these trips was impressive, totaling 2,700 master recordings, and helped New York commercial record companies spark popular interest in American vernacular music. The Columbia hillbilly series alone sold an estimated 11 million records between 1925 and 1932.[7] Drawn by recording opportunities, folk musicians flocked to New York. Clarence Ashley, Uncle Dave Macon, Mississippi John Hurt, Furry Lewis, and Dock Boggs all recorded in the city in the 1920s. Beginning in 1924, the blind guitarist and harmonica player George Reneau recorded dozens of sides for Vocalion Records at its Midtown studio, and Vernon Dalhart, Carson Robison, Arthur Fields, Frankie Marvin, and Frank Luther were particularly active and popular singers. The Carter Family, who initially recorded in Bristol, Tennessee, also made albums at the Victor studios in Camden, New Jersey. Gene Autry, the famous singing cowboy, arrived in the Big Apple from Oklahoma in 1930 to cut his first recordings, and he returned many times over the next five years.[8]

The New York record companies also began to transform rural Southern musical forms. While Southern hillbilly

above: Bessie Smith, 1936. Called "The Empress of the Blues," Smith recorded for Columbia Records in New York in the 1920s. Photograph by Carl Van Vechten.

opposite: On a trip to Lafayette, Louisiana, in June 1934, John and Alan Lomax recorded blues and boogie woogie musician Wilson Jones (aka Stavin' Chain) performing the ballad "Batson," as seen in this photograph by Alan Lomax. An unidentified violinist provides accompaniment.

musicians initially depended on traditional ballads and older fiddle tunes, those recording in the city increasingly had to rely on material written by professional tunesmiths like Carson Robison as record companies built up their hillbilly catalogs with a steady stream of releases. This music generally had a mellower sound than many of the field recordings made in the South and West. While performers crowded the recording studios, they seldom appeared in local concerts or radio programs. (One exception was Vernon Dalhart, who made over 400 recordings between 1916 and 1924 and performed in 1926 on the local WEAF radio station, part of the NBC network, and in 1927 on NBC's "Royal Music Makers" show.)

As the Harlem Renaissance flowered in the 1920s, the interest of New York record companies in African-American musical forms increased, and many blues performers recorded in the city. Mamie Smith's "Crazy Blues," recorded for Okeh Records in 1920, opened the floodgates, and in 1922 Trixie Smith, born in Atlanta, released "Trixie's Blues" on the tiny Black Swan label. She switched to Okeh, which also recorded Ida Cox, a prominent blues singer. Bessie Smith was especially popular, cutting "Down Hearted Blues" for Columbia in 1923; members of Fletcher Henderson's orchestra subsequently backed her in these studio recordings. The often raunchy Lucille Bogan recorded for Brunswick until 1930. While race records in the late 1920s constituted just an estimated five percent of the overall sales of New York labels, they represented a significant part of African-American community life.[9]

Meanwhile, to introduce readers nationwide to folk music, New York publishing firms distributed numerous compilations and anthologies of ballads, most notably Carl Sandburg's *American Songbag*, issued by Harcourt, Brace & Company in 1927. Sandburg, a Pulitzer Prize-winning poet and biographer of Abraham Lincoln, had been a passionate song collector since he was a young man wandering across the country. On a national lecture circuit that took him to universities and civic clubs, Sandburg collected songs from friends, labor leaders, and folklorists. Indefatigable in his efforts, he aimed to illustrate the country's collective heritage to a popular audience through folk songs. *American Songbag* presented 280 songs in an accessible manner, with piano accompaniments for each tune, often embellished with folksy notes and line drawings. In contrast to the commercial record companies, Sandburg did not delineate songs into racial divisions but rather treated African-American music as central to the nation's cultural identity. He did include a section on African-American "Blues, Mellows, Ballets," but in general placed black songs in broad categories such as "Railroad and Work Gangs," "Prison and Jail Songs," and the "Road to Heaven." Other groupings, sometimes whimsically titled, included "Picnic and Hayrack Follies, Close Harmony,

opposite: Members of the Bog Trotters Band, Galax, Virginia, 1937. John and Alan Lomax made over 200 recordings of this group of traditional Appalachian string-band players for the Library of Congress.

above: John Lomax (left) and Uncle Rich Brown at the home of Mrs. Julia Killingsworth near Sumterville, Alabama, October 1940. Photograph by Ruby T. Lomax.

and Darn Fool Ditties" and "Tarnished Love Tales or Colonial and Revolutionary Antiques." *American Songbag*, wildly successful and extensively reviewed, went through many editions. But while Sandburg was a popularizer, he also shunned modern recording technology and relied on the songbook tradition of collecting written texts, transcribing songs, and taking down notes and lyrics as he heard people sing.[10]

FOLK MUSIC DURING THE GREAT DEPRESSION IN NEW YORK

The 1930s signaled hard times for the nascent commercial folk music industry. The Great Depression caused the decline of the record business, including sales of blues and gospel records, which had significantly decreased by 1931: national sales plummeted from $46 million in 1930 to $16.9 million the following year. As the economy collapsed, the Depression inevitably limited the activity of New York record labels. As a result, many Southern rural musicians lost a source of employment and had to return to full-time farm work, coal mining, and factory labor. Economic collapse also led to

the closing of numerous New York nightclubs and theaters. Many composers, musicians, and music publishing companies, lured by the thriving film industry, began to decamp to Hollywood. And yet, the Great Depression political milieu elevated folk music. Against the backdrop of political and cultural trends that celebrated the "common man," New York became a supportive environment for activists seeking to use folk songs to advance their political agenda.[11]

In the 1930s and 1940s, American radicals redefined the genre of folk music from a quaint musical form associated with rural life to "the people's music"—a weapon in the ideological battle to mobilize workers to develop a class consciousness and create an inclusive democratic society based on socialist political principles. During the Depression, leftists were hardly a monolithic group. They included members of the American Communist and Socialist Parties and an array of other activists, who differed widely in age, ideology, social background, cultural outlook, and political commitment. Attitudes evolved as circumstances changed over the course of the decade, particularly around 1935. As the threat of fascism intensified in central and southern Europe, and as the concern of homegrown right-wing populism increased in the United States, the American Communist Party, in line with the Soviet Communist International, changed strategy from a focus on the overthrow of capitalism to the establishment of a "Popular Front," defined as a broad alliance of liberal and leftist forces to combat the menace of authoritarian tendencies at home and abroad. The Communist Party, led by Earl Browder, announced that "Communism is 20th Century Americanism," in effect depicting communist ideas as a central part of American democratic traditions. In this context, the Left developed a cultural agenda to use not only music but also theater, dance, poetry, fiction, and art as tools of propaganda to convey an ideological message. But while 1930s radicals contributed to the trend of popularizing folk music, they never achieved their dream of creating a singing movement of workers.[12]

The Communists' use of music for political purposes dated from the 1920s and early 1930s, when they organized revolutionary choruses to foster class solidarity. Many eastern European immigrant groups in New York incorporated choruses as part of their cultural traditions; these choruses were led by conductors who chose the music appropriate for the masses. It was a hierarchical organizational model based on strict rehearsals meant to instill discipline among the working class. Communist Party members composed and published songs to help foment class rebellion, though with negligible success. The 1932 *Song Book For Workers*, issued by the Red Star Publicity Service, included only 11 songs, such as the stilted "Comintern" and "Stand Guard, The Soviets Are Calling," along with labor activist Joe Hill's

previous: Alan Lomax (center) and Pete Seeger (right) practice for the "Folksong 59" concert at Carnegie Hall, New York, 1959. Photograph by John Cohen.

above: Published in 1932 by the Workers Music League in New York, the *Red Song Book* included several strike songs from Appalachia and elsewhere, such as "Poor Miner's Farewell" by Aunt Molly Jackson. In a review of the book, *The Worker Musician* criticized the "immaturity" and "arrested development" of the Kentucky mining songs, showing the lack of faith that many New York City radicals had in the political utility of folk music in the early 1930s.

THE SPECIAL TASK OF THE WORKERS MUSIC LEAGUE IS THE DEVELOPMENT OF MUSIC AS A WEAPON IN THE CLASS STRUGGLE.

popular "The Preacher and the Slave." The Pierre Degeyter Club, named after the Belgian socialist and composer of "The Internationale" and based in New York, exemplified the revolutionary chorus tradition. The club consisted of composers, writers, and performers and aimed to develop music for the proletariat. The bulk of the music was avant-garde in nature. In 1932 the Pierre Degeyter Club founded the Composers' Collective, which included composers Marc Blitzstein and Charles Seeger, who was also a musicologist. The collective embarked on "the task of writing music of all sorts to meet the needs of the growing mass working class movement." Most of the music was didactic and in general did not resonate with workers during the Great Depression. In 1931 the Communist Party formed the Workers Music League (WML) in New York to create proletarian music. Most members had affiliations with revolutionary choruses, and leaders came primarily from the Pierre Degeyter Club. On the purpose of the league, Charles Seeger observed, "The special task of the Workers Music League is the development of music as a weapon in the class struggle." Like their counterparts in the Pierre Degeyter Club, composers in the WML chose music to elevate workers' tastes and jolt them out of their "false consciousness." In 1934 the WML published the *New Workers Song Book*, for which Charles Seeger and composer Lan Adomian compiled 22 songs with classical structures and proletarian lyrics designed for trained choruses.[14]

Members of the Composers' Collective and the WML, for the most part professional musicians trained at the nation's foremost conservatories, dedicated themselves to edifying workers with "good music." At first they regarded folk music with disdain. As Charles Seeger reflected, "Many folksongs are complacent, melancholy, defeatist, intended to make slaves endure their lot—pretty but not the stuff for a militant proletariat to feed upon."[15]

Aunt Molly Jackson, a ballad singer, union organizer, and political activist from Harlan County, Kentucky, personified the gulf between the Composers' Collective and folk music. Jackson was a participant in the violent "Harlan County War" in 1931 between striking miners and union organizers on one side, and coal firms and law enforcement officials on the other. From a family of miners, Jackson had already experienced tragedy. In 1917 her husband was killed in a mining accident, and later her father and brother were blinded in another. Embattled, she wrote protest songs such as "I Am a Union Woman" and "Poor Miner's Farewell," adding to her repertoire of hundreds of ballads that she had learned from her great-grandmother. In November 1931, as the violent struggle intensified for the rights of miners to organize and press for better wages and working conditions, the National Committee for the Defense of Political Prisoners, headed by writer and activist Theodore Dreiser and known as the Dreiser

Committee, descended upon Harlan from New York City to investigate the conflict and compile a report for the National Committee for the Defense of Political Prisoners under the auspices of the American Communist Party. Jackson, the self-proclaimed "pistol-packin' Mama," testified in front of the Dreiser Committee, which also included the writers John Dos Passos, Lewis Mumford, and Sherwood Anderson. In an account of the living conditions of her fellow Appalachian workers, Jackson told the committee, "The people in this country are destitute of anything that is really nourishing to the body. That is the truth. Even the babies have lost their lives, and we have buried from four to seven a week all along during the warm weather." She proceeded to perform her song "Kentucky Miner's Wife (Ragged Hungry Blues)." Startled, the committee invited her to New York to sing and raise money for the striking coal workers. Faced with threats by local police and the mine owners, Jackson accepted the invitation and moved to the city. The musician Margaret Larkin brought her to the Columbia studio, where she recorded the two-sided "Ragged Hungry Blues." Not surprisingly, the New York political left embraced Jackson. She was a vigorous public orator, at once abrasive and direct, usually colorful and sometimes vulgar, and known to embellish stories about her past. Through her impassioned pleas for assistance for miners in Kentucky, she became a symbol of the struggle of workers in rural America.[16]

Around 1933 Jackson attended several meetings of the Composers' Collective as the group studied the development of music for the proletariat. Presumably, Jackson embodied the connection between song and radical politics. She performed a few of her compositions, in the language and idiom of Appalachia, set to traditional melodies. Most members of the collective were polite but unimpressed. Plain and stark, her hillbilly songs failed to stir them. They preferred the dissonance and complexity of Hans Eisler's choral compositions and marches. Similarly, their music bewildered her. But Charles Seeger acknowledged the vitality of her songs of social struggle. He remarked to her, "Molly, they didn't understand you. But I know some young people who will want to learn your songs."[17]

Seeger and his colleagues came to realize that the compositions in their songbook largely failed to engage workers. As the Popular Front emerged in the middle of the decade and the Left-liberal alliance developed an appreciation for folk art forms, the WML recognized the need to embrace indigenous labor ballads and published several in the second edition of their songbook in 1935. Seeger, folklorist Alan Lomax, composer Earl Robinson, and others involved in political activism pursued a strategy to "discover" folk music that would be appropriate for a leftist political movement. Proletarian writer and novelist Mike Gold, who was editor of the American

Folksinger and union activist Aunt Molly Jackson from Kentucky, shown here ca. 1935, epitomized the connection between music and leftist politics during the Great Depression. Though most New York City radicals were at first indifferent to her songs, they eventually championed her as the voice of Appalachian labor.

JOSH WHITE JR.

My father, Josh White, had recorded more than 90 "race records" with a dozen hits, and had given hundreds of performances on stage and radio between 1928 and 1936 ... but had never been seen in a live performance by a <u>white</u> person! Then, in 1939, he co-starred on Broadway with Paul Robeson in <u>John Henry</u> and was sponsored by John Hammond in Greenwich Village at Cafe Society, the first integrated nightclub in America. The audience loved his artistry, and he became a star to the masses ... black <u>and</u> white. Soon he would have hit records and his own national radio show. He would become popular on Broadway and in films and headline concert halls around the world. But every year he would come back to the Village to play Cafe Society, the Blue Angel, and the Village Vanguard.

In 1940, while co-starring with Woody Guthrie, Lead Belly, Burl Ives, and the Golden Gate Quartet on the national radio show <u>Back Where I Come From,</u> my dad and Lead Belly began a six month run at the Village Vanguard. At the same time, Josh, Lead, Woody, and Burl began helping out some young, socially active folkies in the Village named Pete Seeger, Lee Hays, and Millard Lampell in a group they were forming called the Almanac Singers. The Village was the first place where Josh and Lead (soon to be joined by Sonny Terry and Brownie McGhee) had the opportunity to interact with and share their music with like-minded white folk artists. I believe these multi-racial collaborations became the seeds for the national folk music movement.

In 1944, the same year my dad had his smash hit "One Meatball" (the first million-selling folk record), I began performing at his side and at the feet of the master ... literally. He always performed standing, with his right foot on a chair, guitar resting on his knee. Little four-year-old me stood on that chair and sang with him as loudly and passionately as I could. In 1945 Oscar Brand began hosting his <u>Folksong Festival</u> radio show on WNYC and New York's first public hootenanny shows, on both of which

we regularly performed. It was exciting to come down to
the Village in those years to perform and interact with
Woody, Lead, Pete, Burl, Sonny, Brownie, Oscar, and all
the fascinating people of different races, nationalities,
and beliefs.

Our family lived in Harlem, a very nice area ... but the
only place in 1940s New York where we were allowed to
live. There were unofficial segregation and racial laws
for blacks living in New York. Regardless, if we played at
Carnegie Hall, in Central Park, on the radio, or at a rally
at Madison Square Garden, I never felt threatened in the
city. The Village was particularly special. The atmosphere
was friendly with all the artists. It felt like family. I
felt safe there.

— — —

*Josh White Jr., one of the last artists connected to the
folk renaissance of the 1940s, began his career as a child
star in Greenwich Village, performing and recording with his
legendary father Josh White, who pioneered African-American
folk, blues, spirituals, and songs of social conscience to a
multiracial audience in America and then around the world.
Branching out on his own in 1961, White Jr. has toured the
world's greatest concert stages, recorded 25 albums, starred
in four TV concert specials, written songs for Pete Seeger
and Harry Belafonte, and distinguished himself as a Broadway
actor. Named the "Voice of the PEACE Corps", and VISTA in 1980,
he has sung for presidents, prime ministers, the Pope, the
imprisoned, and the poorest of the poor.*

Communist Party's *New Masses* magazine, also endorsed the use of folk music for radical causes. The transformation in attitudes was not simply the result of the emergence of the Popular Front. These activists took a cue from history, citing not only the case of Aunt Molly Jackson in Harlan County, but also the effective use of folk music in the 1929 strike of textile workers in Gastonia, North Carolina.[18]

Vernacular folk songs and ballads increasingly became part of the Left's cultural and political toolkit in New York City. The local socialist Rand School Press published the *Rebel Song Book* in 1935, featuring mostly older socialist tunes but including the folk labor songs "Hold the Fort," "On the Picket Line," "Solidarity Forever," "We Shall Not Be Moved," and "Casey Jones." In 1935 the New Singers recorded three records for Timely Records that illustrated their leftist labor agenda, and in 1937 Timely issued a folk-oriented three-record set by the Manhattan Chorus that included Joe Hill's "Casey Jones" and "We Shall Not Be Moved." While neither Timely set attracted much interest, they indicated the move towards folk music by New York's musical left.[19]

The arrival of African-American blues musician and guitarist Huddie "Lead Belly" Ledbetter in New York at the end of 1934 diversified the city's budding leftist folk community. Born in Louisiana around 1888, Lead Belly was raised on a small family farm. In his early years, he toiled in fields in different parts of the Deep South and learned an extensive array of songs, including primordial blues, spirituals, reels, cowboy songs, and traditional ballads. Lead Belly also had a fierce temper that led to convictions for murder in 1917 and attempted murder in 1930. He claimed that the 1917 murder was committed in self-defense and eventually received a pardon from Texas Governor Pat Morris Neff in 1925, largely due to his good behavior and a persuasive appeal that included a song.[20]

While serving time for the attempted murder in Louisiana's Angola Prison Farm, Lead Belly was "discovered" by folklorist John Lomax and his son Alan on a field recording trip to the region in 1933. Working for the Archive of American Folk Song of the Library of Congress, the Lomaxes traveled to relatively isolated areas and, using modern recording equipment, collected songs from cotton plantations, cowboy ranches, and lumber camps. John was particularly keen on recording music in segregated penitentiaries, reasoning that these institutions had kept prisoners away from the trappings of modern society, especially the phonograph and radio, and thus maintained, to some degree, the purity of the songs. At Angola Prison, Lead Belly astounded Lomax not only with his vast repertoire of 100 songs, but also with his resonant voice and commanding performance style on the 12-string guitar. For the Lomaxes, Lead Belly's song repertoire was a treasure trove, an affirmation of a rich African-American

On a field recording trip to Louisiana's Angola Prison in 1933, folklorist John Lomax and his son Alan "discovered" the African-American blues musician and guitarist Huddie "Lead Belly" Ledbetter (foreground). Lead Belly astonished the Lomaxes with an extensive repertoire of blues, spirituals, and cowboy songs, prompting them to return for another recording session in July 1934, when Alan took this photograph of prisoners in the compound.

musical tradition. The Lomaxes returned to Angola in July 1934 for another session, recording several numbers that included Lead Belly's seminal versions of "Goodnight, Irene" and "The Midnight Special." Following the visit, the Lomaxes submitted a petition to Louisiana Governor O. K. Allen that called for the release of Lead Belly. The plea included a song by the prisoner, appropriately titled "Governor O. K. Allen." The next month, Lead Belly won his freedom. At first Lead Belly and the Lomaxes believed that the release was a result of the appeal and the song. But the truth was that Lead Belly had gained his freedom under Louisiana laws due to good behavior. The fable of rescue and redemption nevertheless became popular, reinforced by media accounts and by Lead Belly and the Lomaxes themselves.[21]

Upon release from prison, Lead Belly strengthened his ties to the Lomaxes, working as John's chauffeur and field assistant on recording trips throughout the South. In 1934 John and Lead Belly traveled to Arkansas, Louisiana, Alabama, Texas, Georgia, North Carolina, and South Carolina, often stopping at penitentiaries to record. John Lomax was determined to broaden the nation's under-standing of folk music beyond the Anglo-Saxon Appalachian ballads treasured by earlier academic folklorists, such as the Englishman Cecil Sharp. The Lomaxes' *American Ballads and Folk Songs* (1934), published by Macmillan in New York, included songs by miners, lumbermen, sailors, soldiers, railroad men, hobos, and convicts from various regions of the country. It also featured popular songs taken from the radio, commercial recordings, newspapers, magazines, and literary sources. Especially eager to illuminate the range of African-American traditions, the Lomaxes remarked that black singers created "the most distinctive of folk songs— the most interesting, the most appealing, and the greatest in quantity."[22]

Though the John Lomax-Lead Belly relationship was inherently unequal, it was also reciprocal and mutually beneficial in ways. Lomax sought to showcase the talent of Lead Belly in New York and on college campuses and other forums in the Northeast. To Lomax, Lead Belly epitomized a noncommercial, premodern rural past that was quickly fading in an era of expanding urbanization and industrializa-tion. Following his release from prison, Lead Belly desired to embark on a musical career and viewed the institutionally connected Lomax as a valuable resource. But the Lomaxes also arranged an exploitative management contract with Lead Belly, giving themselves two thirds of the singer's earn-ings in an era when a 50 percent commission was common. John Lomax also represented the racist attitudes of the era. Preparing to take Lead Belly to the North, he submitted a letter to the New York media as part of a publicity blitz. "Lead Belly is a nigger to the core of his being," Lomax

ALAN LOMAX

Authority on American Folk-Lore . . . Archivist to the Library of Congress . . . Commentator and Artist on "Columbia's School of the Air"

As assistant in charge of the Library of Congress's Archive of American Folk Song and host of two series on CBS's nationally broadcast *American School of the Air* in the late 1930s and early 1940s, Alan Lomax worked tirelessly to introduce folk songs to a broad portion of the American population. In New York City, Lomax organized concerts and produced recordings, becoming a prominent advocate for a public role for folklore.

Lead Belly performs in front of an interracial crowd in a New York City living room, ca. 1940. Photograph by Weegee.

commented. "In addition he is a killer. He tells the truth only accidentally. ... He is as sensual as a goat, and when he sings to me my spine tingles and sometimes tears come. Penitentiary wardens all tell me that I set no value on my life in using him as a traveling companion."[23]

Arriving in New York on New Year's Eve in 1934, Lomax and Lead Belly immediately gained the attention of the city's intellectuals, artists, and reporters. On the night of their arrival, Lead Belly performed at the Greenwich Village apartment of Macmillan editor Margaret Conklin and New York University English Professor Mary Elizabeth Barnicle. (A labor activist and a professor of folklore and medieval literature, Barnicle assigned *American Ballads and Folk Songs* in her courses and introduced it to New York singers Earl Spicer and J. Rosamond Johnson.) After the party, Ledbetter went to the Rockland Palace in Harlem, where Cab Calloway's orchestra was performing.[24]

Through the Lomaxes, Lead Belly formed artistic and commercial relationships with figures in New York's folk music industry. In 1935 he recorded dozens of sides for the American Record Company and subsequently for Musicraft and Victor, although relatively few were actually released. The Lomaxes also arranged numerous performances for Lead Belly at parties and at John's lectures. Intent on maintaining Lead Belly's persona as the epitome of pristine folk music, John was dismayed to find that the blues guitarist was eager to expand his repertoire with pop and jazz songs. As his "exclusive

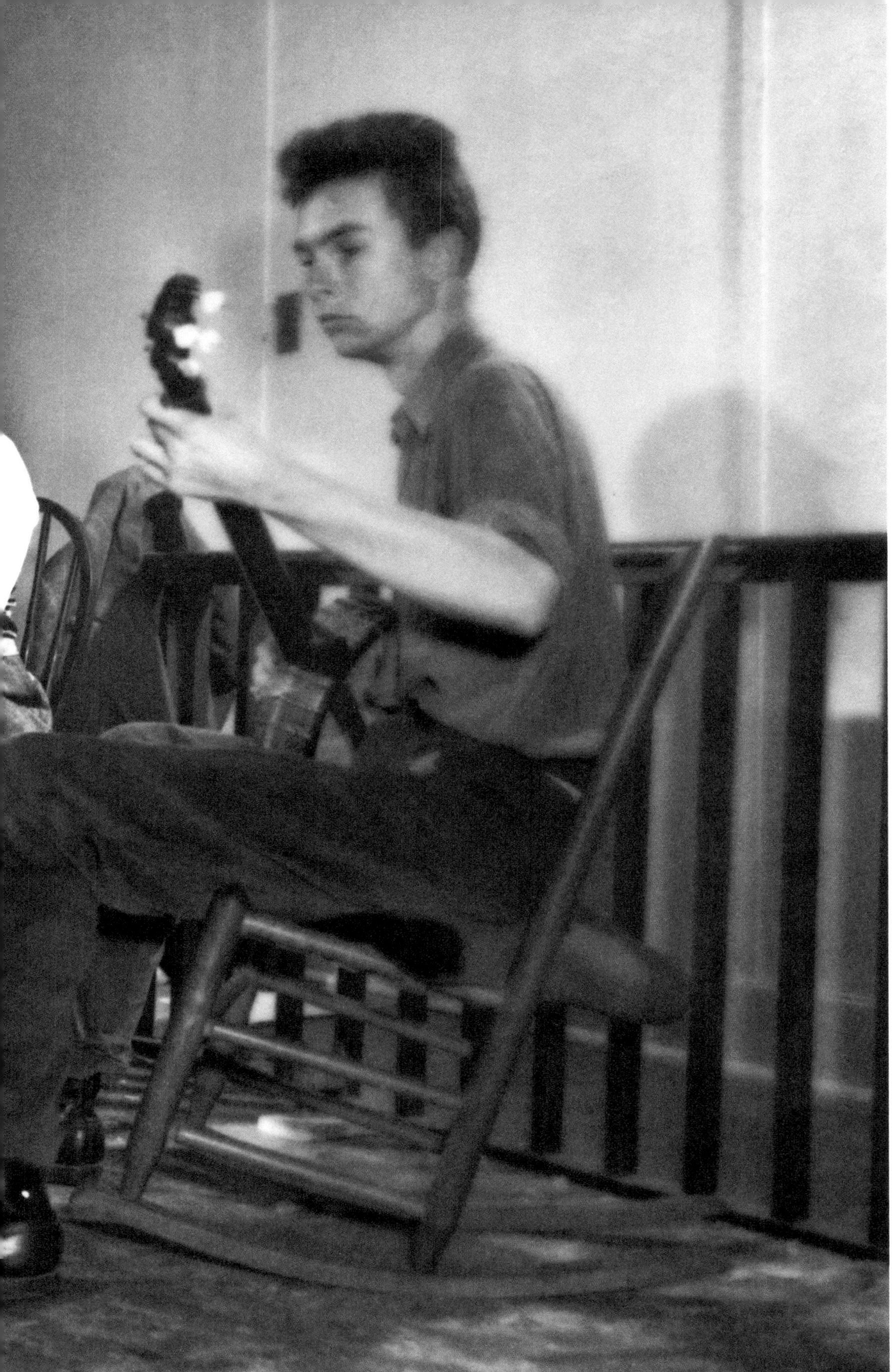

manager, personal representative and adviser," John signed a contract with Macmillan for a book on African-American folk songs based on Lead Belly's catalog. Published in 1936, *Negro Folk Songs as Sung by Lead Belly* featured selections by the Lomaxes that discussed Lead Belly as part of the folk process of transmission of traditional ballads to a larger audience. Only a few songs were Lead Belly originals; most were interpretations of ballads, modified by guitar accompaniments that suggested the influence of ragtime and other popular styles. The book generally received rave reviews, but *New Masses* contributor Lawrence Gellert, a field collector of black spirituals and blues himself, wrote a scathing critique. Gellert, a radical with views that contrasted sharply with those of politically conservative John Lomax, showed special interest in chronicling black protest traditions in the South. He denounced Lomax for exploiting Lead Belly and for a romantic portrayal of black life in the South, overlooking the "peonage, poverty, and degradation" that afflicted African Americans in the region and failing to document the songs that challenged the racial hierarchy.[25]

The New York media covered Lead Belly in sensational articles. *Time* labeled him a "Murderous Minstrel," and the *Brooklyn Eagle* described him as "virtuoso of Knife and Guitar." The *Herald Tribune* announced, "Lomax arrives with Lead Belly, Negro Minstrel" and added the subtitle "Sweet Singer of the Swamplands Here To Do a Few Tunes between Homicides." The CBS radio news program *March of Time* arranged for Lomax and Lead Belly to do a reenactment of the pardon story. The newsreel featured a magnanimous Lomax agreeing to aid an acquiescent and obsequious Lead Belly in obtaining a pardon from the governor. The program aired in January 1935 and reinforced traditional stereotypes of the benevolent master and the helpless, contented slave. Other news coverage was racist even by the bigoted standards of the day. A 1937 *Life* feature titled "Lead Belly—Bad Nigger Makes Good Minstrel" captioned an image with "these hands once killed a man." In articles that evoked depictions of primal savages from non-Western societies in a manner reminiscent of Joseph Conrad's novel *Heart of Darkness* (1913), the New York press portrayed Lead Belly as an exotic "other," characterizing him as untamed, irrational, and unfeeling.[26]

Conversely, the reports repeatedly made allusions to Lead Belly's musical authenticity, juxtaposing his songs with trends in modern popular music. One article commented, "There is but slight resemblance between his singing and that of the stage and radio singers. There is a deep primitive quality to Lead Belly's songs." The *New York Post* noted the "perfect simplicity" of Lead Belly's music. The guitarist seemed to be an outcast on the margins of American society, a victim of oppression, at once earnest and noble. He thus represented an alluring figure to leftist, middle-class New York audiences.

previous: (From left) Josh White, Lead Belly, and Pete Seeger in New York City, March 1941.

opposite: Lead Belly performs in a New York nightclub with Josh White on guitar behind him, ca. 1940. Photograph by Carlo Pappolla.

above: Lead Belly plays guitar, accompanied by his wife on piano, in a New York City apartment. Shortly after he was released from prison in 1934, Lead Belly traveled to New York City with John Lomax and married his girlfriend, Martha Promise, in Connecticut in 1935.

At Lead Belly's New York premiere at a University of Texas alumni event, John Lomax reflected, "Northern people hear Negroes playing and singing beautiful spirituals which are too refined and are unlike the true Southern spirituals. Or else they hear men and women on the stage and radio, burlesquing their own songs. Lead Belly doesn't burlesque. He plays and sings with absolute sincerity. ... I've heard his songs a hundred times, but I always get a thrill. To me his music is real music."[27]

As Lead Belly established a greater presence in the city in the late 1930s, Alan Lomax exerted ever more influence at the Archive of American Folk Song and as a popularizer of the nation's traditional ballads in New York. During the Great Depression, Lomax labored to develop a folk song canon and to solidify the relationship between vernacular music and the Left. In contrast to his father, Alan was active in leftist politics and aimed to promote folk music to a large segment of the American population, not just academic and sophisticated audiences. The younger Lomax believed that the relationship between mass culture and corporate America was particularly pernicious. In his view, it homogenized folk arts and was causing the extinction of the country's vernacular music. He saw the conflict through the lens of class, as the attempt of corporate interests to manipulate, dilute, or embellish the "people's music" and produce mellifluous drivel for profit. Lomax worked tirelessly to collect and preserve vernacular music, scouring the country and contributing thousands of field recordings to the Library of Congress. To achieve his political and cultural objectives, Lomax collaborated with academics, activists, politicians, bureaucrats, performers, journalists, and foundations. He used his CBS radio programs in New York during the Depression to introduce Americans to Aunt Molly Jackson, Lead Belly, Woody Guthrie, Josh White, Burl Ives, Pete Seeger, Sonny Terry, Brownie McGhee, and other respectful practitioners of folk songs. In 1940 he also helped produce Woody Guthrie's *Dust Bowl Ballads* and Lead Belly's *Midnight Special and other Southern Prison Songs*, two landmark albums of the folk music revival issued by RCA. And though Lead Belly's relationship with John Lomax ended badly, primarily over finances, Alan Lomax and the "King of the 12-string guitar" became close collaborators. Lomax worked with New York University Professor Mary Elizabeth Barnicle to book Lead Belly for performances in front of left-wing groups.[28]

Several concerts in New York during this era signaled a turning point in the relationship between folk music and the city and illustrated the trends initiated by cultural entrepreneurs and performers. One performance in particular stood out: "From Spirituals to Swing: An Evening of American Negro Music" presented at Carnegie Hall on December 23, 1938. The show connected progressive politics to vernacular art forms,

above: *Southern Exposure* by Josh White, released by Keynote in 1941, was a controversial protest album containing anti-segregationist blues songs. The album cover art juxtaposes the two worlds of the South: white and black, day and night.

embodying the spirit of Popular Front culture that celebrated the common folk and their songs, legends, and myths. The performers, from the South, Appalachia, the Midwest, and other regions, represented a range of musical and dance traditions, mostly rural but also urban in origins. To a sophisticated New York audience, they seemed to be authentic, unspoiled, rooted in a premodern time and place, almost anachronistic among the modern skyscrapers of Midtown Manhattan where the concert occurred.

Presented by producer and jazz writer John Hammond and dedicated to the recently deceased blues singer Bessie Smith, "An Evening of American Negro Music" was performed for a capacity crowd. The concert featured African field recordings, gospel, blues, early New Orleans jazz, boogie-woogie piano, and swing. Hammond recruited a stellar lineup of musicians from the South and the Midwest, personally traveling to North Carolina and signing up blues harmonica player Sonny Terry and the a cappella gospel quartet Mitchell's Christian Singers. He initially wanted Robert Johnson, but the bluesman had died several months earlier in Mississippi. In Johnson's stead, Hammond landed Big Bill Broonzy, a blues singer based in Chicago. Other performers included the Count Basie Band, gospel singer Sister Rosetta Tharpe, and saxophonist Sidney Bechet.[29]

Hammond aimed to illustrate the rich history of black music to combat racist stereotypes about the impoverishment of African-American culture. He explained that the

occasion "would bring together, for the first time, before a musically sophisticated audience, Negro music from its raw beginnings to the latest jazz." Despite acknowledged omissions, the acts illuminated continuity and change in musical forms over time and across place. The concert booklet's lead article, entitled "The Music Nobody Knows," captured the uniqueness of the moment, as this was music seldom performed in New York and, even less often, in front of an integrated audience. Stressing the obstacles of the musicians, the essay observed, "Most of the people you will hear are absurdly poor." Failing to obtain funding for the event from the NAACP and the International Ladies' Garment Workers' Union, Hammond secured support from the *New Masses*, a publication to which he contributed a column under the pseudonym Henry Johnson. The *New Masses* not only promoted the Congress of Industrial Organizations (CIO), but also advocated sharecropper unions in the South and campaigned against lynching. In case the agenda of the event's producers was still unclear to concertgoers, they needed only to look at the show's other sponsors. Advertisements in the program were for the Medical Bureau and North American Committee to Aid Spanish Democracy, a Clifford Odets play at the Belasco Theatre, Soviet films from the Amkino Corporation, and the Workers Book Shop.[30]

The concert received a largely positive response, though not surprisingly some attacked it as subversive. *New York Times* reporter H. Howard Taubman raved, "An evening of

American Negro music shook the stage, the rafters, and the audience at Carnegie Hall last night." He especially enjoyed Mitchell's Christian Singers and the whoops and hollers and harmonica dexterity of Sonny Terry in his version of the song "Fox Chase." Taubman noted, "They represented, in their concentration, true musical feeling, integrity and unaffectedness, Negro music in its pristine aspects." Alan Lomax was also enthusiastic and liked the idea of presenting different but related musical styles on one bill; he obtained Hammond's permission to record five of the performers for the Library of Congress. Buoyed by the reaction, Hammond staged a second "From Spirituals to Swing" concert at Carnegie one year later, on December 24, 1939. The roster included the Count Basie Band, Sonny Terry, Ida Cox, the Golden Gate Quartet, Big Bill Broonzy, and the racially mixed Benny Goodman Sextet. Emceed by Howard University Professor Sterling Brown, the concert repeated some material from the previous year and received less praise, though the performances were generally solid. In many ways, Hammond was the star of both shows. Not only did he strengthen his reputation as a talent scout and a civil rights activist, but he also set a high bar for presenting vernacular music in New York, luring talent to the city from all over the country.[31]

Hammond's concerts had widespread political and cultural implications and demonstrated the vitality of Popular Front culture in New York in the late 1930s. More than simply a coalition of leftists and liberals that formed to combat the rising tide of fascism, the Popular Front encompassed the convergence of social democratic movements based on racial and labor justice. Popular Front culture dovetailed with the expansion of the entertainment and amusement industries. Increasingly in the 1930s and 1940s, the Left exerted influence on the modern "cultural apparatus," in the establishment of workers theaters, proletarian magazines, and composers' collectives. Radicals and progressives also worked in Hollywood film studios and in radio broadcasting, and many staffed federal government agencies. In these organizations, they developed affiliations and allegiances and formed artistic and social networks oriented around causes of industrial unionism, civil rights, and antifascism. "From Spirituals to Swing" epitomized Popular Front trends, and the impresario Hammond orchestrated performances that challenged prevailing assumptions on race and class. The organizers and the performers by and large considered themselves generic "communists" with a small "c," not ideologues in a party. However, the events were not merely political. Many of the artists already had recording contracts and were part of the commercial fabric of New York folk music. The categories of "protest" and "commercial" singers were not mutually exclusive and did not sufficiently describe the loyalties and commitments of the artists.[32]

Flier announcing Lead Belly's performance at Irving Plaza, May 1947.

Hammond's events and the 1940 "Grapes of Wrath" concert strengthened the association of folk music with New York. But while the principal performers became highly influential in the folk revival in the city and beyond, folk music remained on the artistic margins at the end of the Great Depression, obscure compared to Tin Pan Alley and big band swing music and poorly understood by the public and media at large.[33]

WORLD WAR II
AND ITS AFTERMATH

By the start of World War II, a thriving informal folk culture connected loosely, though not officially, with the Communist Party had emerged in the city. The site for much of the folk activity in the early years of the war was the Village Vanguard. In 1935 Max Gordon had opened the Vanguard on Seventh Avenue, where it quickly became a popular Village nightspot. In 1940, inspired by John Hammond, Gordon featured an integrated lineup that included the Golden Gate Quartet and Josh White. Gordon also featured African-American artists Lead Belly and Josh White in 1941. The Vanguard was one of the few integrated clubs in the city at the time, in addition to Barney Josephson's Cafe Society at 1 Sheridan Square in the Village and his Cafe Society Uptown on East 58th Street.

The Almanac Singers, organized in New York in early 1941, were the embodiment of Popular Front ideals. They were an informal group, loosely organized. Members came and went and barely rehearsed. They lived communally in a loft in Greenwich Village. The core consisted of the founders Pete Seeger, Lee Hays, and Millard Lampell. Woody Guthrie, Bess Lomax (daughter of John Lomax and sister to Alan), and Pete Hawes played frequently with the ensemble. Members were unabashedly on the Left in their politics and champions of the working class, though they themselves were middle-class in background. During the span of their short career, which lasted until late 1942 or so, their topical songs varied in theme depending on the geopolitical circumstances. At times the Almanacs sang antiwar songs, labor ballads, or patriotic tunes. Their main goal, however, was to start a singing union movement. Despite their earnestness and commitment, they were utterly unsuccessful in this regard.[34]

The Almanac Singers included an amalgam of personalities. Son of composer and musicologist Charles Seeger, Pete Seeger played the banjo and showed discipline as the leader of the group. Lee Hays, a skilled group singer, was the son of a Southern minister from Arkansas and an alumnus of the progressive Commonwealth School. Millard Lampell, from a liberal Jewish family in New Jersey, was a fine lyricist. Massachusetts native Pete Hawes sang sea chanteys in

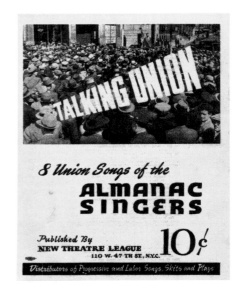

above: Published by New Theatre League in 1941 or 1942, this Almanac Singers songbook included labor songs with militant lyrics. The Almanacs introduced the song "Talking Union" at a rally of some 20,000 striking transit workers on May Day of 1941 at Madison Square Garden.

opposite: Active during World War II and based in New York City, the Almanac Singers, seen here ca. 1940, aimed to create a singing union movement. They blended music and politics to advance leftist ideology.

above: *Songs for John Doe* was the debut album of the Almanac Singers, released in May 1941, when the Soviet Union and Nazi Germany remained at peace. In line with the Soviets' anti-interventionist stance, the album included antiwar songs that were critical of America's peacetime draft. The cover, executed with a hand-drawn quality, depicts a farmer/musician everyman and two laborers—black and white—to whom the Almanac Singers gave a voice.

a baritone voice and had a passion for political theory. Bess Lomax sometimes took weekends off from Bryn Mawr College outside of Philadelphia to sing with the group. Woody Guthrie was the hero of the group, a literary mastermind and on occasion a mentor to other members, but also hard to deal with, especially when he drank too much.[35]

At first the Almanacs sang mostly antiwar and labor songs in line with the Left's stance toward the Soviet Union during the era of the Nazi-Soviet nonaggression treaty. In May 1941, they played at a rally at Madison Square Garden in front of 20,000 striking Transport Workers Union members. Their song "Talking Union" about the struggles of a union organizer won great applause. They also performed an antiwar song from their debut album, *Songs for John Doe*, chiding President Roosevelt for an increasingly militant stance. Their union songs so impressed Mike Quill of the Transport Workers Union that he helped land them a national tour of CIO unions. This would have been the realization of their dreams.[36] However, on June 22, 1941, the Germans invaded the Soviet Union. The event shocked the Almanacs—and the American Left. It was no longer tenable for them to sing antiwar songs as the Red Army mobilized for battle. As *New York Post* journalist Dorothy Millstone recalled, "After hearing that Russia had been invaded, I hung up the phone, and the first thing I did was break my Almanac records." Almost immediately, the group dropped part of their musical repertoire, alienating many supporters.[37]

Their national tour in 1941 was a mixed bag. Some leaders of the CIO cheered them for their commitment to labor causes while others saw them merely as entertainers. Many workers

only mildly appreciated them. It took others a while to warm up to them. Seeger recollected, "When we walked down the aisle of a room where one thousand local members of the [San Francisco] longshoremen's union were meeting, we could see some of them turning around in surprise and even disapproval. 'What the hell is a bunch of hillbilly singers coming in here for? We got work to do.' But when we finished singing 'The Ballad of Harry Bridges' for them, their applause was deafening."[38]

Back in New York, the group moved into a townhouse in Greenwich Village at 110 West 10th Street. Music filled the rooms, and, though group living often led to tension, a communal atmosphere developed. Song sheets, instruments, and wine bottles littered the floor. Sometimes friends such as Lead Belly or Earl Robinson came by for a jam session. They frequently held "hootenannies" on Sunday afternoons in their basement to help raise money to pay the rent. It was a lively scene where friends and acquaintances sat around and sang together.[39]

The Almanacs, though zealous about labor causes, increasingly recognized the chasm between their music and workers in the audience. Most New Yorkers in immigrant

Sonny Terry plays guitar for a crowd including Woody Guthrie and Pete Seeger at a People's Songs hootenanny at Irving Plaza, ca. 1946. People's Songs, an organization founded in New York City at the end of 1945, was committed to promoting the labor movement and other progressive causes, such as civil rights.

communities listened to their own ethnic music or to show tunes and pop hits. Topical songs about labor did not resonate with most workers. Bess Lomax observed, "I think we were in the wrong city. In New York, we sang Appalachian songs to Central European or Irish immigrants in the International Ladies' Garment Workers' and the Transport Workers Unions." To some observers the Almanacs seemed paternalistic in their attempts to transform workers into unionists or radicals.[40]

On December 7, 1941, the Japanese attacked Pearl Harbor, America entered the war, and the Communist Party asked unions for a no-strike pledge. The Almanacs had to drop their labor songs, another large portion of their repertoire. Political circumstances transformed the group yet again. They began to play pro-war songs.[41]

In 1942 the Almanacs enjoyed success with their patriotic songs such as "Reuben James" and "Dear Mr. President." Once labeled "propaganda," a topical political song that supported the war now became an expression of loyalty. In February 1942, a *Life* photographer chronicled one of their hootenannies. The prominent William Morris Agency made an offer to manage them. Guthrie, Bess Lomax, Sis Cunningham, and Seeger sang on the CBS program *We the People*. Some members also performed on the popular CBS program *This Is War*.[42]

In an episode both comical and upsetting, the ensemble auditioned to play at the Rainbow Room, the ritzy nightclub on the 65th floor of Rockefeller Center. A successful performance had the potential to launch them on a nationwide concert tour and a CBS radio series. The setting was sumptuous and the views of Manhattan stunning. Guthrie recalled, "There was big drops of sweat standing on my forehead, and my fingers didn't feel like they was mine. I was floating in high finances, sixty-five stories above the ground, leaning my elbow on a stiff looking table cloth as white as a runaway ghost." Bess Lomax added, "We were absolutely unprepared for success of any kind." Dressed casually in an era when nightclub performers wore formal attire, the Almanacs were the proverbial fish out of water.[43]

The group began with an anti-Nazi song, impressing most of the onlookers. But one manager indicated that the ensemble lacked stage presence. Another proposed that the men wear overalls and the women sunbonnets. Guthrie was deeply insulted. The group changed the lyrics to the next song, Lead Belly's "New York City." They sang:

> At the Rainbow Room, the soup's on to boil
> They're stirring the salad with Standard Oil

The managers laughed, and Guthrie became angrier. The Almanacs left in a huff.[44]

Just as quickly as the Almanac Singers achieved success, their popularity plummeted, in large part due to newspaper articles that referenced their earlier antiwar songs. Damning articles appeared in the *New York Post* and *World-Telegram*. They lost bookings at clubs as well as radio play. On the orders of J. Edgar Hoover, the FBI conducted an investigation of the group for threatening wartime recruitment with their music but did not follow through with any prosecutions. Seeger himself did not care about the loss of money, but the lack of an audience perturbed him. By the end of 1942, the group was on the verge of dissolution in any case due to the wartime service of its members. Seeger received a draft notice, and Guthrie joined the Merchant Marine. Other members left New York for Detroit for jobs in war production.[45]

As the first urban folk music group, the Almanac Singers were pioneers. When Guthrie was front and center, they boasted credentials as authentic folk musicians; without him the other members could only emulate rural ways in their dress and speech. They sang the blues, hillbilly tunes, mountain ballads, and Southern Methodist hymns. Alan Lomax told them, "What you are doing is one of the most important things that could possibly be done in the field of American music. You are introducing folk songs from the countryside to a city audience." They were nonprofessional and noncommercial. In their Almanac House in the Village, they brought a diverse array of people together from different racial, class, ethnic, and regional backgrounds. The Almanacs were at once urban and rural, both cosmopolitan and provincial. And they illustrated the possibility of self-reinvention in the New York political and cultural milieu.[46]

America's entry into World War II had a ripple effect through the New York folk scene. In the absence of the Almanacs, folk music in the city was fragmented but still remained vibrant, with Aunt Molly Jackson, Lead Belly, Richard Dyer-Bennet, the Reverend Gary Davis, and Josh White continuing to perform regularly. There were a few recording sessions during the war as performers drifted in and out. In particular, Moses Asch had begun issuing records in 1939 on the Asch label, and in 1943 he merged with Herbert Harris to create the Asch/Stinson label, located at 27 Union Square. Lead Belly continued to record and appear on radio programs through the war. He released *Leadbelly and the Golden Gate Quartet with Guitar* on Victor in 1940, followed by the Asch albums *Work Songs of the U.S.A. Sung by Leadbelly* and *Songs by Lead Belly,* then the Disc album *Negro Folk Songs as Sung by Leadbelly.* In addition, the all-star lineup of Guthrie, Seeger, Cisco Houston, Burl Ives, and Tom Glazer, under the name the Union Boys, cut the *Songs For Victory* album. Such records had scant circulation but captured the attention of the city's creative folk community. Guthrie, too, recorded on and off during the war period. In

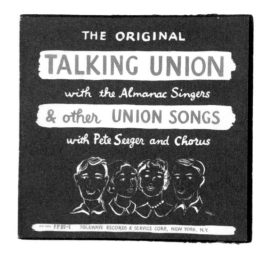

Talking Union was the second album by the Almanac Singers, released in 1941 by Keynote. It featured six labor songs, including "Which Side Are You On?" and "Union Maid." This version, released by Folkways in 1955, included seven additional songs.

The anti-fascist message on Woody Guthrie's guitar illustrates his faith in the power of song to combat authoritarianism and transform society. Guthrie, seen here in March of 1943, wrote numerous anti-fascist songs during World War II, including "Talking Hitler's Head Off Blues." Photograph by Al Aumuller.

mid-1944 he recorded extensively for Asch and Stinson, around the time that Tom Glazer and Josh White recorded the album *Citizen C.I.O.*[47]

By the war's end, numerous folk performers had drifted back to the city and again used folk music to promote their political agenda. In March 1945, Norman Studer, a music teacher at the Little Red School House in Greenwich Village, organized a conference on "Folklore in a Democracy" at the nearby Elizabeth Irwin High School. There were papers by folklorists Benjamin Botkin and Charles Seeger and music by Woody Guthrie, Sonny Terry, and Alan Lomax. A few months later, Margot Mayo's American Square Dance Group sponsored a "home from war" party with Lead Belly, Seeger (just out of the Army), Richard Dyer-Bennet, John Jacob Niles, and Guthrie.

Seeger had lost none of his prewar political passion. In late December 1945, he hosted a gathering at his in-laws' apartment in the Village to organize People's Songs, a musical organization that promoted international cooperation, labor

unions, and racial equality. "In 1945 Americans came home from the war," Seeger later explained. "We dived enthusiastically into long-deferred projects. A number of us who loved to sing folk songs and union songs thought it the most natural thing in the world to start an organization which could keep us all in touch with one another, which could promote new and old songs and singers and in general bring closer the broad revival of interest in folk music, and topical songs which we felt sure would sooner or later take place." For the next three years, Seeger devoted much of his energy to promoting People's Songs.[48]

Seeger also carried on an active recording career. In 1946 he joined Tom Glazer, Hally Wood, and Lee Hays on the album *Songs For Political Action* issued by the CIO-Political Action Committee and recorded *Roll The Union On*, with Hays and others, on the Asch label. In 1948 Seeger toured with Henry Wallace, the Progressive Party's presidential candidate, as People's Songs ran the music desk for the campaign. In 1948 Seeger self-published *How To Play the 5-String Banjo*. "Played

previous: Pete Seeger leads the crowd in "When We March into Berlin" at the opening of the Washington labor canteen, sponsored by the United Federal Workers of America, Congress of Industrial Organizations, February 1944. His audience includes First Lady Eleanor Roosevelt (seated, center). Photograph by Joseph A. Horne.

above: Leslie Scott and chorus at a Yankee Stadium rally for Henry Wallace, the Progressive Party's presidential candidate, 1948. Photograph by Julius Lazarus.

In 1948 Pete Seeger wrote his instructional manual *How to Play the 5-String Banjo*. Many banjo players cite the book as their inspiration for playing the instrument, and the manual went through many versions, including this second edition from 1954.

by hundreds of thousands of Americans 75 or 100 years ago, today this instrument has nearly died out," he explained. "Today, the five-string banjo is almost forgotten; instrument companies produce very few; a hock shop is the most likely place to find a good one." There were indeed few five-string players in New York at the time. It took three years to sell out the first 100 mimeographed copies, but Seeger continued to use his recruiting influence. By the time the booklet's professionally printed second edition appeared in 1954, issued along with the Folkways 10-inch instruction album, interest in the instrument had expanded.[49]

People's Songs' national board of directors included Seeger, Lee Hays, Alan Lomax, Woody Guthrie, Millard Lampell—the stars of the city's folk community. The first issue of the monthly *People's Songs* bulletin appeared in early 1946. While People's Songs was a national organization, New York remained its organizational base. Seeger and his colleagues were heartened by the upsurge of labor activism at the war's end and the fleeting promise of a peaceful world. Along with a spate of national strikes in various industries, New York experienced a wave of strikes even before Seeger had returned from his Army duty on Saipan at year's end. In late September 1945, the city temporarily ground to a halt with 1.5 million workers on strike, followed by the longshoremen's temporary walk-out in October. The national steelworkers strike in early 1946 hardly affected the city, however, since few workers in New York were employed in large factories.

Following the war, besides the numerous folk concerts and square dances throughout the city, there were various local (and national) radio programs devoted to folk music, in particular Oscar Brand's *Folk Song Festival* that launched in 1945 on the public station WNYC. Born in Canada, Brand served a stint in the United States Army and then settled in New York, where he quickly became a major promoter of folk music as well as a prolific recording artist. Tom Glazer's *Ballad Box* national show aired on ABC from 1945 to 1947, while Elaine Lambert Lewis's *Folk Songs of the Seven Million* began in 1944 on WNYC. Alan Lomax briefly resumed his radio career in 1948 with the weekly show *Your Ballad Man* on the New York-based Mutual Broadcasting Network. He featured a wide selection of music, including country, blues, and jazz. During 1948 Lomax also served as head of the music program for Henry Wallace's Progressive Party presidential campaign, an extension of his work for People's Songs.

Following Henry Wallace's defeat in 1948—Seeger and Paul Robeson had performed with the candidate at numerous rallies—People's Songs briefly limped along. "New York, A Musical Tapestry," an eclectic show at Carnegie Hall in 1949 that featured jazz pianist Art Hodes, Brownie McGhee, the young Harry Belafonte, Yma Sumac and her Inca Trio, and the Weavers, was intended to raise needed funds but lost

money instead. "We had envisioned a singing labor movement spearheading a nationwide folksong revival," Seeger
lamented. "How our theories went astray. Most union
leaders could not see any connection between music and
pork chops. As the cold war deepened in '47 and '48 the split
in the labor movement deepened. 'Which Side Are You On'
was known in Greenwich Village but not in a single miner's
union local." People's Songs collapsed in early 1949 due to
financial problems as well as the mounting federal and local
anticommunist crusade.[50]

Despite the demise of People's Songs and the increased
charges of communist taint as the decade ended, folk music
still seemed alive and well in New York. Both popular and
traditional folk musicians passed through to perform in
concerts and make records, and the continuing presence
of local artists such as Oscar Brand, Pete Seeger, Woody
Guthrie, Tom Glazer, Josh White, Reverend Gary Davis,
Lead Belly, Susan Reed, and Alan Lomax, along with newcomers like Harry Belafonte, kept the movement vibrant.
People's Songs' booking agency, People's Artists, located at
13 Astor Place, continued to function. It held a hootenanny
on August 26, 1949, and, in conjunction with the Harlem
chapter of the Civil Rights Congress, planned a concert on
August 27 in Peekskill, up the Hudson River from New York.
A violent mob prevented the concert from taking place, but
a second attempt with actor and activist Paul Robeson on
September 4 was a success. However, aided by the police,

African-American singer and
activist Paul Robeson speaks
at a concert benefitting the
Harlem chapter of the Civil
Rights Congress, September
4, 1949. Held in Peekskill, New
York, the performance triggered
anti-communist riots tinged
with racist and anti-Semitic
undercurrents. Following the
performance, a mob largely
comprised of members of local
Veterans of Foreign Wars and
American Legion chapters threw
rocks at departing vehicles of
concertgoers and performers,
including one that contained
Woody Guthrie, Lee Hays, and
Pete Seeger, his wife Toshi, and
their infant children.

a vicious attack by right wing zealots on those leaving the concert grounds vividly exposed the heated anticommunist political atmosphere.

After Lead Belly's death (December 6, 1949), Alan Lomax organized a Lead Belly memorial concert at Town Hall on January 28, 1950. Drawing upon his eclectic musical interests, it included Woody Guthrie, Tom Paley, the jazzmen Hot Lips Page and Sidney Bechet, Pete Seeger with the Good Neighbor Chorus, Sticks McGhee, W. C. Handy, Jean Ritchie, Count Basie, Tom Glazer, calypso performer Lord Invader, Reverend Gary Davis, Sonny Terry and Brownie McGhee, and the Weavers. The evening embodied the city's rich musical landscape. As Oscar Brand recalled, "American music today is almost a direct reflection of the kind of amalgam which Town Hall provided that night—blues, ballads, calypso, and jazz, mingled in what is now popular song."[51]

As the decade ended, New York's musical scene was complex and vibrant, including jazz, blues, pop, opera, and folk music in the city's clubs and concert halls and also, on warm Sunday afternoons, in Washington Square Park in Greenwich Village. "Everyone likes to go walking in the park on a Sunday afternoon, and nearly everyone likes to sing," the article "Sidewalk Hootenanny" in the February-March issue of *People's Songs* bulletin announced.[52]

Meanwhile, the Weavers, a new quartet, emerged in late 1948. Its members included Seeger and his colleague in the Almanac Singers Lee Hays, along with Fred Hellerman and Ronnie Gilbert. "I had met Fred Hellerman right after World War II," Seeger recalled. "He and Ronnie Gilbert had both started singing folk songs before the war, as counselors at the same summer camp. ... So now Ronnie, with her exciting contralto, and Fred, a gifted guitarist who could sing either high or low, joined their voices with my split tenor and Lee's big gospel bass." They kept busy through 1949, recording Hays's song "Wasn't That a Time" (which remained unissued) on the Charter label, and Seeger and Hays's "The Hammer Song" for the tiny Hootenanny Records. The songs expressed the group's antiwar and pacifist ideals. The Weavers also released on the Charter label a two-sided single, "The Peekskill Story," with songs and narration by Paul Robeson and Howard Fast. Following appearances at the Panel Room and the Penthouse on Astor Place, the fledgling quartet appeared with the Grito de Lares Youth Club at the "Peace On Earth" hootenanny on Christmas Eve 1949 at Webster Hall, 119 East 11th St. "We helped put on some of the world's best little hootenannies," Seeger remembered, "but in late '49 we were ready to break up. We had never intended to be a professional group. We were dead broke and about to go our separate ways."

Why not be good and commercial?

Lee Hays, The Weavers[1]

MAKING
A
BUSINESS
OUT
OF IT

Pete Seeger told the story over and over again. It was 1949, and the Weavers, newly formed, had reached a crossroads. In the Greenwich Village home of Seeger's parents-in-law, the group discussed their future. Playing political rallies and benefits was meaningful, but their following was small. After the violence of the Peekskill Riots, Seeger argued to his bandmates, Ronnie Gilbert, Lee Hays, and Fred Hellerman, that they needed to reach a broader audience to communicate their messages of civil rights and peace. If their impact remained minimal, he maintained, they had no reason to continue. He even made the bold suggestion that they consider performing in nightclubs and becoming professional singers. The others were unconvinced. They understood that they could not survive outside the commercial realm, but playing in swank nightclubs seemed too great a compromise to their identity as respectful practitioners of folk music. Undeterred, Seeger pressed on. Recalling his wife Toshi's idea, he proposed, "Look, I think Max Gordon would have me back at the Village Vanguard. Rather than go there by myself, let's go in as a group. If we split my salary four ways, we'd each get fifty dollars a week." Silence. The meeting ended after the quartet agreed to mull over the matter and reconvene.[2]

Then came the moment of truth. An American Labor Party (ALP) representative phoned People's Songs executive secretary Irwin Silber with a request: The party was planning a benefit concert and asked Silber to help them get Richard Dyer-Bennet, a traditional balladeer, to perform. Dyer-Bennet, a Decca artist, was popular and commercially successful, unlike most folksingers associated with People's Songs. Surely, he would draw a big crowd and help the party with fundraising. "Perhaps I can help you get him," Silber responded. "But in case he can't make it, how about getting Pete to do the concert?" The ALP representative replied, "Oh, we know Pete. He's sung on our sound truck for years. We need someone who can bring a mass audience. We need to raise money."[3]

Izzy Young outside the Folklore Center, October 1963. Described by Dave Van Ronk as a "clubhouse for the folk scene" and by Bob Dylan as the "citadel of Americana folk music," Young's Folklore Center on MacDougal Street sold records, books, and accessories. Young also posted notices about folk happenings, allowed itinerant musicians to pick up their mail at the store, and hosted informal jam sessions in his back room, creating a rendezvous in the epicenter of the revival for singers, journalists, agents, managers, producers, activists, and folkies alike. Photograph by David Gahr.

Making a Business Out of It

Seeger became irate as Silber relayed the conversation. "Here I was," he recalled, "trying to follow what I thought was a tactical, strategic course, and yet Dick Dyer-Bennet—who was making a career in traditional fashion—was of more use than me. That taught me something." Seeger realized that he needed to gain recognition to attract large crowds and make an impact in American society. He could still play in front of progressive groups in union halls and other local venues, but he would no longer shun the expanding folk music market-place.[4] "I decided to stop congratulating myself on not going commercial," Seeger declared. He and the other Weavers, along with Toshi, began to arrange bookings at nightclubs in the city.[5]

- - -

Business and consumer trends in New York reshaped the folk music industry from the late 1940s to the late 1950s, transforming the genre from an art form largely associated with leftist politics to a popular craze with mass appeal nationwide. The period also witnessed the establishment of numerous record companies and other commercial music organizations. Record labels included Folkways, founded by Moses Asch in 1948; Vanguard, by brothers Maynard and Seymour Solomon in 1950; Elektra, by Jac Holzman in 1950; and Riverside, by Orrin Keepnews in 1953. Other developments included the birth of *Sing Out!* magazine, founded by Irwin Silber, Pete Seeger, and Alan Lomax in 1950, and the opening of the Folklore Center in Greenwich Village by Izzy

opposite: The Weavers enjoyed commercial success for a brief spell during the early Cold War, playing in major nightclubs in New York City and eventually throughout the nation. The quartet, pictured here in Greenwich Village's Cafe Society in July 1951, appealed to large audiences with catchy renditions of traditional ballads and became a model for other folk music groups interested in attaining popularity.

below: *Sing Out!* founding editor Irwin Silber at his desk in the Folkways Records office in New York, ca. 1958. As co-founder and editor, Silber worked for *Sing Out!* from 1950 to 1967; he was also Associate Producer of Folkways Records from 1958-64. In 1968 he began to write on more directly political subjects for the radical left-wing newspaper the *Guardian*. Photograph by Diana Davies.

Young in 1957. Although these were all modest organizations at first, targeted at a niche audience, they nourished folk music in different ways and created a groundswell of interest by recording a variety of artists, producing albums, sponsoring concerts, and stimulating provocative debates about the role of songs in politics and culture writ large.

These were distinctively New York institutions, developing with the city's ascent as the international cultural capital of the world. Following World War II, New York supplanted Paris as the world's preeminent artistic center. Literature and the arts, both established and experimental, flowered in Midtown and Downtown. In publishing and radio, in journalism and television, in painting and jazz, in dance and theater, New York became a magnet for performers, writers, and artists. Folk music was an integral part of this heady brew. It represented, on one hand, an alternative set of values, widely regarded as an "authentic" antidote to a banal mass culture. On the other hand, during and after the Red Scare, folk music, to some, reflected an oppositional stance in politics, linked to leftist causes. Undoubtedly, by the late 1950s it was increasingly a component of show business. And therein was the tension.[6]

The expansion of the folk music industry also illuminated the growing entrepreneurial presence of Jews in the city. Asch, the Solomons, Holzman, Keepnews, Silber, Young, and other folk music businessmen and journalists, such as Harold Leventhal, Art D'Lugoff, and Robert Shelton, were all Jewish, though they were hardly a unified group. In fact, they often competed with each other and clashed over prevailing trends in the industry, demonstrating the values of dissent and argumentation that typified postwar Jewish culture in New York. For the most part second-generation in background, they also reflected a creative and sometimes paradoxical blend of the capitalist economic spirit and progressive political commitment that characterized Jewish culture in the city. Despite their differences, folk music captivated them. Their allegiance was profound and intense, and their institutions made New York the epicenter of the nationwide folk music revival by the late 1950s.[7]

THE BUSINESS AND POLITICS OF THE WEAVERS, 1948–1952

The Weavers made their nightclub debut during Christmas week of 1949 at the Village Vanguard, located at 178 Seventh Avenue South. Toshi Seeger, the quartet's temporary manager, brought them to Robert Hall Clothes for a fashion makeover, insisting that they wear dapper outfits. But it was hard to find suitable attire for the portly Hays. "We were wearing corduroy jackets and blue washable pants," Hays recalled. "I think that Toshi went out to the army-and-navy store and found something to fit me. ... I remember being a little baffled by the nightclub life, which was new to me." Toshi also negotiated the group's contract with Vanguard owner Max Gordon. The initial deal was $200 a week and free hamburgers. But when Gordon saw the number of hamburgers they were eating, he revised the terms to $250 a week and no free hamburgers.[8]

The Weavers were an immediate hit, and their early appearances marked a watershed not only in New York nightclub culture, but also in the folk music industry in general. The Village Vanguard had previously featured solo acts by a few folk performers, including Lead Belly, Josh White, Richard Dyer-Bennet, and Pete Seeger himself, but a quartet represented a change. For several weeks crowds filled the Vanguard to capacity, and critics were enthusiastic. *World-Telegram* columnist Robert W. Dana applauded Gordon for the audacious move and lavished praise on the Weavers, describing them as an entertaining group with an eclectic repertoire of blues, ballads, hoe-downs, work songs, prison songs, and originals. The quartet played the basement club every night except Mondays, captivating audiences with rousing renditions of Lead Belly's "Midnight Special" and the Spanish Civil War fighting song "Venga Jaleo." Dana singled out Seeger's banjo skills and stage presence: "Like a schoolboy fresh off the farm, when it's his turn to accentuate the positive with his instrument, he holds the drum part up to the microphone

Noted for his beautiful tenor voice, the minstrel Richard Dyer-Bennet gained the attention of New York audiences and critics alike with artistic interpretations of traditional English ballads and European and American folk songs. In 1949 Dyer-Bennet recorded *Richard Dyer-Bennett: Twentieth Century Minstrel* for Decca, helping to inspire the Weavers to become professional singers and shed their misgivings about the commercial marketplace.

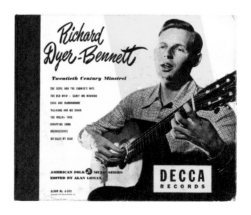

The Weavers made their breakthrough on the nightclub circuit during Christmas week of 1949 at Max Gordon's Village Vanguard, the jazz and comedy club in Lower Manhattan. Their lively shows at the Vanguard stirred crowds and earned them a contract with Decca, a prominent folk music label. Photograph by Steven Pinker.

following: The Weavers at Carnegie Hall, 1963. Photograph by Joe Alper.

and strums away." He also noted the crowd's involvement and the communal feeling. "Customers can't keep their feet still when the Weavers sing 'When the Saints Go Marching In,'" he remarked. In the *Daily Compass*, Jay Russell commended the quartet's "distinctive type of artistry" and observed that seven encores were typical. "Here is solid humanity bursting out in song. Here is down-to-earth stuff done with honesty, with buoyancy and sparkle," wrote Russell. The highest praise came from the Pulitzer Prize-winning writer, poet, and folk-song anthologist Carl Sandburg, brought to the Vanguard by Alan Lomax. "The Weavers are out of the grassroots of America. I salute them," Sandburg commented. "When I hear America singing, the Weavers are there."[9]

During the Vanguard performances, Harold Leventhal, a former promoter of Irving Berlin's songs, met the group backstage one night and, at Seeger's request, agreed to manage them. A child of Orthodox Jews from eastern Europe, Leventhal was raised on the Lower East Side and the Bronx. Formerly active in Zionist youth groups and, like Seeger, once a member of the Young Communist League, Leventhal was a veteran of labor battles in the 1930s and 1940s who developed an interest in folk music by reading Woody Guthrie's column in the *Daily Worker*. His stint with Irving Berlin gave him experience in the music industry and helped prepare him for a management position.[10]

In another coup for the Weavers, in 1950 bandleader Gordon Jenkins, staff musical director for Decca Records, based on the Upper West Side, visited the Village Vanguard and, immediately smitten, offered the group a recording

contract. Jenkins was an authoritative figure in pop music who had worked with such prominent musicians as Frank Sinatra, Louis Armstrong, and the Andrews Sisters. Decca, a premier folk music label since its establishment in 1934, boasted a stable of fine artists, including Burl Ives and Josh White, along with other popular entertainers, such as Bing Crosby and Gene Austin. In 1947 Alan Lomax became the editor of Decca's Folk Music Series and began reissuing earlier folk releases in the newer 33 1/3-rpm format.[11]

The Decca contract raised questions about the appeal of the Weavers. At a glance, the quartet seemed plain and unpolished, not the typical Decca group, but they possessed numerous qualities that contributed to their success. For one, the Weavers exhibited excellent chemistry. The members included a bass (Hays), a baritone (Hellerman), a split-tenor (Seeger), and an alto (Gilbert), and their personalities complemented each other. Hays, from Arkansas, was wry and irreverent. Hellerman, a guitarist and Brooklyn College graduate, was studious and affable. Gilbert, a Brooklyn native like Hellerman and formerly a secretary at CBS, was outgoing and magnetic. Seeger, a Harvard dropout, lanky and steady, tended to avoid social situations but showed a knack for involving audiences in sing-alongs. On stage they were decidedly unglamorous in style and appearance, but they were likable and radiated warmth. Their songs' simple arrangements, creative power, and robust content resonated strongly with audiences. Despite their disdain for material rewards, the musicians were fiercely competitive. "Performing commercially is something that makes you want to see if you can do it as well as the next fellow," Seeger told Hays.[12]

In May 1950 the Weavers recorded the 1941 Israeli soldiers' tune "Tzena, Tzena" and Lead Belly's "Goodnight, Irene" at Decca Studios. The group pruned out Lead Belly's verse about taking morphine from "Goodnight, Irene" and modified the chorus from "I'll get you in my dreams" to "I'll see you in my dreams." The songs skyrocketed on the charts. "Tzena, Tzena" reached number two the first week of July, and "Goodnight, Irene" became number one the following week, where it remained for four months, selling two million copies. Rave reviews poured in from national publications. Gilbert Millstein observed in *The New York Times*, "The most overpowering phenomenon in the music business these days is a lorn, whining ballad about a marriage gone sour, set in waltz tempo and called 'Goodnight, Irene.' . . . Some people in the trade believe that no other song ever sold so fast in so short a time." *Time* magazine commented, "Professional folk singing in the U.S. is mostly the province of a few long-haired purists who rarely get a hearing outside the clubs and recital hall where their small but fervent public gathers. Last week a group of four high-spirited folksters known as the Weavers had succeeded in shouting, twanging, and crooning

THE SUMMER OF 1950, NO AMERICAN COULD ESCAPE [GOODNIGHT, IRENE] UNLESS YOU PLUGGED UP YOUR EARS AND WENT OUT INTO THE WILDERNESS.

above: The Weavers on a New York City rooftop, December 1958. Photograph by David Gahr.

opposite: The Weavers achieved national popularity in 1950 with recordings of the Israeli soldiers' song "Tzena, Tzena" and Lead Belly's "Goodnight, Irene." Decca released these songs and two other hits on an EP in 1953, pictured here.

folk singing out of its cloistered corner in the commercial big time." Recordings of "Goodnight, Irene" were made by Frank Sinatra (Columbia, 175,000 sold), Dennis Day (Victor, 147,000), Jo Stafford (Capitol, 68,000), and the country singing duet Red Foley and Ernest Tubb (Decca, 95,000). "Goodnight, Irene" seemed to be on the radio all the time. "The summer of 1950, no American could escape that song unless you plugged up your ears and went out into the wilderness," Seeger recalled.[13]

The summer of 1950 saw the Weavers at the pinnacle of their commercial success. NBC offered them a weekly national television spot, and they were booked by the country's top nightclubs. They played Ciro's in Hollywood and the Shamrock in Houston and headlined ritzy joints in Los Angeles and Reno. In New York, the quartet moved uptown from the Vanguard to the tonier Blue Angel. At the Strand Theater on Broadway they did four or five sets a day and made $2,250 a week. "Although the Weavers had not lost their 'singing for the hell of it' quality," *Time* observed, "they looked back a little wistfully at the not-so-old Greenwich Village days." Fame affected each member differently, but, with the exception of Seeger, they all welcomed success to some degree. "While the rest of us were sleeping off the work (or excesses) of the night before," Hays quipped about their time on the road, "Pete would go out to historical sites." Seeger kept his distance from show business temptations. "People came up to me and asked, 'How does it feel to be a success?'" he noted.

"I felt kind of silly. To me, I was a bigger success nine years before, when the Almanacs sang for the Transport Workers Union in Madison Square Garden."[14]

As the Weavers rode high on their newfound popularity, the anticommunist Red Scare intensified in the nation, and, just as their commercial rise was sudden, their blacklisting and fall from stardom were abrupt and ruinous. After a brief hiatus, the group began to incorporate some of their political material, particularly Spanish Civil War songs, into concert performances. Audiences continued to applaud and ask for more, but not everyone approved. A paid government informant, Harvey Matusow, advised the FBI to monitor the Weavers. The Bureau already had a file on the quartet, filled with army intelligence reports and articles from the anticommunist magazine *Counterattack*. Pete Kameron, music business veteran and assistant to Harold Leventhal, urged Seeger to avoid performing at hootenannies tinged with left-wing politics. "Right now we've got a real problem to get you cleared and give you a good reputation. A brand new one. Your old reputation has got to go," Kameron coun- seled Seeger. The group's appearances at political events decreased, and some of their old allies on the Left criticized them for their shifting stance. They were also scolded by *Sing Out!* editor Irwin Silber for singing the songs of black America without having a black member.

Personal circumstances worsened for Seeger in the months following *Counterattack*'s June 1950 publication of *Red Channels: The Report of Communist Influence on Radio and Television*, a tract that destroyed the careers of hundreds of individuals. *Red Channels* listed Seeger 13 times—the only Weaver to be named. Though the group still had many hits on the national charts, the backlash against them commenced. They lost a television contract. Concerts were canceled. The *New York World Telegram* published an article on their earlier political activities, and the FBI put them under surveillance. In February 1952, Matusow, encouraged by *Counterattack*, testified as a friendly witness before the House Un-American Activities Committee (HUAC) that three of the Weavers were members of the Communist Party. (He reported that Hays had quit the party.) The quartet lost radio play and Decca termi- nated their contract. "Then we went lower and lower as the blacklist crowded us in. Finally, we were down to places like Daffy's Bar and Grill on the outskirts of Cleveland," Seeger remembered. The Weavers disbanded in 1952.[15]

The Weavers' rise and fall was spectacular, a mirror of the fluidity in the music industry and the anxiety in the polit- ical sphere. "The Weavers had been propelled into fame so quickly that they never quite understood what hit them," commented Oscar Brand, who championed the group on his local WNYC radio show. Brand, also named in *Red Channels*, was particularly sympathetic. "They never really sought the

Published in 1950 during the Red Scare, *Red Channels: Communist Influence on Radio and Television* named Pete Seeger as a "subversive" political figure in the music industry. The listing led to the temporary demise of his group, the Weavers, by 1952, resulting in lost radio play, cancelled concerts, and the termination of their Decca contract.

OSCAR BRAND

There is no question that folk music in the early days after World War II had become left-sponsored, and that folk performers often appeared at political action committee meetings, labor party rallies, and Communist party functions. A cruel anti-communist joke described two party members arranging a meeting: "You bring the Negro, I'll bring the folksingers." Why did the folksingers appear? Usually, it was the promise of remuneration, or to keep the goodwill of the people who provided the bookings. Whatever the reasons, including sincere left-wing sympathies, the record shows an uncommon number of folksingers, and their songs, peopling the activities of the left wing.

By 1948 a derogatory mention in Counterattack was enough to cause a performer to lose his or her jobs. Mention in Counterattack, coupled with a few letters or postcards to the networks, usually resulted in the end of a career in mass communications. Soon American Business Consultants provided the entertainment world with an extremely serviceable publication, perfect for organizing a permanent blacklist.

On June 22, 1950, they published the 213-page booklet called Red Channels, The Report of Communist Influence in Radio and Television. The effect of this compilation was immediate and devastating. As the Saturday Review pointed out, in commenting about Red Channels, "To accuse is enough."

It is possible that I am one of the few performers extant who was blacklisted by both the Left and the Right. I was among the chosen 151 listed in Red Channels for having appeared before many left-wing groups as a performer, along with many of my friends, including Josh White, Paul Robeson, Pete Seeger, and Burl Ives. Having my then-ample weekly income cut to "$0," I was fortunate enough to have royalty income from "A Guy Is a Guy," which was my Doris Day hit at the time, and which enabled me to take off for

Canada, and then Europe, until the doors began to open
again for me. I escaped being compelled to testify before
the investigating committees largely because I was able to
convince them that I could not give them the information
they wanted of me.

I had also started broadcasting my "Folksong Festival"
program in December 1945, for which I celebrated my 69th
continuous year on the air in December 2014. Even during
my traveling days, I managed to ensure that the program
was broadcast week after week, month after month, and year
after year.

Throughout my career, countless other programs and
performances came and went, but the Folksong Festival, for
which neither I nor any of my guests has ever been paid,
remained a home base for me and a haven for all of my guests
who found no other platform on which to perform during the
late 1940s and into the 1950s. Blacklisting is a despicable
art. To its enormous credit, at no time did WNYC attempt
to censor either the content or the guests on my program.
If for that alone, WNYC will always have my respect and
appreciation.

Oscar Brand © 2014

– – –

*Oscar Brand was an intimate of Woody Guthrie, Lead Belly, Josh
White, Burl Ives, Alan Lomax, and Pete Seeger, whose collaborations, beginning in New York in 1940, provided the inspiration for the national folk music revival. The Folksong Festival
radio show, now in its 70th consecutive year, began airing on
WNYC in 1945. Virtually every major folksinger has made his or
her first New York radio appearance on his program, including
The Weavers, Odetta, Joan Baez, and Bob Dylan. Oscar, co-founder and curator of the Songwriters Hall of Fame and a two-time
Peabody Award Honoree, inaugurated the first weekly Hootenanny
Concerts in New York in 1946, recorded more than 100 record
albums, produced some 75 documentary films, hosted dozens of
national radio and television shows, composed music for Broadway and film, authored 11 best-selling books, and served on the
board that created Sesame Street. He has delighted audiences in
countless concerts throughout North America, and his songs are
sung throughout the world. The Canadian version of his signature song, "Something to Sing About," is beloved as the second
national anthem of Canada.*

blinding limelight which illuminated them. They accepted the rewards with hesitation and with ceaseless introspective questioning. And when they were finally struck down in full flight by the blacklisting apparatus of the mass communications industry, they may even have been a little relieved—although regretful that their public would be deprived of their spirited wares."[16]

Despite their plummet, New York folk music entrepreneurs immediately recognized the economic significance of the Weavers. As *Time* observed, they were "the most imitated group in the business." The Weavers created a model for commercial success. Their catchy and smooth renditions of old songs showed the potential of folk music in a growing marketplace. As folklorists continued to collect and preserve songs from different regions of the nation, the Weavers aimed to make them popular. In the process, they introduced Americans to part of their cultural heritage. The Weavers were the filters and conduits between Library of Congress field recordings and millions of Americans listening to songs on the radio or to vinyl albums on phonographs. But in making songs appealing to large audiences, they manipulated melodies, changed lyrics, and refashioned arrangements, effacing regional accents and ironing out the subtleties and rawness of traditional ballads. The Weavers made songs modern, and, as the quartet gained a measure of fame and fortune, they generated some resentment. As mass culture expanded in the prosperous 1950s, debates continued in New York about the effect of commercial institutions on folk music.[17]

THE ENTREPRENEURIALISM AND IDEALISM OF NEW YORK'S FOLK MUSIC RECORD COMPANIES

The success of the Weavers stemmed from the support of a nexus of entrepreneurs and enthusiasts in New York. But their bestselling albums also illustrated broader consumer trends. Folk music was part of an expanding market for recorded music. National record sales of all genres climbed in the early 1950s, sparked by the growth of middle-class purchasing power, along with the emergence of smaller labels serving niche markets, such as rhythm and blues, country, gospel, jazz, and polka. After the demise of the Weavers, Decca retained an interest in folk music, recording marine biologist turned folksinger Sam Hinton for their Children's Series, for instance. But to a considerable extent, the ongoing appeal of folk music was the result of initiatives by new record

following: (From left) Folkways Records founder Moses Asch with Ed Badeaux and Irwin Silber, May 1966. Photograph by David Gahr.

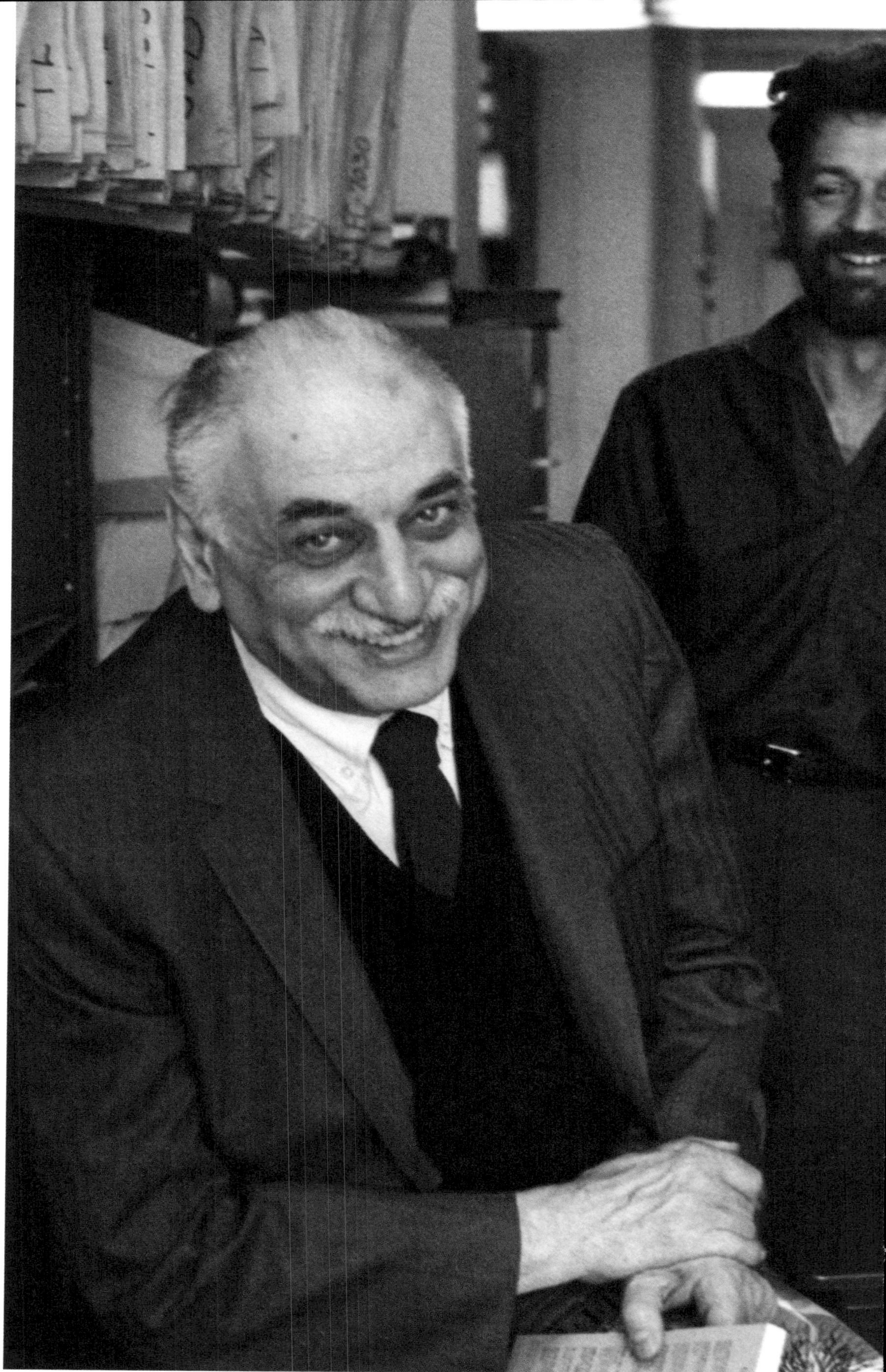

companies in New York City established by Moses Asch, Maynard and Seymour Solomon, Jac Holzman, and Orrin Keepnews.

Moses "Moe" Asch was a critical figure in the folk music revival. Born in Warsaw, Poland, in 1905, Asch was the son of Yiddish novelist Sholem Asch. His family moved to the suburbs of Paris in 1912 and then to New York during World War I. In the 1920s Asch studied electronics in Germany and returned to New York to begin a career as an audio engineer. After opening a radio repair shop during the Great Depression, he took a position at New York's leftist radio station WEVD recording programs on acetate disks for broadcast. In 1940 physicist and humanitarian Albert Einstein, a friend of his father, encouraged him to pursue a career that involved his recording machine. Asch embarked on a mission to create an "encyclopedia" of the world's sounds. At first, to address a gap in the marketplace and the requests of WEVD listeners, he specialized in Yiddish recordings on his own label, Asch Records, founded in 1940. During the war years, Asch developed relationships with Lead Belly, Woody Guthrie, and Pete Seeger, and he became their patron and critic, friend and producer. To some degree he shaped their careers, and they all expressed their indebtedness. Soon Asch's operations included both the Asch and Disc labels, as well as Asch-Stinson, launched in 1943 with Herbert Harris and his Stinson Trading Company. In a 1946 interview with *Time*, Asch criticized the strategy of major record labels and discussed his own outlook. "I'm not interested in individual hits," he remarked. "To me a catalog of folk expression is the most important thing." But, overextended, Asch Records declared bankruptcy in 1948. Under the name of his secretary, Marian Distler, Asch soon inaugurated the Folkways Records and Service Corporation. Though his bankruptcy prohibited him from starting a new label, he in effect ran the company from its establishment in 1948 until his death in 1986.[18]

The objective of Folkways Records was to document and record the sounds of the world. The Folkways philosophy was fundamentally egalitarian and the method anthropological. In the spirit of an ethnographer, Asch did not rank individual musicians or cultures in a hierarchy, but rather embraced artists with talent, integrity, and vision and sought to chronicle the expression of all groups, not just American and European, but also Asian, African, and Latin American. Albums included detailed liner notes that provided synopses of the singers and cultures. Asch particularly liked to work with mavericks and individualists, iconoclasts and dissidents. Not surprisingly, he became close to Pete Seeger and ultimately recorded more than 50 of his records. But the Folkways catalogue contained little explicitly political material. Asch viewed himself as a product of the Popular

below: Niche folk music record companies, such as Folkways, Vanguard, and Elektra, produced albums for a coterie of dedicated "folkies." Nationally prominent labels like Decca targeted a larger audience of both devoted fans and casual listeners, manufacturing polished fare in competition for market dominance. Occasionally Decca issued "best of" albums that compiled notable songs by a particular singer or group, as this 1964 brochure illustrates.

above: Moe Asch in his
New York office, ca. 1950.
Photograph by Diana Davies.

opposite below: Unlike
executives of major record
labels, who tended to focus on
popular albums with top hits,
Folkways Records founder Moe
Asch embraced a cosmopolitan
view of music exemplified by
this 1958 bulletin.

Front tradition that celebrated the humanity of all: to record and present the musical expression of common people, he believed, was in effect a political statement.[19]

Above all, Asch believed in the importance of service to specific communities. As mass culture forms of expression—hit songs, radio serials, pulp fiction, television sitcoms, and Hollywood movies—targeted large and anonymous audiences in the 1950s, Asch tailored his albums to particular groups and discriminating individuals. His method represented a challenge to the major record labels that endeavored to create a homogeneous listenership. Asch explained, "The man [who] ... will render service in exploiting local talent and issuing records for that community finds a customer for his product, by servicing that community." He added, "New customers cannot be developed by the archaic method of standardizing performer and composition as the [major labels] tend to do."[20]

In his relationship with artists, Asch stressed the value of collaboration while he respected their individual creativity. Like William H. Whyte in his bestselling *The Organization Man* (1956), Asch was critical of the dominant approach in corporate America that valued the organization over the individual in the decision-making process. He sometimes spoke of Folkways contributors as an extended Jewish family. As they pursued a common goal, they argued and debated relentlessly. Through dispute, they refined their thoughts. Asch oriented the company around personal relationships and trust, and, though he lacked the finances to lure major musicians, he gave his contributors autonomy. Folkways represented a blend of communal and individualistic ideas, similar to eastern European Jewish progressive values.[21]

In his sales and marketing strategies, Asch aimed at specific audiences. Though he collaborated with music retailer Sam Goody, he understood that wholesale outfits generally lacked interest in his esoteric catalog. Indeed, it was hard to find Folkways albums in record stores outside of major cities. Instead, he appealed to scholars, librarians, and music educators, and several times a year attended major academic conferences to sell his material. For example, he sold records at gatherings of the Music Library Association, the Society for Ethnomusicology, the American Anthropological Association, the American Library Association, and the Modern Language Association. To librarians, his primary clients, he promoted recordings of spoken word, language instruction, and children's music; to teachers at the elementary and secondary school levels, he encouraged the use of specific albums in curriculum development, teacher training, workshops, conventions, and exhibits. He also reached out to aquariums, science and natural science museums, and art museums. No one accused Moe Asch of pandering to a mass audience.[22]

In a catalogue that boasted records of outsized importance by Guthrie, Lead Belly, and Seeger, no Folkways album was as significant as Harry Smith's *Anthology of American Folk Music*, issued in 1952. Born and raised in the Pacific Northwest, Smith was an eccentric painter, filmmaker, anthropologist, and folklorist with a collection of thousands of early 78-rpm recordings from the 1920s and 1930s. He showed special interest in the music of Appalachia, the Mississippi Delta, and the North Carolina Piedmont. At the encouragement of Asch, Smith selected and arranged material from his collection into an anthology with the goal of providing a sweeping document of American music. He eschewed prevalent trends in the industry to categorize songs by race into African-American "blues" and white "hillbilly" catalogs. Inspired instead by the unifying power of music, Smith classified recordings into "ballads," "social music," and "songs," and in the process eliminated racial distinctions and culturally constructed musical genres. The arrangement of the songs blurred differences among spirituals, work songs, field hollers, and ballads from different regions of the nation, illuminating aspects of the cross-fertilization of styles between races and a broader common heritage. The result of Smith's labor was a three-volume anthology comprised of six records that included a total of 84 songs. The tracks, commercially recorded by black and white musicians between 1927 and 1932 for smaller markets, became part of the canon

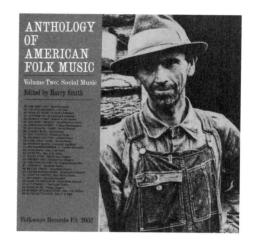

Released by Folkways in 1952, Harry Smith's *Anthology of American Folk Music* became a seminal work in the folk music revival. In six albums, Smith compiled 84 folk songs, all originally commercially recorded between 1927 and 1932, that illustrated the rich musical traditions of Appalachia, the Mississippi Delta, and the North Carolina Piedmont.

of the nationwide folk music revival at the end of the decade.[23]

Smith's *Anthology* was seminal. It reintroduced many notable blues and old-time music artists, including Dock Boggs, Mississippi John Hurt, Clarence "Tom" Ashley, Blind Willie Johnson, and Charlie Poole and the North Carolina Ramblers. Smith selected some of their finest recordings, introducing New Yorkers and other Americans to their work. Because of the rather steep price tag, the set was mostly purchased by libraries and for scattered personal collections. The anthology had an immeasurable effect on many owners, such as citybillies Mike Seeger, John Cohen, and Ralph Rinzler. They studied it intensely and performed tracks faithfully in their groups, the New Lost City Ramblers and the Greenbriar Boys, in effect becoming anthologists themselves.[24]

As Moe Asch expanded Folkways' impressive catalog, often recycling earlier releases, Seymour and Maynard Solomon launched Vanguard Records in 1950 at 80 East 11th Street, initially specializing in classical music albums. Vanguard branched out to include jazz, show tunes, and a smattering of folk albums. In 1954 the Solomons released two albums by folk- and gospel singer Brother John Sellers, *Brother John Sellers* and *Sings Blues and Folk Songs*. These records straddled the permeable lines between folk, blues, and jazz. On *Brother John Sellers*, jazz musicians Walter Page, Ruby Braff, Freddie Greene, and Jo Jones backed Sellers. "In the rich contribution of the Negro people to American music, there have been constant cross-currents between gospel songs, blues, and what have come to be known as folk songs," producer John Hammond explained in his album notes. "A great achievement of John Sellers is that he has brought these traditions together, and yet does each with the deepest feeling and most authentic style." In 1954 Vanguard released another Sellers record, *Jack of Diamonds (and other folk songs and blues)*, but did not become fully identified with folk music until the release of the Weavers' 1955 Christmas reunion concert at Carnegie Hall.[25]

While the Solomons initially had scant interest in folk music, Jac Holzman, founder of Elektra Records in 1950, showed a commitment from the start. Raised in New York, Holzman dropped out of St. John's College in Annapolis, Maryland, to open a record store in Greenwich Village. "Greenwich Village was the symbol of free living and free loving," he reflected. "I longed to live there. I walked the narrow streets, some of cobblestone, and found a room for $5 a week in a walkup at 40 Grove Street in the residential part of the West Village." His first Elektra album was *New Songs* by John Gruen in 1951. His store, the Record Loft, became an outlet for Elektra Records as well as other folk music labels. "Sooner or later everyone in the very narrow world of city folkdom came into the store, singers, guitar players, collectors, aficionados like George Pickow, a photographer, whose

above: Columbia Records largely disassociated from folk music between World War II and the early 1960s, but this 1952-53 catalog includes some folk music albums issued by the label in the interim.

following: (From left) Fred Gerlach, Dave Van Ronk, Sonny Terry, and Brownie McGhee perform for a live studio audience on George Lorrie's radio show on WNCN, August 3, 1959. In the late 1950s and early 1960s, New York City radio stations, including WNYC and WBAI, broadcast an increasing number of folk music shows. Hosted by Oscar Brand, Henrietta Yurchenco, Bob Fass, and others, they provided a critical forum for folk musicians. Photograph by Aaron Rennert.

wife [Jean Ritchie] was from a family of Kentucky mountain singers," Holzman continued. "Ken Goldstein dropped by, and that was the start of a long friendship. Ken was far more knowledgeable than I about traditional folk music—he knew all the Folkways titles, advised me to get an index of the Library of Congress collections, and generally pointed me in useful directions." Captivated by the traditional sound, Holzman issued 10-inch albums by artists from Appalachia and the Piedmont region including Jean Ritchie, Frank Warner, and Sonny Terry. Elektra's recording of Tom Paley's *Folk Songs from the Southern Appalachians* (1953) became a landmark in the introduction of a Northern audience to Southern white vernacular music.[26]

In 1954, after producing seven or eight records, Holzman decided to focus on record production rather than retail, so he closed the Record Loft and moved Elektra around the corner to larger offices at 361 Bleecker Street. Needing extra financing, he invited wealthy former classmate Leonard Ripley to become a partner, and Elektra became a center for gatherings of folk musicians. "Folkies would meet with cheap wine and beer and no eats, smallish rooms, just large enough to have some elbow room so you could play a guitar or banjo, and most everybody played and sang," recalled Theo Bikel, an Elektra artist. Though it quickly became a premier folk music label with national distribution, Elektra was not able to break even on its balance sheet until 1956.[27]

The city's jazz scene provided another launch pad for folk music. Numerous record company executives combined folk and jazz, not unusual for such nightclubs as Cafe Society, the Village Vanguard, and, later, the Village Gate. In 1953 Orrin Keepnews and Bill Grauer founded Riverside Records, located at 553 West 51st Street, as a blues and jazz label. They began with reissues of recordings by Jelly Roll Morton, Ma Rainey, and King Oliver, and then expanded to jazz contemporaries like Randy Weston, Cannonball Adderley, and Charlie Byrd. Within a few years, they started to feature albums by such folk artists as Ed McCurdy, Cynthia Gooding, and Peggy Seeger. Similarly, Prestige Records, founded by Bob Weinstock in 1949 as a jazz label and located at 446 West 50th Street, also began including folk music in the early 1960s.

Another important folk label was Tradition Records, formed by Patrick "Paddy" Clancy, with his brothers Liam and Tom, in 1956 in Greenwich Village. Originally from Ireland, Paddy and Tom had immigrated to Canada in 1947, and moved to Greenwich Village in 1951 as stage and television actors. To raise money for their small theater production company, they began staging "Midnight Special" concerts at the Cherry Lane Theatre, where they performed upbeat Irish drinking songs. Their younger brother Liam joined them in New York in early 1956. Funded by the wealthy Diane Guggenheim Hamilton and advised by Kenneth Goldstein, an army veteran who had

above: Patrick "Paddy" Clancy served as president and director of Tradition Records, a label that specialized in folk music from 1955 to 1966. He also joined with his brothers, Liam and Tom, and Tommy Makem to form the highly popular Irish group the Clancy Brothers and Tommy Makem. The group helped spark broad interest in Irish folk music and played in major venues, such as Carnegie Hall, as this 1963 concert poster shows. Photographed by John Halpern.

opposite: *Sing Out!* magazine, co-founded in New York by Irwin Silber in 1950 as the successor to *People's Songs*, embodied the connection between folk music and leftist politics and published many activist songs in support of civil rights, pacifism, and other progressive causes. The publication's title came from the third verse of the "The Hammer Song," by Pete Seeger and Lee Hays, which was published on the cover of the first issue in May 1950.

done market research for Fairfield Publications and would soon become one of their record producers, the Clancys decided to launch their own label, Tradition Records. Liam explained, "An office was rented at 131 Christopher Street, a half block from Paddy's apartment. ... It all seemed too easy, but then, with Guggenheim money, many things seem easy." They began by releasing their own album of traditional Irish folk songs with fellow Irishman Tommy Makem, and soon after they produced Odetta's first solo LP, *Odetta Sings Ballads and Blues*. (Bob Dylan later cited this album as his inspiration to choose folk music over rock n' roll.)[28] Other artists recorded by Tradition included Alan Lomax, Ed McCurdy, Paul Clayton, and Oscar Brand. The Clancy brothers sold the Tradition catalog to Everest Records in 1966, several years after their own folk group, the Clancy Brothers and Tommy Makem, was signed to Columbia Records.

FOLK MUSIC TAKES ROOT

The initiatives of New York record companies expanded folk music culture in the city. The press played an important role: just as the Weavers were launching their career at the Village Vanguard, the folk magazine *Sing Out!* emerged from the ashes of People's Songs. Sponsored by People's Artists and located at 106 East 14th Street, the monthly magazine's first issue (May 1950), 16 pages in a small format, promised to connect folk music and radical politics. "We propose to devote ourselves to the creation, growth and distribution of something new, yet not so new, since its beginnings have been visible, or rather—audible, for some years now. We call it 'People's Music,'" editor Robert Wolfe explained. "In these pages each month we intend to include union songs ... songs of the Negro people ... songs of other nations," and much else. The sheet music for "The Hammer Song" graced the first cover. Irwin Silber, a mainstay of People's Songs, emerged in late 1951 as the editor and continued as the magazine struggled through the decade.[29] Under his leadership, the publication combined music and politics with a particular interest in civil rights and the peace movement as the Korean War continued until 1953. Although financial problems forced cancellation of three issues during the summer of 1953, after another publishing hiatus during 1954, Silber decided to switch to a 32-page quarterly format with the fall issue, which enabled *Sing Out!* to continue into the next decade.

The non-folk press also played an important role in spreading the word about the events in the Village. *The Village Voice*, founded in late 1955, covered the local culture, but had little interest in the folk scene. Soon, however, reviewers for *The New York Times*, in particular Robert Shelton, would fill the gap. Born in Chicago in 1926, Robert

WE PROPOSE TO DEVOTE OURSELVES TO THE CREATION, GROWTH AND DISTRIBUTION OF SOMETHING NEW, YET NOT SO NEW, SINCE ITS BEGINNINGS HAVE BEEN VISIBLE, OR RATHER— AUDIBLE, FOR SOME YEARS NOW. WE CALL IT 'PEOPLE'S MUSIC.'

opposite: Pete Seeger and Irwin Silber in the offices of *Sing Out!* magazine, March 1962. Photograph by David Gahr.

Shelton Shapiro arrived in New York in 1951 and began work as a copy boy at *The New York Times*. Using the simple byline "Shelton," his writings began to appear in the paper in 1956. In 1958 he began to review concerts, records, and festivals under the name Robert Shelton.

New venues for performances also began to open. In 1950 Columbia University's Institute of Arts and Sciences staged a series of concerts, part of their Folk Song Festival, at McMillin Theater, starting with Burl Ives on October 1st, followed by Josef Marais and Miranda in December. The next year, Josh White, Susan Reed, and Richard Dyer-Bennet performed.

Throughout the 1950s, as the market for folk music grew, Lou Gordon, a veteran of the Spanish Civil War and a labor organizer, began organizing folk concerts for professional musicians at the Cherry Lane Theatre, 38 Commerce Street, at midnights following a play by the Clancy Brothers. The initial show on March 5, 1954, known as "Swapping Song Fair," featured Oscar Brand, Jean Ritchie, and Robin Roberts, followed by Trinidad Steel Band, Cynthia Gooding, Sonny Terry, Brownie McGhee, and Reverend Gary Davis. The shows later moved to the Circle-in-the-Square at 5 Sheridan Square (Seventh Avenue and West 4th Street), where they included Martha Schlamme, a calypso show with Lord Invader, Ed McCurdy, the Kossoy Sisters (Irene and Ellen), Tune Tellers, Theo Bikel, and the Clancy Brothers. Swapping Song Fair, a concert series started by the Clancy Brothers, organized "'Bound for Glory': A Musical Tribute to Woody Guthrie" at Pythian Hall in March 1956, with Pete Seeger, Lee Hays, Ed McCurdy, Reverend Gary Davis, and other folk musicians. In 1956 Swapping Song Fair moved uptown to 305 West 44th Street and staged concerts by Josh White, Richard Dyer-Bennet, and Pete Seeger. Around the same time, producer Art D'Lugoff staged "The Midnite Special" evenings at the Actor's Playhouse (Seventh Avenue off Sheridan Square), then at Circle-in-the-Square, with Earl Robinson, Betty Sanders, Leon Bibb, and the Wayfarers. D'Lugoff also organized a flamenco night with 'Nita Scheer and Company.

D'Lugoff also organized a series of calypso concerts throughout the city in 1956, taking advantage of the calypso fad, and later included Brooklyn-born Lord Burgess (aka Irving Burgie, the author of early Belafonte hits) in his mammoth "The Whole World Sings" midnight event at Carnegie Hall in November 1958. The program included Leon Bibb, Theo Bikel, Pat and Tom Clancy, Billy Faier, Cynthia Gooding, Vince Martin, the Tarriers, and various other prominent local performers, indicating the diversity of folk styles. "Folkniks of New York had themselves an aural hall at Carnegie Hall Saturday night with 'The Whole World Sings,' one of the most showmanly ideas ever presented in the folk music concert field," according to a review by Len Levinson.[30]

THE FOLKLORE CENTER

"Israel G. Young, a young bookseller with ideas (and possibly idioms) will soon issue his second catalog of folklore and folk song from his office at 782 Broadway, New York City," Benjamin Botkin and William Tyrrell wrote in their column in *New York Folklore Quarterly* in the spring of 1957. "From his observation as a bookseller, publisher (The Folklore Press), and teacher of traditional longways dances, he has a feeling that there are going to be 'some changes (and not just square dance changes) made' and that new forces and movements are about to burgeon in the American folklore field. Such progress we can always use." Their prophecy would quickly become reality, with important consequences for the folk revival.[31]

Israel "Izzy" G. Young was born in 1928 on Manhattan's Lower East Side and grew up in the Bronx. As a student at the Bronx High School of Science, he became involved with Margot Mayo's American Square Dance Group, which connected him with members of the city's developing folk music scene, including Pete Seeger, Tom Glazer, Lead Belly, Woody Guthrie, and Oscar Brand—although he had no interest in the politics of the Communist Party that many of those musicians shared. As a young man, he worked at his father's Brooklyn bakery and at a Catskills resort during the summers; he briefly studied pre-med at Brooklyn College, but never graduated. In the mid-1950s, Young met folk producer Kenneth Goldstein— it was this connection that steered him to collecting folklore books, and he issued his first catalog in 1955. In 1957, nearing the age of 30, he opened his own store specializing

below: (From left) Dave Van Ronk, Bob Yellin, and Roy Berkeley at the Folklore Center, November 1957. Photograph by Aaron Rennert.

opposite above: Izzy Young inside The Folklore Center, August 1960. Photograph by David Gahr.

opposite below: Catalog of folksong books in paperback, published by the Folklore Center, ca. 1960.

in folk music material. "For many years folk song fans have said, 'Wouldn't it be wonderful if there were one place which sold everything available in the folk song field?' Now, a young man in New York has come along and answered the question," Irwin Silber happily announced in *Sing Out!* in early 1957. "Israel G. Young, a bookseller and publisher, has just opened The Folklore Center at 110 MacDougal Street, in New York City. The Center, at present, is primarily a bookshop, although Young also stocks some folk records and eventually hopes to carry a full line of everything which might interest the folk song lover." Young kept a detailed record of his comings and goings, writing in late February 1957: "I signed the lease for my new store last week and I am all ready to open up on April 6—[Bob] Harris will get rid of his 10-inch [Stinson] LPs (he is switching over to 12-inch LP) in my store and I will be able to sell them for $1.00—this should be a tremendous beginning offer that will make me many friends and also see who is on my side in Folk Music. ... I love the future."[32]

Izzy might have had some initial thoughts of making money, but he was mostly interested in promoting folk music in all forms—books, records, instruments, concerts—and the Folklore Center quickly became the heartbeat not just of the local folk scene, but also of the nation's. Liam Clancy recalled dropping by the Folklore Center "where the banjos and guitars were going at it. Paul Clayton was there singing whaling songs with his friend Jo El. It turned into a party as it always did at Izzy's place." In early 1959, Young began his regular column, "Frets and Frails," in *Sing Out!,* which was basically a gossip column that kept the readers informed about the developing scene. "When Izzy opened that little hole, there was suddenly a place where everyone went, and it became a catalyst for all sorts of things," Dave Van Ronk observed. "There were picking sessions, and Izzy even held a few concerts there to help out singers who needed a gig and couldn't find one elsewhere."[33]

The Folklore Center became the main outlet for more new folk magazines, including *Caravan* and *Gardyloo.* Folk enthusiast Lee Hoffman had developed an interest in science fiction, and in early 1957, she edited a special folk music issue of the science fiction magazine *CHOOG,* which evolved into *Caravan* with its August issue. Hoffman featured articles by local folk performers, including Dave Van Ronk, who began with a highly critical essay about Elektra Records and its stable of performers that included Theo Bikel, Josh White, and Cynthia Gooding. "*Caravan* became our forum," Van Ronk later explained, "with page upon page of theoretical argument about the current stance of the modern urban folk musician or listener." Hoffman relinquished *Caravan* to banjo player Billy Faier in early 1959, when it became more of a scholarly publication, until it folded in mid-1960. Meanwhile, in April 1959, Hoffman initiated the mimeographed *Gardyloo,* which also had a Greenwich Village focus and served as a fanzine for the emerging old-time string band, the New Lost City Ramblers.[34]

Folk music in Greenwich Village was becoming more eclectic and dynamic, with new performance venues opening in rapid succession. In 1957 Van Ronk and a few Village friends launched the Folksingers Guild at 13 West 17th Street when they got tired of working for free at Rick Allmen's Cafe Bizarre, one of the first local folk clubs. "The obvious problem with forming a protective organization for workers in the folk industry was that at that point Rick Allmen was the sole capitalist on the scene, and even he was only rather fecklessly exploiting anybody," Van Ronk explained. "We were basically a trade union with no bosses, and we realized pretty quickly that we would have to be our own bosses, and began putting on concerts." Their first concert in late December at Adelphi Hall, 74 Fifth Avenue, included Roger Abrahams, Van Ronk, Roy Berkeley, Gina Glazer, and Bob Yellin. A number of other concerts soon followed, along with a series of symposiums with Tony Schwartz, Jean Ritchie, and Margot Mayo at the Old Chelsea School in 1958. On April 24, 1958, the Folksingers Guild organized a concert at Mills College Theater, 66 Fifth Avenue, with Frank Hamilton, Tony Saletan, Harry and Jeanie West, and the Greenbriar Boys. In late June, Tom Paley and John Cohen joined Berkeley for "Folkmusic at Midnite" at the Sullivan St. Playhouse, 181

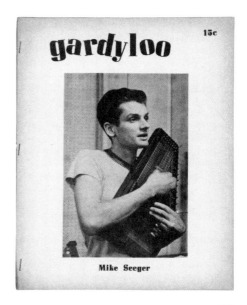

Mike Seeger

THE SHANTY BOYS

above: Formatted like a fanzine, *Caravan* was founded in 1957, also by Lee Hoffman. It served as a forum for modern urban folksingers, running articles, letters, reviews, concert announcements, advertisements for guitar and banjo lessons, and polemical columns by Dave Van Ronk, Barry Kornfeld, and Roger Lass. The magazine's circulation peaked at an impressive 2,000 just before Shaw sold it to banjo player Billy Faier in 1959.

Sullivan Street. "One way and another, the Guild was a way for us to pick up a few bucks to establish ourselves, and to learn our craft," Van Ronk recollected. "There were a lot of fans and amateurs involved, but there was a core of people who really wanted to be professional folksingers, and the Guild was essentially our support group."

By the end of the 1950s, folk music was established as a pillar of New York City's music scene. And the business of folk both encouraged and fed off the continuous influx of new talent like Baltimore-born, upstate New York-bred guitarist Erik Darling. Darling, who moved to New York to live with his mother at the age of 16, soon began visiting Washington Square with his guitar on Sunday afternoons. "The singers of folk songs were New Yorkers, all ages, all colors, all sizes," he recalled. Darling soaked in such local influences as Brand's WNYC radio programs and shows at Town Hall and the Village Vanguard, along with mambo bands at the Palladium. "We were constantly picking up new kinds of songs: calypso, blues, Elizabethan ballads, old mountain tunes. ... It was like getting to experience different parts of the person I was going to be." He also hung around Peter Carbone's guitar shop at Bleecker and MacDougal. A skilled banjo and guitar player, Darling appeared on various records as one of the few local session folk musicians. He joined Roger Sprung and Bob Carey as part of the interracial Folksay Trio, who recorded for Stinson in 1953, and also teamed with Mary Travers and

opposite above: Started in 1959 by folk music fan Lee Hoffman, *Gardyloo*, a mimeographed magazine distributed in Izzy Young's Folklore Center, exemplified the do-it-yourself, nonprofessional spirit of the folk music revival. It lasted only six issues and served in part as a promotional tool for the "citybilly" group the New Lost City Ramblers, the trio that initially consisted of Mike Seeger, Tom Paley, and John Cohen.

below: Lee Hoffman Shaw, editor of Village folk magazines *Caravan* and *Gardyloo*, 1957-60. Photograph by Aaron Rennert.

Tommy Geraci as the Song Swappers on a few albums for Folkways. Then in 1955 he joined the Tarriers with Carey and Alan Arkin (later of screen fame). Originally a quartet known as the Tunetellers, the Tarriers were New York's first commercially successful folk trio.

With the assistance of local concert promoter Art D'Lugoff, who became their manager, the Tarriers signed a recording contract with Philip Rose, who owned the small Glory label, located on 47th Street between Fifth and Madison Avenues. They first recorded "Cindy, Oh Cindy" with singer-songwriter Vince Martin. Written by Robert Nemeroff, who was married to playwright Lorraine Hansbury, and Burt D'Lugoff (Art's brother)—under the names Robert Barron and Burt Long—the record reached number nine in late 1956 and remained on the pop charts for 19 weeks; Eddie Fisher also had a hit with his cover version. The group began to tour and also played at the Village Vanguard. Their recording of the "Banana Boat Song" peaked at number six in early 1957, spurring cover versions by Steve Lawrence, Sarah Vaughan, the Fontaine Sisters, and a satirical interpretation by Stan Freberg. "We had begun the calypso craze, however, and would be typecast as a calypso group, not as singers of folk songs," Darling later recalled with bitterness. "The T.V. show 'Your Hit Parade' had production numbers of the song for eight weeks with dancers in costumes and sets suggesting bananas and Bahamian vacations." (Darling would remain with the popular Tarriers until he replaced Pete Seeger in the Weavers in 1958.[35])

The Tarriers were not the first to record "The Banana Boat Song." Harry Belafonte had included his version, known as "Day-O," on his 1956 album *Calypso*. Born in New York in 1927, Belafonte had grown up in Harlem and Jamaica, and, after a stint in the military, he launched an acting and singing career, with some involvement in People's Songs; his musical and political role model was Paul Robeson, the singer and actor active on issues of civil rights, anti-fascism, and anti-imperialism. Belafonte's professional life was slow to take off, and for a short time he was co-owned the Sage, a small restaurant in Greenwich Village. But in late 1951, he appeared at the Village Vanguard for three months, followed by major venues around the country. He soon began recording for RCA. "With all these concert dates, and all that applause, I felt sure I'd peaked. But then my third album, *Calypso,* became a phenomenon, an album, truly, for the history books: the first ever to sell a million copies," Belafonte would later write. In September 1956, *Calypso* reached number one on the album charts—challenging Elvis Presley's popularity—and soon RCA issued the single of "Day-O" from the album. The record was a hit in early 1957, overlapping with the Tarriers' popularity. The calypso craze led by Belafonte lasted through the year, then just as quickly collapsed, while his career continued to soar.[36]

previous: The audience at a *Sing Out!* Concert in New York City, February 12, 1973. Photograph by Diana Davies.

below: Harry Belafonte, "King of Calypso," achieved international fame with his landmark album *Calypso* (1956) and helped ignite the nationwide folk music revival by the late 1950s. At once a pop star and sex symbol, as well as an actor and a civil rights activist, Belafonte adorned the cover of many magazines in the 1950s.

above: The Tarriers in Greenwich Village, June 1960. Inspired by the success of the Weavers, the Tarriers embodied commercial trends during the boom of the folk music revival in the late 1950s and early 1960s. Despite a couple of hit songs, they did not achieve the stardom of groups such as the Kingston Trio. Photograph by David Gahr.

The growing popularity of folk music was visible in September 1954, when country music briefly moved to the 48th Street Theatre in the show "Hayride: A Hillbilly, Folk Musical" staring Sunshine Sue; Joe and Rose Lee Maphis; Lester Flatt, Earl Scruggs, and the Foggy Mountain Boys; and the Coon Creek Girls. While the headliners were popular stars on the various barn dance radio shows around the country, the show lasted for only 24 performances. Flatt and Scruggs would soon promote the national popularity of bluegrass music, but there was not yet much of an audience in New York.

Folk music, broadly defined, had begun reaching a local as well as national market when the Weavers returned to Carnegie Hall for their reunion Christmas concert in 1955. Harold Leventhal had tried to secure Town Hall, which refused the booking due to the political shadow still associated with the group, but Carnegie Hall had no knowledge of their past troubles. "In 1952, at the height of the cold war, the Weavers ended a meteoric singing career," Irwin Silber wrote in *Sing Out!* in early 1956. "Three years later, on Christmas Eve of 1955, the Weavers came together again in a Holiday Concert at Carnegie Hall in New York. Apparently their three-year absence had been felt by many thousands. More than two weeks before the concert, the 3000-seat hall was completely sold out." Believing there was a thaw in the Cold War, Silber noted that "if proof were ever needed that peace is the indispensable ally of culture, the Weavers' concert is a small but important documentation." Silber had earlier been critical of their commercial success, but now warmed to the Weavers' triumphant return. Vanguard soon issued an album of the concert's highlights. According to the album's notes, "there was a bit of singing and much applause, cheering and even a few whistles, which you may hear on this record if you listen closely. We have been forced to cut the audience acclaim to a minimum: otherwise the disc would have contained 'Darling Corey' [the opening song], applause, and that's all." For Seeger, this "concert was received so well that the Weavers were in business again. With Harold's cooperation we now made freer choices about where and how we wanted to sing, and audiences responded to the informal give-and-take which we ourselves enjoyed. ... The TV industry wasn't noticing us, but we seldom looked at them either." Vanguard soon followed with other albums, including *The Weavers on Tour, The Weavers At Home,* and *Travelling On with The Weavers.*[37]

The decade of the 1950s had been marked by a complex mix of the commercial folk stylings of various groups and individuals—such as the early Weavers, Harry Belafonte, and the rise of the Kingston Trio and its many imitators—with those who attempted a more authentic sound, such as the calypso groups featured by Art D'Lugoff, the Shanty Boys, the New Lost City Ramblers, Dave Van Ronk, and members of the Folksingers Guild. There was no folk purity, no clear line dividing commercial and authentic performers, with most falling somewhere on the spectrum as the folk music revival expanded. The Kingston Trio's hit "Tom Dooley" in late 1958 marked the escalation of a national folk revival. Although the trio was based in San Francisco, New York would remain the center of the folk music world as the decade ended.

Folk music became popular in the late 1950s, driven partly by an expanding mass consumer culture and, to some extent, by the youth market. "The American teenagers have emerged as a big-time consumer in the U.S. economy," *Life* reported in 1959. "Counting only what is spent to satisfy their special teenage demands, the youngsters and their parents will shell out about $10 billion this year, a billion more than the total sales of GM." Teenagers themselves were earning millions of dollars a year; record players were affordable to them, and 45-rpm vinyl disks were cheap. Of course teenagers were diverse in their interests and pursuits, but an upsurge of advertising and public relations firms, centered in New York, targeted them with sophisticated sales techniques. As important as young teens were, college students and adults constituted the majority of the audience for folk music. In 1958 Pete Seeger observed that classical LPs comprised 25 percent of the record market, other LPs (popular, jazz, folk, and other genres) 40 percent, children's records and country and western singles 8 percent, and pop singles 27 percent. But pop had outsized influence with the Hit Parade.[38]

above: Arranged by Harold Leventhal and recorded by Vanguard, the Weavers' reunion concert at Carnegie Hall on Christmas Eve in 1955 was a pivotal event. The sold-out show marked the quartet's return to critical and public acclaim, even if the taint of the blacklist lingered in some quarters, particularly the television industry. Photographed by John Halpern.

At the end of the Eisenhower era there were myriad entertainment alternatives to folk music, but the dominant mass culture seemed stale and trivial to many observers, particularly leftist critics like Dwight Macdonald, who charged that it was tasteless and mindless and encouraged conformity. After a surge of excitement in the mid-1950s, rock 'n' roll appeared to lose direction and inspiration, burdened in part by payola scandals. Other social and political trends during the period had a demoralizing effect on an increasingly alienated and dispirited middle class. The growth of white-collar employment and the expansion of government and corporate bureaucracies left many people with a decreasing sense of control in their lives. The Cold War and the nuclear arms race intensified anxiety and cast a chill in the culture.[39]

Folk music seemed to be an antidote to the blandness of mass culture and the anomie of modernity. It signified a seemingly authentic mode of expression. To many, it represented a search for understanding, linking the past and present and commenting on serious social and political matters. The songs contained depth of meaning and feeling. At hootenannies folkies often bonded socially in the collective experience of singing together. The music explored themes of work, play, love, death, loss, amusement, misfortune, deprivation. Pete Seeger reflected, "Compared to the trivialities of most popular songs, the words of these songs had all the meat of human life in them. ... They seemed frank, straightforward, honest."[40]

Washington Square Park was a good 75
percent of helping me hone my technique.
I would practice all week, and then on
Sundays I would go to the park and see if
I could do it in front of people. I'd go
there for hours and hours and do the same
things over and over all day, because the
crowds would constantly change.

Eric Weissberg, banjoist and member of the
Greenbriar Boys and the Tarriers[1]

THE

BATTLES

OF

WASHINGTON

SQUARE

PARK

Washington Square Park, ca. 1956. Photograph by Nat Norman.

Folksinger Happy Traum remembered taking the subway from the Bronx to Greenwich Village as a teenager in 1954 to play his guitar in Washington Square Park. For him, the Village was the epitome of cool. Abstract Expressionist painters showed their work in local galleries. Experimental Off-Off-Broadway companies presented European plays too dicey for Broadway. Modern jazz musicians performed in neighborhood clubs. This was the waning period of the Red Scare, after the spectacular rise and fall of the Weavers and before the craze for folk music became a nationwide phenomenon. The park was decidedly informal and casual. It was crowded but not teeming with people. There were few opportunities for commercial success, just kindred spirits enjoying the musical and social scene. Traum saw familiar faces every week. The enthusiasm was palpable. He was learning to play the guitar and getting good at it. "We felt like we were part of a real something happening," Traum recalled. "In the forefront of something, sort of in the vanguard of some kind of movement, but only we knew about it. It was something very special."[2]

- - -

Sunday afternoon folksinging in Washington Square Park exemplified the communal spirit of the revival. But the tradition of "Square singing," increasingly popular in the 1950s, also became the source of conflict. Opponents—ranging from New York University officials, longtime South Village residents, and lower Fifth Avenue patricians, to the New York City parks commissioner himself—squared off against a multicultural coalition of folksingers and their allies, including beatniks, African Americans, and gays.[1] The conflict was in essence a cultural one. Folk music culture—nurtured in lofts, cafes, hootenannies, private parties, political rallies, and concert halls, and tinged by leftist politics—had come to represent the Village's counterculture and cooperative ethos. To Parks Commissioner Newbold Morris, also chairman of the board of Lincoln Center for the Performing Arts, the quirky

Washington Square scene contrasted sharply with his notion of culture, associated with opera, the symphonic orchestra, and classical music. The fight over folksinging in the park, then, represented not only a disagreement about the use of public space, but also sparked a discussion of folk music revival culture in the city. In fact, it triggered a debate about the notion of culture itself.[3]

above: Washington Square, ca. 1957-60. The Washington Square folk music scene transcended generations; professionals played with amateurs, and parents taught children, creating a dynamic atmosphere at once serious and fun. Photograph by Aaron Rennert.

THE WASHINGTON SQUARE PARK SCENE

The tradition of Washington Square singing had begun after World War II and became popular in the 1950s as New York emerged as the epicenter of the folk music scene. Adjacent to the coffeehouse district in Greenwich Village, Washington Square teemed with folkies belting out tunes and relishing the convivial scene. Sunday afternoons from spring to fall were spirited times in Washington Square Park. Folksingers, accompanied by enthusiasts, would perform for several hours in the public space, playing their guitars, banjos, and mandolins and singing tunes like "Michael Row the Boat Ashore," "Blue Tail Fly," and "Hey Lolly, Lolly Lo." They were mostly white, middle-class young adults, liberal in their politics. Some had cultivated their skills and sensibilities as teenagers at progressive summer camps established under the New Deal (in particular, Camp Woodland in the Catskills).

below: (From left) Mike Seeger, Ralph Rinzler, and Bob Yellin perform in Washington Square, 1957-60. These quintessential "citybilly" musicians were committed practitioners of traditional Southern music. Seeger, with the New Lost City Ramblers, and Rinzler and Yellin, in the Greenbriar Boys, introduced a multitude of New Yorkers to old-time and bluegrass music. Photograph by Ralph Rinzler.

Professionals and amateurs congregated and exchanged ideas in the Square, creating a synergy that honed the skills of many. Folksinger Theo Bikel marveled, "Where else could young—or not so young—singers test their mettle in a public place?" Regulars of the 1950s jam sessions included members of the Tarriers, the New Lost City Ramblers, and the Shanty Boys. A Washington Square tradition started by several friends in the mid-1940s, folksinging was an integral part of the park's multihued fabric.[4]

When the gatherings in Washington Square Park began drawing noticeable crowds by the late 1940s, the Police Department started requiring musicians to get permits from the Parks Department. The ordinance allowed license holders to play only "stringed instruments," which in effect excluded percussionists. Though resentful of the regulation, most folksingers were glad not to compete with noisy bongo players, who descended on Greenwich Village in large numbers in the 1950s. Until 1952 George Sprung, brother of banjo player Roger Sprung, organized the events, securing the permits for fellow players. Bassist Lionel Kilberg subsequently assumed this responsibility and persuaded the Parks Department to expand the playing time from two to four hours, from 2:00 to 6:00 p.m.[5]

On a typical warm Sunday during the late Eisenhower era, six or seven groups of musicians would gather in the

park, the majority of them by the Washington Square Arch at the foot of Fifth Avenue or on the rim of the central fountain. Though divisions were never rigid or fixed, folksingers usually gravitated toward others with similar interests. For example, there were the Zionists, who were conspicuous as they danced to songs like "Hava Nagila" in the square's southern part by Sullivan Street. The Loyal Youth Leaguers, a Marxist-Leninist organization, featured guitarist Jerry Silverman and sang union songs such as "Hold the Fort." The bluegrassers, led by Roger Sprung and Lionel Kilberg, staked out another area. The colorful assemblies became a launch pad for several careers. As folksinger Dave Van Ronk recalled, "That Washington Square Sunday afternoon scene was a great catalyst for my whole generation."[6]

THE FIRST BATTLE OF WASHINGTON SQUARE PARK, 1955–1959

In the late 1950s, as city planners redeveloped vast portions of Manhattan and identified Washington Square as a site for modernization, the park assumed greater cultural import, not only for folksingers but also citizens concerned about the direction of development in New York. The conflict stemmed from the plan of Parks Commissioner Robert Moses to construct a roadway through Washington Square. The project—called Washington Square Southeast—was slated to transform nine blocks into three superblocks of high-rise educational, residential, and commercial buildings. Bounded by Washington Square South (West 4th Street) to the north, Houston Street to the south, West Broadway to the west, and Mercer Street to the east, the "blighted area," as *The New York Times* described it, contained 191 buildings—175 industrial or commercial, 16 residential. According to the Slum Clearance Committee tenant survey, only 132 families, or from 400 to 450 people, resided in the area. Most were working-class Italians. From Moses's perspective, the residential relocation was manageable, and the displacement of some 650 industrial or commercial establishments was not cause for concern—many of his Title I projects expedited postwar deindustrialization. From the viewpoint of Moses and his sponsors, particularly New York University, Washington Square Southeast epitomized growth, progress, and efficiency, strengthening the city as a center for higher education by helping a small commuter campus transform into a major research university with modern facilities and dormitories.[7]

The proposal galvanized the community. Two dozen Village groups confronted Moses and his allies. In speeches,

opposite: Save Washington Square Rally, ca. 1958. This image captures the spirited local opposition that met Parks Commissioner Robert Moses's ultimately unsuccessful plans to expand Fifth Avenue through Washington Square Park. Photograph by Ray Sullivan.

below: Washington Square Southeast demolition, 1957. Slum clearance chairman Robert Moses spearheaded the Washington Square Southeast Title I project, which aimed to redevelop a large swath of Greenwich Village south of Washington Square Park and led to the bulldozing of blocks of tenements and factories. While Moses and his supporters viewed the project as a sign of progress in the city, his opponents argued that urban renewal undermined the character of neighborhoods, destroying communal spaces and social networks.

rallies, essays, cartoons, and letters to editors, protesters expressed their view of the park in symbolic and imaginative terms, evoking the character and nature of Washington Square in an effort to win over the public to their vision of the area and for the city's future in general. Echoing a growing chorus of critics of modern urban planning, opponents equated the roadway and superblocks with a trend toward alienation and monotony. They predicted the destruction of their cherished park and of the neighborhood as a whole. The opposition movement gained momentum and media attention as powerful political and civic leaders joined, including Tammany Hall boss and Village district leader Carmine De Sapio, foundation consultant Raymond Rubinow, former First Lady Eleanor Roosevelt, New York University law professor Norman Redlich, *Village Voice* editor Dan Wolf, and real estate investor George Popkin.[8]

Villagers stressed the cultural importance of Washington Square, drawing on folk music revival sentiments, beliefs, and language, as well as ideology that pitted nature against modern development. They focused their critique on what they saw as the dehumanizing nature of the roadway and the new projects. In contrast to the uniform landscape of a geometric superblock, they contended that Washington Square was an idiosyncratic and authentic environment that offered a sense of place in a transient city. Especially on Sunday afternoons, the park was a place where Villagers could experience feelings of community.[9]

previous: Musicians in Washington Square, April 1962. Photograph by Frederick Kelly.

below: The demolition of an artist's studio in Greenwich Village, May 1960. Photograph by Fred W. McDarrah.

After a lengthy battle against Robert Moses and his allies, Village community groups defeated the plan to extend Fifth Avenue through Washington Square Park in 1958, which led to a trial period of closing the park to automobile traffic. Here, local activists celebrate the occasion of the "last car" to drive through Washington Square.

In a widely publicized Board of Estimate hearing on the controversy in 1958, Carmine De Sapio distilled the concerns of the road's opponents in an impassioned speech. De Sapio led the opposition in demanding that the park be closed to traffic. He portrayed Greenwich Village as a distinct entity in the city. To De Sapio, the Village was not simply a physical locality but a web of social relations. Villagers had a sense of identity and an attachment to their neighborhood. "And just as Greenwich Village is a way of life, so Washington Square Park is Greenwich Village," mused De Sapio, a lifetime Villager. "To change the character of this beloved central symbol of the Village would be, ultimately, to eradicate the essential character of this unique community."[10]

The anti-road advocates carried the day. They not only turned back Moses's Fifth Avenue extension plan, but made Washington Square a vehicle-free zone. Following the hearing, the Board of Estimate ruled to temporarily close the existing road in the park to all traffic but emergency vehicles and Fifth Avenue buses. In 1959, after a successful trial period, the Board of Estimate endorsed a plan to take the emergency road out of the square. Jubilant, Villagers held a "grand closing" ceremony in the park. Politicians, on the eve of an election, posed for pictures and took credit in speeches.[11]

The result of this clash was a triumph for local roadway opponents in 1959 and, in a larger sense, critics of modern urban planning, including Lewis Mumford and William H. Whyte. The outcome also marked a victory for folksingers. The closing of Washington Square Park to automobile traffic

Members from Save the Village arrive at City Hall in a "sightseeing train" to attend a public hearing by the City Planning Commission regarding the Zoning Law, February 1960. Greenwich Village's association with artistic creativity and social activism earned the neighborhood nationwide fame in the early 1960s. Political and cultural movements frequently merged, as they did in 1960 with "Save the Village," an initiative led by a coalition of artists and activists against the massive redevelopment of the neighborhood. Photograph by Phil Stanziola.

signified the ascent of their vision of the Square as a communal space. It also translated into larger crowds for Sunday afternoon folksinging.

THE FOLK MUSIC REVIVAL AND THE TRANSFORMATION OF THE SOUTH VILLAGE, 1959–1961

The expanding folk music scene was rapidly transforming the character of Greenwich Village in the late 1950s. This was especially true in the largely Italian-American South Village, where coffeehouses were cropping up—a development that was met with concern by some longtime residents. As folksingers streamed in, so did their devotees, as well as hordes of tourists. The MacDougal block between Bleecker and West 3rd Streets was especially frenetic, teeming with pleasure seekers. Occupants of apartments above the cafes and bars complained to authorities about loud noise and pedestrian traffic. To appease neighbors in units above his Gaslight Cafe, John Mitchell banned conventional applause at shows. At the end of a performance, appreciative audience members snapped their fingers instead of clapping their hands.[12]

South Village youths occasionally harassed and even attacked visitors to the neighborhood. African Americans in general, and interracial couples in particular, were primary targets. Pejoratively called "A-trainers," a term for Harlem

RECOLLECTIONS

HAPPY TRAUM

It was 1954, and I was 16 years old, living in the Bronx.
I can't overstate the sense of anticipation that I felt on
fair-weather Sundays as I boarded the downtown D train and
rode to West 4th in the heart of Greenwich Village, guitar
in hand. A short walk east brought me to Washington Square.
I could hear the echoes of guitars, banjos, and fiddles
before I reached the park. For the next several years I
played and sang, made life-long friends, and started a
musical journey that has informed my life, music, and
career ever since.

"The Square," as we called it, was more than just a gathering of folk singers. It was an unorganized, free-form kind
of social club, with a revolving set of "members" centered
around some stalwart regulars. There was Roger Sprung, big
and stern-looking, with his derby hat and driving bluegrass banjo; Lionel Kilberg, the affable, gentle washtub
bassist (and holder of the police permit); Roy Berkeley, a
tall, acerbic topical songwriter; Tom Paley, whose finger-
picking guitar skills influenced and inspired many learning players (myself included); Eric Weissberg, Marshall
Brickman, Jim Gavin, John Herald, the Kossoy Sisters, Dave
Van Ronk, and many others.

Arriving at the park, I'd make my way through the crowds
of on-lookers and tourists to find the musical group that
I felt most comfortable joining. There were bluegrass jam-
mers, old-time music aficionados, blues shouters, Pete
Seeger/Woody Guthrie acolytes, calypso singers, jazzers,
and other musical cliques that inhabited their own spots
around the central fountain, under the arch, or in the
park's other areas. The first few times I stood shyly on
the edges of the crowd, getting up the nerve to join in, but
after a few weeks I got my confidence and started playing
my guitar, singing and making music—and friends—with the
players, some of whom I am still close to 60 years later.

On rainy days, when we couldn't take our instruments out, we'd retreat to the Labor Temple on 14th Street, where they let us use a big, echoing gymnasium-type room. Sometimes we'd make our way to lofts or apartments in the Village for song-swapping parties that went into the night.

For a kid from the Bronx in the 1950s, Greenwich Village was a revelation. It was exciting, exotic, mysterious, and mind-expanding (before drugs); a place you could see bongo-playing beatniks, interracial couples, homosexuals openly walking hand-in-hand, and all kinds of artistic types in berets, beards, and sandals. The folk music that we played there, and that eventually made its way into the Village coffeehouses, clubs, and concert venues, started out being played by enthusiasts who had no concept of the music as a commercial, professional endeavor. We did it for fun and for the love of it, but as the fifties became the sixties, the music and its intentions morphed into careers, contracts, and the phenomenon that made "folk" a pop culture craze.

– – –

Happy Traum, a renowned folksinger, guitarist, author, and teacher, came of age in the Greenwich Village folk revival of the 1950s and 1960s. He studied blues guitar with Brownie McGhee; performed and recorded with major figures in the folk music world (including Bob Dylan); taught guitar at leading camps, clinics, and workshops; was editor of Sing Out! *magazine; and has produced more than 500 instructional CDs, DVDs, and books for his company, Homespun Music Instruction. For the past 47 years, he and his wife and business partner, Jane, have made their home in Woodstock, New York.*

Italian-American espresso shop on MacDougal Street, August 1940. The South Village was a predominantly working-class, Italian-American neighborhood in the mid-20th century. The area's many espresso shops preceded an influx of coffeehouses in the 1950s that provided venues for the Beat poetry movement and the folk music revival and heralded the community's transformation from quiet residential enclave to vibrant artistic center. Photograph by Marjory Collins.

residents who traveled downtown via the subway, African Americans were increasingly hanging out in the Village in the late 1950s, embodying to many South Villagers the disruptive local changes. The tension occasionally led to violence. For example, Len Chandler, one of the few African-American folksingers on the scene, was attacked outside the Gaslight by a group of Italian toughs "attempting to clean up the neighborhood." Dave Van Ronk recalled, "There was a lot of that shit going down back then." In 1959 the *Village Voice* reported a series of assaults on black people in the South Village. As a result, the Sixth Precinct added patrolmen to the area, especially on Friday and Saturday nights.[13]

Folk music venues became a lightning rod for the growing social tensions. On several occasions, youngsters vandalized new cabarets and restaurants, concrete symbols of the South Village in transition. Although most proprietors were loath to discuss the matter, the *Village Voice* learned that incidents occurred in 1959 at the Village Gate, Rienzi's, Punjab, and Port O' Call. Village Gate owner Art D'Lugoff was repeatedly the victim of vandals. He suspected the attacks happened just before dawn and estimated the damage at several hundred dollars for broken windows, a smashed showcase, and a stolen flag.[14]

The conflict stemmed in part from the stress between old-timers and newcomers. For some longtime residents, the influx of a diverse population into the South Village represented an encroachment on their traditional ethnic community. Though their enclave was already in demographic decline due to the trend toward suburbanization, driven by the GI Bill, many Italian Americans were intent on maintaining their political and cultural influence in Greenwich Village. A new business owner observed, "This was once an established neighborhood and now it is threatened. Many people feel that their whole way of life is in danger, and naturally they resent it."[15]

The strife was also a consequence of rising property values. The growth of the tourist district led to higher rents on Bleecker, Thompson, and Sullivan Streets. Unable to compete, some Italian coffeehouses closed down. A supermarket replaced a butcher and a grocer. Other developments also caused displacement. The expansion of New York University, for instance, was uprooting many residents and businesses. The recently completed Washington Square Village, Robert Moses's Title I urban renewal project, drove up prices for residential units. The new trends disquieted many in the community.[16]

Of the many countercultural spaces in Greenwich Village, the liveliest and most integrated was Washington Square Park, especially during Sunday afternoon folksinging. After the Board of Estimate closed the park to traffic in 1958, Washington Square gained cohesion as an enclosed area and attracted larger and more diverse crowds. As *The New York Times* reporter Michael James observed in 1959, "Musicians, many with guitars, some with banjos, a few with mandolins and one or two with bass viols, share the fountain with Greenwich Villagers, tourists, cats and dogs and a clicking corps of photographers." Beatniks amassed in the park on Sundays. African Americans and gays attended the events in increasing numbers. Many New York University students spent their leisure time in the park. New Yorker Robert J. Silverstein described the scene in 1961 as "one place in America where people of whatever race or color could mingle and be with whomever they wished."[17]

THE SECOND BATTLE OF WASHINGTON SQUARE PARK, 1961

At the end of the Eisenhower era in New York, folk music culture blended with other social trends in Greenwich Village. Beatniks, blacks, and gays increasingly attended the weekly gatherings, not necessarily to sing but to mingle in the budding countercultural milieu. Single people often looked for dating partners. Parents sometimes brought their children. To some viewers, including many members of the South Village community, the events were disorderly and many of the participants antisocial. But to others, the park was a patchwork of diversity

opposite: Elevated view of Washington Square Park, May 1959. Photograph by Fred W. McDarrah.

opposite below: Lincoln Center for the Performing Arts, ca. 1965. Parks Commissioner Newbold Morris deemed the Lincoln Center plaza the quintessential public space, recognizing that its modernist interpretation of a classical Italian piazza was intended to edify visitors. Emblematic of American power and prosperity at the height of the Cold War, the plaza sharply contrasted with quirky Washington Square Park, though both featured centrally located fountains. Photograph by Morris Warman.

that fostered social encounters and interactions and reduced racism. These tensions came to a head in a debate that represented not only a disagreement about the use of public space, but also the significance of the folk music revival culture in New York.[18]

Key to this debate was Newbold Morris, who had been appointed parks commissioner by Mayor Robert Wagner in 1960. Morris was a prominent figure in Robert Moses's urban renewal coalition, as well as a member of Manhattan's cultural elite. Descended from the city's Knickerbocker aristocracy, Morris counted among his ancestors Founding Fathers Lewis Morris and Gouverneur Morris. Morris received his education at the elite Groton School and, in keeping with family tradition since the colonial era, attended Yale, where he became a member of the Scroll and Key secret society. He was active in New York politics, serving as president of the New York City Council under Mayor Fiorello La Guardia from 1938 to 1945 and on the City Planning Commission from 1946 to 1948.[19]

As chairman of the board of Lincoln Center and a founder of City Center Theater in 1943 and the New York City Opera in 1944, Morris worked actively to bring high culture to the public at a reasonable price. Mayor Wagner described him as an "aristocrat in the noblest sense of the word."[20] From Morris's perspective, folk music in Washington Square signified the antithesis of the Lincoln Center ideal. As parks commissioner, Morris disdained Washington Square folksinging. He saw nothing of artistic, cultural, or social value in the Sunday afternoon events.

In an internal memorandum circulated on March 13, 1961, Morris announced his decision to stop giving permits for the playing of musical instruments in the square, revealing his attitudes toward high and low culture:

> I want to emphasize I am not opposed to the wonderful symphony concerts, bands, quartets or chamber music [in Washington Square Park]. What I am against is these fellows that come from miles away to display the most terrible costumes, haircuts, etc. and who play bongo drums and other weird instruments attracting a weird public.

> I patrolled the area on Sunday and I was shocked. Conditions are much worse than when we were down there last year. You cannot call it a park anymore. It is so heavily used, not by the neighborhood, but by these freaks, that there literally was not room on the walks.[21]

Part of Morris's concern involved the regulation of public space and the maintenance of social order. In this regard, he shared the attitude of his predecessor, Robert Moses. (It was

below: Izzy Young in New York City, ca. 1960. Folklore Center owner Izzy Young, along with Judson Memorial Church minister Howard Moody, formed the "Right to Sing" Committee and led the 1961 protests against the ban of folksinging in Washington Square Park. Young contended that the ban infringed upon the civil liberties of folksingers. Photograph by Diana Davies.

above top: The folk music ban in Washington Square by Parks Commissioner Newbold Morris triggered a clash between protesters and the police on April 9, 1961 that was labeled a "riot" by some media outlets, including *The New York Times* and the *New York Mirror*. In this film still from *Sunday*, Dan Drasin's short documentary about the incident, officers apprehend Robert Easton of the Bronx as he plays his autoharp in defiance.

above bottom: Izzy Young in Washington Square Park on April 9, 1961, from Dan Drasin's documentary *Sunday*. "We have been singing here for 17 years and never have had any trouble," Young declared to fellow demonstrators. "We have a right to sing here." Photograph by Harvey Zucker.

rumored that Moses still controlled the parks and that Morris was his puppet.) During his tenure as commissioner from 1934 to 1960, Moses envisioned parks as sites for recreational activity. Throughout the city he directed the construction of swimming pools, baseball diamonds, tennis courts, skating rinks, playgrounds, and other athletic facilities in public spaces, but he limited political and cultural events within them. He clashed with Shakespeare Festival founder Joseph Papp, for instance, about the value of Shakespeare in Central Park (though he eventually relented). Morris adopted a similarly restrictive view.[22]

Morris's decision divided the neighborhood, pitting a multicultural coalition of folksingers, beatniks, blacks, and gays against New York University officials and wealthy lower Fifth Avenue and longtime South Village residents. The ban against folksinging in the park also represented a reckoning of revival culture in New York. It was an early culture clash in the 1960s.

After *The New York Times* reported the ban two weeks later, outraged New Yorkers sent letters to the parks commissioner and the mayor. Villager and WNYC radio broadcaster Oscar Brand, whose Sunday show was a crucial platform for folksingers, promised to Wagner, "I intend to join wholeheartedly in any active mass protests against this action." In a letter to Morris, Judson Memorial Church Reverend Howard Moody predicted a local movement against the ban. "If you need community support, it can be aroused," he commented.[23]

Despite the objections, the parks department began denying permits to event organizers, including the Folklore Center's Izzy Young. Young requested a permit for "folksinging with stringed instruments" every Sunday in April. The parks department rejected the application without any explanation. In an internal communication, one staff member warned, "I feel certain that refusal to grant the requested permit after so many years, when they were allowed to play, will be questioned and possibly be aired in the press." In fact, musicians and their supporters were already planning a demonstration.[24]

Passions predictably erupted in Washington Square Park the following Sunday afternoon, April 9, 1961, as folksingers confronted police for several hours. At 2:00 p.m. approximately 50 demonstrators entered the park from the southwestern corner, carrying a cello as a mock coffin and signs that read "Keep the Sound of Music in the Square" and "Comm. Morris, Don't Stop Us, Join Us." Local Sixth Precinct Captain Adrian Donohue and 15 of his men met the group and allowed them to march silently around the fountain. Hundreds of supporters joined the procession as perplexed tourists looked on. Inspired by the occasion, some sang Woody Guthrie's "This Land Is Your Land." When officers spotted a youth, Robert A. Easton of the Bronx, age 18,

singing while playing his autoharp, they apprehended him and whisked him away to a patrol car. Seconds later, police arrested two more players. The incensed crowd, estimated at 2,000, heckled the authorities.[25]

At 3:00 p.m. protesters with guitars, directed by Izzy Young, occupied the dry fountain. Taking their cue from civil rights activists, they started singing "We Shall Not Be Moved." Art D'Lugoff ridiculed Morris's latest pronouncement that folksingers and their audiences destroyed the park's grass and shrubbery, pointing out that performances occurred on asphalt by the fountain and the Arch. Addressing the crowd, Young cited the tradition of folksinging in Washington Square. "We have been singing here for 17 years and never have had any trouble," he declared. "We have a right to sing here."[26]

At 3:30 Inspector Patrick MacCormick ordered police to leave their nightsticks behind and clear the demonstrators from the fountain. Riot squad cops, reinforcing the Sixth Precinct, pushed occupants of the basin toward the rim. A *Village Voice* reporter observed, "A few of the officers reacted as if they had 1917 Union Square Bolsheviks as adversaries." Fights broke out, combatants exchanged blows, and police knocked down demonstrators. There was shoving, kicking, and wrestling. The police ultimately arrested 10 individuals. At least 20 people were injured, including three officers. As patrol wagons hauled off protesters, demonstrators yelled "fascists" and gestured with their arms in a mock Nazi salute. Village Independent Democrat (VID) district leader

previous: A man (at right) films the scuffle as police officers and riot squad cops clear demonstrators from around Washington Square's central fountain, April 9, 1961. Many local leaders accused the police of employing excessive force during the confrontation. Photograph by Fred W. McDarrah.

below: The socially conscientious Judson Memorial Baptist Church, seen here ca. 1975, the socially conscientious Judson Memorial Church had anchored Washington Square South since 1893, and in the mid-1950s, it began to support a vibrant "arts ministry" under the leadership of Senior Minister Howard Moody. Along with Izzy Young, Moody led the Right to Sing Committee in 1961. Photograph by Edmund V. Gillon.

Stills from Dan Drasin's
17-minute, 16-millimeter
documentary film *Sunday*, 1961.

candidate James Lanigan told *The New York Times*, "I saw evidence of police brutality. As a citizen and attorney I believe in order. But the expulsions from the park and methods used were unnecessary."[27] VID vice president, attorney Ed Koch, offered to provide legal representation to the arrested demonstrators.[28]

During the mêlée and after, scores of protesters found refuge in Judson Memorial Church. Essentially the front yard of the church, Washington Square Park was especially dear to the church's pastor, Howard Moody. Moody had been an influential voice against Moses's roadway plan in his roles as Judson minister and VID president. The native Texan sometimes attended Sunday afternoon gatherings after his church service and sang along in his sonorous drawl. Moody was livid at the behavior of police and collected signed statements of nearly 100 people who claimed they had witnessed acts of brutality. He gave many reporters interviews and was widely quoted in the Monday newspapers. He received numerous letters from sympathizers, encouraging him to champion the cause of the musicians. Like Izzy Young, Howard Moody was becoming a key figure in the dispute.[29]

The day after the clash, Newbold Morris issued a statement defending his policy. He stressed his concern for the park's greenery and blamed folksingers for drawing large crowds that trampled the natural features. Moody, his adversary, wryly recalled, "He wanted to turn Washington Square Park into an English garden." Morris professed that as parks commissioner, he aimed to make Washington Square "an attractive area for both passive and active recreation," and he contended that attaining this goal was impossible due to Sunday festivities. To accommodate the musicians, he advised that they apply for permits to play in the spacious East River Park amphitheater off Grand Street, on the eastern-most border of the Lower East Side.[30]

The parks commissioner received support from New York's mayor and the media establishment. Daily newspapers vilified the protesters and defended the police. Front page headlines in *The New York Times* exaggerated, "FOLK SINGERS RIOT IN WASHINGTON SQ." The *New York Mirror* related in two-inch type that "2000 BEATNIKS RIOT IN VILLAGE." The *Daily News* reported, "Embattled beatnik musicians, joined by friends and veteran anti-cop shouters, turned peaceful Washington Square Park into a wrestling ring yesterday afternoon." *The New York Times* editorialized that Morris "treated the crisis with intelligence and restraint" and implied that his East River Park proposition was fair and reasonable. From Florida, where he was on vacation recuperating from an operation, Mayor Wagner weighed in with approval of Morris's ban on folk music in Washington Square Park and his relocation initiative.[31]

below: Social activists, folksingers, and Village community leaders and residents joined forces in this 1961 "Right to Sing" rally. After several weeks of vigorous demonstrations, held in the park and in local institutions and venues such as Judson Memorial Church and Art D'Lugoff's Village Gate, Mayor Robert Wagner repealed the ban against folksinging.

THE RIGHT TO SING COMMITTEE AND WASHINGTON SQUARE CULTURE

To folksingers, if Washington Square represented Shangri-La, East River Park meant Siberia. The battle intensified as Howard Moody and Izzy Young formed the Right to Sing Committee. Many Villagers joined the committee, including VID leaders James Lanigan, Ed Koch, and Sarah Schoenkopf, Village Gate owner Art D'Lugoff, WNYC broadcaster Oscar Brand, and New York University law professors Edmond Cahn and Norman Dorsen. Other influential residents, such as Jane Jacobs and *New York Times* writer Gilbert Millstein, backed the group. The New York Civil Liberties Union aided their cause by filing a petition in the State Supreme Court to direct Morris to issue folksingers a permit.[32]

Neighborhood organizations dominated by longtime residents overwhelmingly backed Newbold Morris in his ban on folksinging in the park. Four days after the demonstration, representatives of more than 25 Greenwich Village civic, religious, veterans, and cultural associations met at the Church of Our Lady of Pompeii to form the Committee to Preserve the Dignity and Beauty of Washington Square Park. The groups—collectively known as the Washington Square Dignity organizations—included the Chamber of Commerce, the Washington Square Association, two American Legion posts,

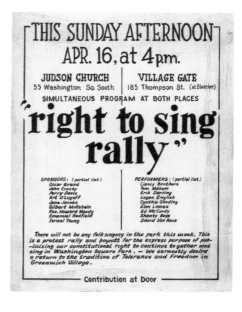

above: Community organizer and urban theorist Jane Jacobs at a press conference at the Lion's Head Restaurant in Greenwich Village, December 1961. Jacobs led a local movement to defeat a plan to redevelop a large section of the West Village in 1961, in part by amassing evidence about the area's vitality and presenting it at public hearings and at press conferences. Her book *The Death and Life of Great American Cities* (1961) became a seminal work in urban planning. Photograph by Phil Stanziola.

the Marquette and Knickerbocker Councils of the Knights of Columbus, the Pompeii Parent-Teacher Association, the Village Temple, the Village Business Men's Association, the Mothers' Club of St. Anthony, the Catholic Youth Organization (CYO) of Pompeii, and Cub Scout Pack #325. Chaired by William King, head of Pompeii's Catholic Youth Organization, the committee endorsed the Morris relocation plan and disputed Izzy Young's claim that the ban infringed upon the civil liberties of folksingers. In a statement released to the press, the committee argued that the park should be "a quiet oasis for proper and peaceful recreation," not criticizing folksinging per se but rather the effect of the events. The coalition contended, "The Sunday gatherings have attracted crowds from all over the Metropolitan District, creating overcrowded, unsanitary, and disorderly situations. This situation has gotten beyond the proper control and supervision of both the police and Parks Departments."[33]

Numerous Villagers who resided in luxury apartments just north of the park on lower Fifth Avenue, a choice New York address, joined South Village residents in this coalition that transcended barriers of class and ethnicity. Most directly affected by the Sunday events, they above all wanted a tranquil Washington Square Park. In encouraging missives, Fifth Avenue residents Sydney F. Spero, Daniel A. Shirk, and John W. Frost informed the parks commissioner that they and most of their neighbors supported him. E. Camoin de Bonilla of 19 Fifth Avenue articulated his desire for the park to Morris, "It would be most pleasant and comforting to sit again under its trees surrounded by some green and perhaps some flowers." Mrs. Abraham Starr of 33 Fifth Avenue rejoiced at the folksinging ban and recommended to Mayor Wagner, "The best strategy would be to rehabilitate the park, remove the hideous and useless fountain and replace it with flower beds, install new, modern benches, re-seed the lawns and enforce a strict KEEP OFF THE GRASS law."[34]

Morris's supporters argued that their longtime residency in Greenwich Village gave them priority in determining the use of Washington Square Park. In letters to the parks commissioner, they underscored their neighborhood roots and characterized Sunday attendees as trespassers. Marie Di Giorgio of Sullivan Street stressed that she was a "native Villager," Alma Maravelo of the Pompeii CYO noted that she had "lived in Greenwich Village all her life," and Eugenia O'Connor of Bedford Street indicated, "I was born in the Village on Hancock Street and have never lived anywhere else. My children were born here too." These Villagers maintained that they could not relax and enjoy the park with their families as a result of the commotion caused by the jamborees. "To listen to bongo drums at 2 o'clock on Sunday afternoon," proclaimed a Bleecker Street lifetime resident at a community planning board meeting, "is degrading to my mother and father."[35]

The Washington Square Dignity organizations and their allies cited "misbehavior" in the park and usually singled out "beatniks" as the culprits. In their appeals to Morris and Wagner, they condemned beatniks as slovenly and unclean, listless and effeminate, and vulgar and licentious. Echoing critiques heard in popular culture around the nation, New York University education professor F. Thrasher spewed invective at "degenerate beatnik rabble," which had "absolutely NO regard for the moralities of normal, decent people." Charles Rao, president of Tiro A Segno (Rifle Club) of New York, Inc. on MacDougal Street, expressed to Morris, "We of Tiro, the oldest American club of Italian origin in the States, wish to compliment you in the action to do away with the ridiculous display of beatnicks [sic] in Washington Square Park which degrades this fine community."[36]

The conflict was essentially cultural. "Beatniks" embodied the values of the nascent counterculture, not only in their use of marijuana, but also in their unconventional attitude toward work. Disdainful of the 1950s American Dream, beatniks shunned the trappings of suburbia and gravitated toward college towns and bohemian areas in cities. "There is nothing wrong with material possessions," remarked Village Beat poet Ted Joans. "But you should use them and not let them use you." Beats often decried the depersonalized nature of work and leisure and their desire to avoid the "rat race." A feature story in LOOK commented, "The goals of the Beat are not watching TV, not wearing gray flannel, not owning a home in the suburbs, and especially—not working." In his study of 300 Village Beats in the summer of 1960, sociologist Ned Polsky reinforced some of the claims made by the scandalized media and in the popular culture. Polsky found that 35 percent of the Beats were working class in background, 60 percent were middle class, and 5 percent upper class. Blacks, women, and gays were all part of the subculture. Most beatniks got by through temporary jobs and a combination of panhandling, borrowing money, living off their girlfriends or parents, selling marijuana, or moving from one apartment to another to avoid paying rent. Some slept on the floor of a friend's loft; a few became homeless. Beat writer Lawrence Lipton referred to this lifestyle as "holy poverty." In an era when a generation of Americans attained middle-class status, the beatniks of Greenwich Village represented downward mobility.[37]

In a letter to Morris, one critic used the oxymoron "beatnik folksingers." While there was some overlap, these were two different cultures. The Beat and folk music movements flourished simultaneously in Village coffeehouses. There was cross-fertilization of ideas between the artists. The poetry of Allen Ginsberg and the novels of Jack Kerouac, for instance, influenced folksinger Bob Dylan. But in terms of audiences, styles, and politics, the artistic movements were largely distinct. As Dave Van Ronk observed, "The real Beats liked cool

Beat poet Allen Ginsberg was an early advocate of the legalization of marijuana. Outside the Women's House of Detention in January 1965, he led this group of demonstrators to demand the release of prisoners arrested for marijuana use or possession.

THERE IS NOTHING WRONG WITH MATERIAL POSSESSIONS... BUT YOU SHOULD USE THEM AND NOT LET THEM USE YOU.

Musicians in Washington Square Park, 1955-65. Photograph by Nat Norman.

jazz, bebop, and hard drugs, and the folkniks would sit around on the floor and sing songs of the oppressed masses."

Moreover, folksingers and their followers, in contrast to the Beats, tended to be politically active and to support bolder liberal policies, particularly in civil rights. Nevertheless, the conflation of folksingers and beatniks shaped the viewpoint of Newbold Morris and strengthened his sense of righteousness. A particularly damning assessment of folksingers came from one of the most powerful figures in the Washington Square area, New York University President Carroll V. Newsom. In a letter to Morris, Newsom reflected:

> There was a time when a folk singer was a person who sang folk songs; most people enjoyed his contribution to community life. Now a folk singer may or may not be able to sing. Sometimes he is a hoodlum; many believe he indulges in abnormal sexual behavior. Judging by his conduct in Washington Square Park, he dislikes little children, and likes to disrupt life in the community. He seems to be especially happy when he can gather with others of his ilk.[38]

The Washington Square Dignity leadership also complained that folksingers lured unsavory elements to the park. In the early 1960s, the most popular downtown gay cruising areas were Greenwich Avenue, Eighth Street, and Washington Square Park. Despite the Sixth Precinct's crackdown, more and more gays hung out in these Village locales. On Greenwich Avenue, gay men sat on doorsteps or car hoods and watched promenaders until cops dispersed them. Their favorite gathering place in the park was a railing known as the "meat rack" along Washington Square West. In a letter to the editor of *The New York Times*, J. Owen Grundy, *Greenwich Village News* editor and public relations chairman of the Committee to Preserve the Dignity and Beauty of Washington Square Park, fulminated about the changing nature of the Village:

> During the past two or three year[s] the community has experienced an extraordinary invasion of homosexuals and professional beatniks, mostly from outside, who seem to take especial pride in appearing in public in the dirtiest and most unkempt attire conceivable. To this is added irregular and shocking conduct. This motley mob attracted by so-called folk singing has made the fountain in Washington Square Park its Mecca each and every Sunday.[39]

The park conflict also fueled racial tensions in the neighborhood. Though Greenwich Village liberals endorsed a strong civil rights plank in the Democratic Party platform, most were more comfortable denouncing racism in Birmingham than on Bleecker Street. One prominent exception was Howard Moody. In a sermon at Judson Church during the controversy, Moody spoke frankly, "There is some prejudice in Greenwich Village. There are Italians that do not like Negroes, but there are non-Italians that don't like Negroes and there are Negroes who think all Italians belong to the Mafia, and there are Anglo-Saxons who think that neither of the aforementioned ought to be allowed in the park." The Committee to Preserve the Dignity and Beauty of Washington Square Park vehemently denied that race was a factor in the dispute. But incidents were too numerous and hate mail to Morris and Moody too extensive to discount the issue. Investment advisor Harwood Gilder, of 29 Washington Square West, urged Morris to rid the park of "Bronx A-trainers" (although there was no A train from the Bronx). Mrs. Forrest Rutherford of 33 Fifth Avenue berated Moody:

> Please allow me to assure you that the residents of Washington Square do NOT want to see this lovely, traditional, refined community become a skid row for beatniks, degenerates and negro mongrels masquerading as "folk singers."

> We are 100% behind the Police Commissioner and the Mayor and we will wipe out this blot on the fair name of Fifth Avenue. If you are so much in favor of

interracial activities, why don't you invite them to meet in your so-called church?[40]

In response, folksingers and their supporters put forward a defense of the Washington Square scene in cultural terms. In contrast to Morris's elitist interpretation of culture, linked to the fine arts and tied to notions about education, background, and propriety, they viewed culture from an anthropological perspective, drawing on strands of 20th-century thought that embraced the value and integrity of local traditions. Folklorists such as Alan Lomax and Zora Neale Hurston had adopted similar anthropological methods in the 1930s as they studied the customs and practices of groups in the South and made field recordings of rural folk music. By the postwar period this ethnographical approach became increasingly influential in surveys of both rural and urban communities. In the 1950s in New York, for instance, groups displaced by highway construction and slum clearance in neighborhoods like East Tremont in the Bronx and Lincoln Square in Manhattan in effect developed their own local ethnographies as they battled against the urban renewal coalition—in vain—to keep their homes. As critics such as Robert Moses characterized their communities as "slums" that impeded progress in the city, they countered with descriptions of the complex ways of life and vital networks of social relations in their neighborhoods. Coalitions of Villagers and their allies embraced this model of resistance with great success, first against the Moses roadway and second against the Morris folksinging ban.[41]

The Right to Sing Committee mobilized neighborhood groups and made strong arguments about the cultural and economic value of the Washington Square scene. The committee received support from many local organizations, such as the VID, the *Village Voice*, numerous coffeehouses, Cinema 16 film society, and the Eighth Street Bookshop. At turns incensed and reflective in notes to Morris, area political and business leaders counted the benefits of Washington Square folksinging. Eli Wilentz, co-owner of the Eighth Street Bookshop, observed that while central city locations throughout America were in economic decline, Greenwich Village remained vibrant, in part due to the Sunday tourism that bolstered community establishments, including his store. Amos Vogel, executive secretary of Cinema 16, contended that the racially integrated gatherings represented the best of an expanding, yet imperfect, American democracy. Dan Wolf, editor of the *Village Voice*, chided Morris for allowing the Fifth Avenue Coach Company to idle its buses around the square and emit fumes and noise while claiming to care about the park's greenery and the quality of experience of local residents.[42]

Carmine De Sapio's backing of the folksingers was a surprise to many Villagers. With his district race against the VID's James Lanigan just five months away, De Sapio was

Folk music and political activism frequently converged in Greenwich Village in support of both national causes, such as civil rights and pacifism, and neighborhood endeavors, such as the "good government" movement. This flier advertises a 1962 benefit concert at the Village Gate to aid the Village Independent Democrats (VID) in a campaign against their party rivals from the Tamawa Club, run by Tammany boss Carmine De Sapio.

DAN DRASIN

In 1961 I was 18 years old, living in a cheap apartment in Greenwich Village a couple of floors above Izzy Young's Folklore Center, where, according to legend, 1960s counter-culture was born. Parks Commissioner Newbold Morris had just banned folk musicians from nearby Washington Square Park in an attempt—driven by local real-estate interests—to erase a funky, joyous tradition that dated back to the late 1940s. In response, the Folklore Center announced a protest event to take place on Sunday, April 9th.

Everyone knew <u>something</u> was going to happen that day, but no one knew exactly what. So it occurred to me that this just might make a good subject for a documentary. Fortunately I was then employed by D. A. Pennebaker, Richard Leackock, and Albert Maysles, pioneering documentary filmmakers who had designed their own highly portable 16mm filming gear (a rarity at that time) and generously allowed their employees to borrow it on weekends. So I commandeered some friends, three cameras, a briefcase-size portable tape recorder, and some expired black & white film that I'd hacked out of the my employers' freezer with an icepick, and off we went to the park.

When we arrived, about 100 folksingers had already come to defend their right to sing freely. Musicians, writers, artists, and activists debated with and confronted the police, eventually joining hands in solidarity until suddenly the police were ordered to clear the square, violence broke out, and many were arrested. Luckily we'd brought <u>just</u> enough film to cover the gist of the event.

$800 later (all the money I had in the world), I'd edited the footage into a finished 17-minute documentary that went on to earn nine international festival awards and became widely recognized as one of the first social-protest films of the turbulent 1960s.

In the end, the protest succeeded. There were no convictions
save one, of novelist Harold "Doc" Humes (seen being
wrangled into the paddy wagon at the end of <u>Sunday</u>), and the
parks commissioner agreed to reissue the license for weekly
musical gatherings in the square.

At its core, the protest had been a manifestation of the seed
that was to grow into a generation's struggle to address social issues across the board. Dissatisfaction with the status quo runs in cycles, with each generation having to learn
its social lessons anew. But it always comes down to the same
polarities: hierarchy vs. democracy, secrecy vs. transparency, opportunism vs. accountability.

Now, a half-century later, <u>Sunday</u> has been restored and
preserved at the UCLA Film and Television Archive, thanks to
the generosity of Martin Scorsese's Film Foundation.

– – –

*Dan Drasin is a media producer—filmmaker, photographer, and
writer—whose career spans five decades and whose films have
earned over two dozen international awards. His 1961 documentary* Sunday *is part of the permanent film collection at New York's
Museum of Modern Art.*

Washington Square Park, ca. 1956. Photograph by Nat Norman.

especially deliberate in his actions. Though his base included the South Village and lower Fifth Avenue, he broke from his constituents while acknowledging their concerns. His maneuver represented his recognition of the formidable Right to Sing movement. In an interview with the *Village Voice*, De Sapio explained, "I have no hesitancy in encouraging entertainment if it is not offensive and if performed in an orderly fashion." A lower Fifth Avenue resident himself, he added, "I have never witnessed any of the objectionable acts in Washington Square that I have read or heard about." De Sapio urged both sides to make concessions.[43]

Folksinging advocates described Sunday afternoon gatherings as wholesome and fun events. They characterized folksingers as respectful high school and college students, young urban professionals, and established musicians. For many attendees, the jams served as weekly social occasions. Historian David Rosner recalled that as a teenager from the Upper West Side, he looked forward to enjoying the free entertainment on Sundays with friends, some of whom were fellow alumni of the progressive Camp Thoreau in upstate New York. Many observers condemned Morris for banning an activity that was a positive outlet for youngsters at a time of high rates of juvenile delinquency.[44]

Local activist Jane Jacobs also backed the Right to Sing Committee. At this same time, Jacobs was leading the

community battle against Mayor Wagner's plan to redevelop 14 blocks of the West Village. She contended that neighborhood parks, such as Washington Square, became exuberant as a result of the creative ways that people used them. The Morris ban represented the kind of autocratic approach to urban policy that she railed against. In reply to the claim that the Sunday gatherings were morally depraved, Jacobs, the mother of two children, affirmed, "I have never seen anything or heard any song in Washington Square Park that would corrupt or hurt a child."[45]

Supporters of folksingers, like their adversaries, expressed concern about antisocial acts in the park, but they largely attributed the incidents to the growing homeless population in the area, not to musicians. The city's demolition of the Third Avenue elevated railway in 1956 had led to the displacement of numerous Bowery derelicts to Greenwich Village, where many slept on benches in Washington Square Park, flaunted liquor bottles in public, used drugs in broad daylight, or panhandled aggressively. The increase in vagrancy contributed to a rise in the number of petty narcotics dealers in the square. At a community meeting, *New York Times* writer and Villager Gilbert Millstein voiced his sorrow for the addicts and his antipathy towards the pushers. But he distinguished folksingers from lawbreakers. "In five years, I've yet to see one fight or arrest among the singers," he noted.[46]

One week after the April 9 demonstration, the Right to Sing Committee held a rally in Judson Memorial Church. More than 500 folksingers and their allies jammed into the building, as rain poured down outside. The featured speakers were Howard Moody, Gilbert Millstein, Ed Koch, Izzy Young, and Art D'Lugoff. Moody delivered the opening remarks, pledging to use all legal means to overturn the ban on folk music in Washington Square. D'Lugoff announced that Congressmen John Lindsay and Leonard Farbstein and City Councilman Stanley Isaacs offered their assistance to the folksingers. Excitement rose to a feverish pitch between speeches as popular musicians sang protest songs. Performers included Ed McCurdy, the Clancy Brothers, Logan English, Erik Darling, and the Shanty Boys. The event ended with a mass singing of Woody Guthrie's "This Land Is Your Land."[47]

The Right to Sing Committee staged another protest on Sunday, April 23. Approximately 2,000 demonstrators filled a block of Thompson Street, just south of Washington Square, on that beautiful spring day. Someone tacked a banner on a fence that scoffed: "Don't trample the asphalt." Protesters performed a musical between police barriers, portraying Morris as a villainous blockhead. Folksingers strummed guitars and banjos on the street, changed lyrics to tunes, and gibed "Newbold Morris is a grizzly bear" and "There ain't no Morris in this land." Dozens of people even picketed Morris's home on the Upper East Side. They carried signs quoting

previous: Jane Jacobs (center) in Washington Square Park, August 24, 1963. Photograph by Fred W. McDarrah.

opposite: Howard Moody in front of Judson Memorial Church, ca. 1963. In addition to forming the Right to Sing Committee with Izzy Young, Moody was a prominent Greenwich Village community leader active in civil rights, narcotics rehabilitation, Democratic Party reform, and the campaign against the expansion of Fifth Avenue in Washington Square.

Goethe (in German), Coleridge, and Emerson, and sang
a mocking rendition of "The Battle Hymn of the Republic."
Throughout the rally, Howard Moody urged cooperation and
restraint from the demonstrators. With 50 policemen on
duty, this time there were no incidents.[48]

The following Sunday's protesters were once again
orderly, though more restive. As 60 policemen kept watch,
more than 2,000 demonstrators amassed outside the
park. Early on, some people tried to evade barricades on
Washington Square South, but they were pushed back by
police on foot and horseback. Later, hundreds of protesters
skirted the blockade and gathered near the fountain. They
held hands in a circle and started singing "This Land Is Your
Land." As police moved to disperse the assembly, Chief
Inspector William F. Real intervened and lectured the group.
Noting the pending court case on the ban, he admonished,
"If you want to act up you're going to make a mess out of
everything and probably spoil the decision." Someone then
broke into a song, and the police approached. A skirmish
occurred between Detective David Yanolotos and New York
University freshman William French. As Yanolotos hustled
French away, the crowd booed and shouted. The student
was charged with disorderly conduct and felonious assault
for allegedly kicking the officer in the shin after being
ordered to move away from the fountain. The demonstrators
left Washington Square riled up.[49]

Days later the Right to Sing Committee suffered a legal
setback when State Supreme Court Justice William C. Hecht
Jr. upheld the city's ban against folksinging in Washington
Square. Persuaded by Morris's contention that the events
interfered with those who desired to use the park for sitting,
resting, and meditating, Hecht ruled that the court "may not
substitute its own judgment for that of the Commissioner
of Parks." Before the decision, Izzy Young had sent tele-
grams to President John F. Kennedy and Attorney General
Robert F. Kennedy exhorting them to lend "moral support."
Preoccupied with the disastrous Bay of Pigs Invasion, the
President and his staff had no time for Washington Square.
Despite the ruling, folksinging advocates pressed on. The
New York Civil Liberties Union announced it would appeal
the verdict with the Appellate Division. And the Right to Sing
Committee planned another protest.[50]

Hours before the next demonstration, Moody, in his
weekly sermon, articulated a defense of folksinging that was
in effect an expression of the multicultural ethos that defined
Greenwich Village and a distillation of communalism in folk
music revival culture. Reprinted that week in the *Village
Voice*, the homily was titled "Folksingers, Factions, and Our
Faith." Moody identified the "problem of pluralism" as the
essence of the park conflict and challenged his congregation, "Can we as a people of very diverse ethnic and religious

WHETHER YOU ARE 'IN' OR 'OUT,' BLACK OR WHITE, RICH OR POOR, 'SQUARE' OR 'BEAT,' WE ARE CHILDREN OF GOD CREATED TO LIVE TOGETHER IN THE NEIGHBOR-HOOD OF HIS WORLD.

backgrounds live together with some degree of accommodation so as not to force legally on others our mores and manners?" He blasted Morris and his supporters for trying to impose their ways on others and praised protesters for meeting the decree with spirited resistance. In a meditation on his church's involvement in the controversy, Moody discussed reasons relating to "justice" and "values." For Moody, like his contemporary Martin Luther King Jr., the concept of justice transcended the laws of man. "Even a law that is legal may be unjust," he observed. Moody stressed that social justice was the central concern of his church. In Greenwich Village, Judson Church demanded justice not just for folksingers, but for narcotics addicts ignored or criminalized by society, for Verrazano Street tenants threatened by an urban renewal project, for coffeehouse owners harassed by the Mafia and corrupt police. On the subject of values, he lambasted long-time residents for their hostility toward visitors to the community. Moody eloquently culminated his discourse:

> We are all immigrants that live or work or play in the Village whether we or our father came on a boat from Naples, or a bus out of Birmingham, or a flight from Dublin, or an A train on the IND. There is an equality that underlies all our differences. Whether you are "in" or "out," black or white, rich or poor, "square" or "beat," we are children of God created to live together in the neighborhood of his world.[51]

After the service, Moody and Izzy Young led 600 folksingers and their allies, singing a cappella, back into Washington Square Park without obstruction from the police. Moody informed Deputy Chief Inspector John E. Langton that the parks department banned "minstrelsy," or singing with instruments, but not without them. Langton agreed and allowed the folk enthusiasts to sing in the park. The demonstration was lively, though the choral group was reportedly frequently off-key. Around the fountain they sang "The Star-Spangled Banner" and a few ditties that lampooned Morris. They altered the lyrics of "This Land Is Your Land" to "This Park Is Your Park."[52]

After five weeks of protests, Mayor Wagner acceded to the demands of the Right to Sing Committee. In a press conference at City Hall, the mayor, Police Commissioner Michael J. Murphy, and Parks Commissioner Morris announced that folksinging with musical accompaniment would be permitted in the square "on a controlled basis." Appealing to both advocates and critics of the musicians, the mayor explained that the revised policy represented a compromise. Folksingers would be allowed to perform from 3 p.m. to 6 p.m., restricted to the area between the fountain and the Arch. During the trial period, no permits were necessary. The singers and their supporters were jubilant. A delighted Izzy Young proclaimed that the originally scheduled Sunday rally would be converted into a "Thank you, Mayor Wagner" demonstration.[53]

On May 14, folksingers returned to Washington Square with their guitars and banjos and played for three hours, as a crowd of more than 4,000 enjoyed the sunny day in the park. At a short rally held that day, Howard Moody announced the dissolution of the Right to Sing Committee. After the reading of appreciative telegrams sent by the committee to the mayor, parks commissioner, and police commissioner, Kelsey Marechal—co-owner of the theatre One Sheridan Square—quipped to folksingers to "keep in tune and keep your beards combed." The event took place without incident, as 55 policemen stood by.[54]

Furious with the mayor, the Washington Square Dignity committee submitted a petition to City Hall with 2,200 signatures protesting folksinging in the park. Members of the committee met with the mayor and deputy mayor and described alleged acts of immorality in the Square area after songfests. On subsequent Sundays, the crowds were considerably smaller, and the clamor and publicity died down. Still, the battle for Washington Square Park left many longtime residents resentful that their concerns about law and order and family values were disregarded. They bristled with indignation at Democratic Party leaders for submitting to the demands of agitators, beatniks, blacks, gays, and multiculturalists.[55]

In July the folksingers achieved their victory, as the Appellate Division of the State Supreme Court unanimously reversed the Hecht ruling. The court ordered the parks commissioner "to receive and reconsider" applications for permits for Sunday singing. A disingenuous Morris remarked, "I never had the slightest hostility toward folksinging or folksingers. I'm a singer myself." Playfully, Izzy Young extended an olive branch to his nemesis, "We all hope that Commissioner Morris will come down to the park and lead us in some songs."[56]

The Right to Sing movement was successful as a result of compelling arguments bolstered by energetic demonstrations. Of 11 people arrested during the five rallies, only one was found guilty of a crime: novelist Harold Humes Jr. was convicted of making a speech in the park without a permit. The demonstrations attracted extensive media coverage in New York and beyond. Articles with photographs often made the front pages of newspapers. Television reports were broadcast as far away as West Germany. The movement showcased the organizational talents of Howard Moody and won him praise throughout the nation. *The New York Times*, whose coverage eventually became sympathetic to the musicians, ran a glowing feature on the "folk-singing pastor." The Judson minister's plea for racial and ethnic pluralism made him the conscience of not only the folksingers, but also a society struggling with the ideas of democracy and equality.

above top: Film still from *Sunday*, 1961.

above bottom: Demonstrators sing Woody Guthrie's "This Land Is Your Land" in this film still from Dan Drasin's *Sunday*.

In a letter to Moody, City College of New York student David Roberts observed, "Through your actions you provided those protesting with the skilled leadership, purpose, and sense of being right which is so very vital in making protests of any kind effective and meaningful."[57]

When I first came to the Village, I played
at Gerde's; and I met Bob Dylan there and he
told me about the other places to play, like
the Gaslight. So I began playing the different
clubs. I used to come to Gerde's and see the
hoot. I liked to hear the things that the new
people were writing. During those first few
weeks in New York I was approached by lots of
managers and agents. I was overwhelmed by all
the success I was having.

Singer-songwriter Buffy Sainte-Marie[1]

THE
VILLAGE
SCENE IN
THE
EARLY
1960S

R ecalling the peak years of the folk music revival in Greenwich Village, singer-songwriter Tom Paxton reflected on the importance of the clubs, taverns, and coffeehouses in the Washington Square vicinity. These venues mattered, he noted, for both artistic reasons and social purposes. Paxton singled out the two preeminent Greenwich Village folk music clubs in the early 1960s: Gerde's Folk City and the Gaslight. They booked many of the same acts but had distinct identities. While the Gaslight, a coffeehouse, did not sell alcohol, it was in a central location on MacDougal Street between Bleecker and West 3rd Streets. Folk City was several blocks away, on the corner of West 4th and Mercer Streets. For drinks and conversation, some folksingers ventured to the White Horse Tavern, on Hudson Street in the West Village. The Lion's Head on Christopher Street and the Limelight on Seventh Avenue South were other preferred destinations for banter and beer. "But it was really the Kettle of Fish where all the ideas, gossip, songs, and friendships were exchanged," Paxton recalled about the bar next to the Gaslight. Folksingers often relaxed at Kettle of Fish between sets at the Gaslight. "There were constant comings and goings, and the cast of characters included Bob Dylan, Phil Ochs, Dave Van Ronk, Eric Andersen, and David Blue."[2]

- - -

Many people romanticized the intellectual and artistic atmosphere of Greenwich Village. "Going to the Village for the first time in 1952 was like walking into a dream," writer and Indianapolis native Dan Wakefield reflected. "It not only looked different from the rest of New York ... it sounded different too." Wakefield spoke poetically about the local aura. "The special quiet of the Village suggested creation rather than commerce and conveyed a tone of mystery," he mused. In 1963, during the peak period of the folk music revival, a local resident asked, "And where else in this city can you go to a bar and find an intelligent conversation going?" In the early

A crowd gathers outside Rick Allmen's Cafe Bizarre on West 3rd Street in Greenwich Village, November 1959.

1960s, an observer drawn to the area arts scene wondered, "With an artist, there's so much to talk about. Beauty, for instance. What can you talk about to an athlete? How far he swims?" But Greenwich Village was never actually the idyllic landscape that some commentators made it out to be. These accounts overlooked the organized crime, narcotics abuse, racial strife, and juvenile gangs that also characterized the neighborhood.[3]

Beneath the provincial ruminations and triumphal boasting of Village partisans lurked a bigger story about artistic creativity. Greenwich Village was a conduit of ideas, made possible by the concentration of performance spaces around Washington Square Park. These began to sprout up in the late 1950s and proliferated in the early 1960s, especially after folksingers and their allies won the battle of Washington Square in 1961. If observers wondered why the folk music revival flowered in Greenwich Village, they needed only to walk down MacDougal Street from West 4th and make a left onto Bleecker. Numerous clubs lined these colorful streets. The density fostered creative interactions as well as collaboration and competition, and the Village became an incubator of artistic innovation. Skilled and striving artists in close proximity challenged traditional boundaries in lyrics and style in folk music. In the words of David Amram, a jazz composer, multi-instrumentalist, and folksinger: "There was a cross-pollination of music, painting, writing—an incredible world of painters, sculptors, musicians, writers, and actors, enough so we could

View down MacDougal Street, 1966. Greenwich Village's rich intellectual, cultural, and artistic associations radiated a powerful allure in the postwar era, even as the federal government and the media touted the suburbs as the future of American society. At night and on the weekends, visitors flocked to the neighborhood's coffeehouse district and particularly to MacDougal Street. Photograph by Robert Otter.

be each other's fans. When I had concerts, painters would come, and I'd go play jazz at their art gallery openings, and I played piano while Beats read their poetry."[4]

As a result of the artistic ferment in the Greenwich Village coffeehouse district, by 1960 the neighborhood had become the epicenter of the national folk music renaissance. In contrast to the 1950s, when many folksingers—such as Happy Traum, John Cohen, and Dave Van Ronk—arrived from the outer boroughs or the suburbs, the Village in the early 1960s attracted songwriters from points near and far in a manner reminiscent of the 1930s, when the revival first burgeoned in the city. Notable arrivals included Tom Paxton from Oklahoma, Len Chandler and Phil Ochs from Ohio, Carolyn Hester from Texas, Patrick Sky from Georgia, Mark Spoelstra from California, Judy Collins and Judy Roderick from Colorado, Bonnie Dobson and Ian and Sylvia Tyson from Canada, and Bob Dylan from Minnesota. Folksingers found ample work in approximately 20 clubs in a five-block area. Troubadours made little money in the smaller rooms, and talent agents rarely scouted them, but they saw the "holes in the wall" as starting points that would lead to the big time of the Gaslight and Gerde's Folk City.[5]

The multiple Village venues allowed folksingers to hone their skills. The clubs afforded musicians opportunities to experiment with new material and make mistakes in front of sympathetic yet discerning audiences. They learned methods to hold a crowd's attention and had a chance to gain a following. In the better clubs, they encountered agents, managers, and record company executives. Critics, notably *The New York Times* music columnist Robert Shelton, reviewed performances in the premier Village venues. Folksingers launched records in clubs, and, in some cases, solo acts or groups developed a special association with a particular venue.

Dave Van Ronk, 1957-60. Before the folk music revival's commercial boom in the late 1950s brought musicians to New York City from all over the nation, many Greenwich Village folksingers hailed from the city's outer boroughs. Dave Van Ronk, a Brooklyn native, earned the moniker "Mayor of MacDougal Street" for his pervasive presence in the area and for his role as a mentor and friend to numerous folksingers. Photograph by Aaron Rennert.

THE GREENWICH VILLAGE POSTWAR ARTS SCENE AND THE FORMATION OF FOLK MUSIC CLUBS

Painters, poets, actors, and musicians from all over the nation moved to Greenwich Village in the postwar era, drawn by the neighborhood's bohemian character. They settled in low-income areas, especially in tenements southwest of Washington Square Park on MacDougal Street and Minetta Lane. This area, the South Village, was a predominantly working-class Italian district, but an area undergoing demographic change at this time. By the middle of the 1950s, nearly 100

artists resided in this enclave. Their local haunts included Minetta Tavern, Kettle of Fish, and the San Remo.[6] The Village lured reformers, radicals, and artists intent on changing the nation's political and cultural order. They understood the neighborhood's iconoclastic history and wanted to leave their own mark there. As *Village Voice* co-founder and publisher Ed Fancher declared in the late 1950s, "A lot of people think the Village died 50 years ago. We don't. Those are the great days; this is the Golden Age."[7] In his memoir *Kafka Was the Rage* (1993), *New York Times* book critic and columnist Anatole Broyard recalled the attraction of the neighborhood after the war:

> The Village, like New York City itself, had an immense, beckoning sweetness. It was like Paris in the '20s—with the difference that it was our city. We weren't strangers there, but familiars. The Village was charming, shabby, intimate, accessible, almost like a street fair. We lived in the bars and on the benches of Washington Square. We shared the adventure of trying to be, starting to be, writers or painters.[8]

As Broyard recounted, many Greenwich Village taverns in the 1950s resembled literary salons. Artists and intellectuals congregated in bars to talk, drink, smoke, argue, and pontificate. The San Remo, on the corner of Bleecker and MacDougal Streets, for example, was the favorite haunt of actor and director Julian Beck, actress and director Judith Malina, composer John Cage, choreographer Merce Cunningham, writer and social critic Paul Goodman, and writer and poet James Agee. Malina described the Remo as "gay and intellectual, rather close to my notion of a Paris cafe." In contrast to most New York bars, the Remo welcomed interracial couples and gay men. Beat novelist John Clellon Holmes based his roman à clef *Go* (1952) partly on the habitués of the Remo, including Allen Ginsberg and Jack Kerouac. Kerouac, too, found inspiration at the bar and incorporated Remo hipsters into *The Subterraneans* (1958), a tale of interracial love.[9]

The White Horse Tavern, on Hudson Street in the West Village, was a stomping ground for literary figures Dylan Thomas, Norman Mailer, James Baldwin, Clement Greenberg, and Delmore Schwartz. Jack Kerouac frequented the White Horse while he wrote *On the Road* in a nearby apartment. The White Horse also served as a forum for debates on politics and culture. After Friday night meetings at the office of the newspaper *The Catholic Worker*, editor Michael Harrington held informal seminars on topics ranging from leftist labor leaders to factions of the Spanish Civil War. Over pints of beer, crowds joined the Clancy Brothers in songs of the Irish rebellions.[10]

previous: Bob Dylan at the Kettle of Fish bar, July 1964. Situated in the heart of Greenwich Village at 114 MacDougal Street, Kettle of Fish was a favorite place for folksingers to relax, socialize, and have a drink before or after performances at the neighboring Gaslight Cafe. The concentration of coffeehouses, taverns, and restaurants on the MacDougal-Bleecker axis just south of Washington Square Park facilitated the exchange of ideas among artists and the formation of social relationships that nurtured and expanded the folk music revival. Photograph by Douglas R. Gilbert.

below: The *Village Voice* office and Cedar Tavern, ca. 1975. The *Village Voice* and the Cedar Tavern were two iconoclastic neighborhood institutions in the 1950s. The former, a weekly newspaper founded in 1955, promoted advocacy journalism and alternative arts criticism, while the latter became a hangout for Abstract Expressionist painters and Beat poets and novelists. Photograph by Edmund V. Gillon.

DAVID AMRAM

In 1955, at the age of 24, I moved to New York. During those days almost everything south of 14th Street was different than the Asphalt Jungle of Midtown Manhattan. Greenwich Village was a universe unto itself. It felt like an oasis where people from all over the world came to commune. Poets, visual artists, novelists, classical composers, playwrights, jazz musicians, folksingers, college professors, comedians, chess champions, bartenders, waiters and waitresses, moving men, short order cooks, numbers runners, actors, and a wild assortment of <u>bon vivants</u> all felt at home. They could finally be in a place where they could fit in because the Village was actually a joyous community of misfits.

We all had an audience for whatever we were doing, whether it was a jazz or classical musician performing, or an opening for an off-off-(WAY-off) Broadway play, or a reading from a book or a poetry recital, or folk musicians having a hootenanny. The comedians were there, too, reminding us of our shared foibles. They found the Village to be an endless source of inspiration—a playground for all us nut cases. That's what Lenny Bruce told me one night outside the Village Vanguard. When comedians performed in coffeehouses or by park benches or at the "Bring your Own Bottle" parties hosted by painters in their spacious lofts, they could break in new material.

It was at one of these loft parties that I met and became friends with and the musical collaborator of Jack Kerouac. I also played with the folk pioneers of the late '50s, including Ramblin' Jack Elliott, the Clancy Brothers, Jean Ritchie, Logan English, and many others. Pete Seeger, Odetta, and I all played with musicians from every style because there were no cultural commissars telling us what was Correct and what was <u>Verboten</u>.

I was introduced to Woody Guthrie through Ahmed Bashir, a devout Muslim who was a friend of Charlie Parker, Sonny

Rollins, and Charles Mingus, and with whom I was playing at the time. Two weeks later, at a tiny Lower East Side church, I met Joe Papp. It was a year before he began his New York Shakespeare Festival in Central Park. I subsequently collaborated with Joe for 12 years as his composer. Some of the actors who worked with the Festival, like Jerry Stiller, Ann Meara, George C. Scott, Colleen Dewhurst, and Crystal Field, would sometimes come downtown after their shows and join us in our jam sessions.

It was an informal community of malcontents, dreamers, and fun-lovers. The Village was a place of constant stimulation and inspiration. With low rents, no expectations of becoming a superstar, scarcely any pressure to become a financial titan, most of us just pursued the dream of becoming some kind of an artist. We had the space to enjoy life and appreciate one another's company and celebrate each other's work.

– – –

David Amram is acknowledged as one of America's most prolific composers of classical music, as well as a virtuoso multi-instrumentalist and pioneer of the jazz French horn, spoken word, and world music. His endless collaborations include recordings with folk icons Pete Seeger, Odetta, Ramblin' Jack Elliott, and Bob Dylan. Now in his ninth decade, he remains a tireless advocate for the lasting power of the world's folkloric treasures, which he is known to share with anybody and everybody.

The atmosphere of the San Remo bar, on the corner of Bleecker and MacDougal, evoked a literary salon and drew a diverse clientele to converse, drink, eat, and smoke. Among the diners pictured here are actor Montgomery Clift (far left) and novelist Jack Kerouac (far right).

On University Place between 8th and 9th Streets was the Cedar Tavern, a favorite haunt of the Abstract Expressionists, in particular Jackson Pollock, Franz Kline, Willem de Kooning, and Philip Guston. Rugged in appearance and cool in demeanor, the painters styled themselves as rebels and, along with some Beat writers and New York School poets, gave the nondescript bar a reputation for heavy drinking. Their conduct was at times outrageous. In a fit, Jackson Pollock once kicked in the men's room door, and Jack Kerouac, in a stupor, urinated in an ashtray. Demanding attention, Pollock was usually the focal point. He boasted about his paintings, insulted other patrons, and scuffled occasionally with his friendly rivals Kline and de Kooning. On August 12, 1956, the day after his death in a car accident, dozens of painters gathered at the Cedar Tavern to mourn the loss of their volatile comrade.[11]

The folk music revival thrived in this rebellious context in the late 1950s. As the Sunday afternoon gatherings in Washington Square Park increased in size and intensity, a number of performance venues that welcomed folksingers (among other entertainers) opened in the neighborhood. "The folkniks are on the move as never before," Ren Grevatt announced in *Billboard* in 1959. Grevatt cited a variety of record releases, the Newport Folk Festival, and folk concerts throughout the nation. He also noted that the Folklore Center's Izzy Young had observed the rapid increase in sales of folk discs by companies such as Folkways, Elektra, Tradition, Audio-Video, and, to some extent, Riverside.[12]

Though Grevatt's *Billboard* article made only passing reference to folk music in New York clubs, a few venues were starting to appear in Greenwich Village, notably Art D'Lugoff's Village Gate, which opened in 1958 on the corner of Thompson and Bleecker Streets. D'Lugoff was already knowledgeable about the music business, with extensive experience as a concert promoter and the Tarriers' manager. But opening a 450-seat cabaret was a new type of venture. To gain advice from other proprietors and to learn the tricks of the trade, D'Lugoff visited some of the premier folk music venues nationwide, including the Gate of Horn in Chicago and the hungry i in San Francisco. He converted a deteriorating flophouse into a spacious and professional performance venue. Following in the footsteps of the Village Vanguard and the earlier Cafe Society, the politically progressive D'Lugoff featured a wide range of musical styles at the Village Gate, including folk, blues, jazz, comedy, and even musicals; he also hosted political events. As *Caravan* magazine noted in May 1958, "The New York Scene is a busy one these days, what with [Washington Square] open every Sunday afternoon, [American Youth Hostel] Song Fests

The Village Gate, ca. 1967.
Photograph by Avital D'Lugoff.

right: Odetta performs at the Village Gate, July 1966. Village Gate owner Art D'Lugoff demonstrated a strong commitment to social activism, hosting numerous political events, rallies, and fundraisers at his nightclub. Odetta was often called "The Voice of the Civil Rights Movement." Photograph by Diana Davies.

below: D'Lugoff showed a knack for booking unlikely artistic combinations, as he did in this 1960 bill with folk singer Pete Seeger and blues pianist Memphis Slim. The Gate's eclecticism became a trademark, attracting patrons from diverse backgrounds.

following: White Horse Tavern, ca. 1975. On Hudson Street in the West Village, the White Horse Tavern developed a reputation as a gathering place for folksingers such as the Clancy Brothers, Bob Dylan, and Richard Fariña, as well as for many literary figures, including Seymour Krim. Photograph by Edmund V. Gillon.

-Limited Engagement-

TWO WEEKS ONLY!

STARTING TUES., APRIL 12 THRU SUNDAY, APRIL 24

PETE SEEGER

Pete Seeger records exclusively for Folkways Records

AND MEMPHIS SLIM ON PIANO

TWO SHOWS NITELY • 9:30 and 11:30

THREE SHOWS • FRI., SAT. • 9:30, 11:30, 1:30

Art D'lugoff's **VILLAGE GATE**

Thompson St., Cor. Bleecker St. • 2 Blocks South of Washington Square Park

MAKE YOUR RESERVATIONS NOW • GR 5-5120

Coming Attractions to the Village Gate:

APRIL 26 • Marais & Miranda

MAY 17 • The Limeliters

(Lou Gottlieb, Glen Yarbrough, Alex Hassilev)
THE HOTTEST FOLK SONG TRIO IN THE COUNTRY
DIRECT FROM SAN FRANCISCO'S HUNGRY i

---

every Sunday evening, upwards of eight or ten folk-singing parties a month, a [New York] Folksingers Guild concert along about the last week in each month, The Shanty Boys regular shindig the first Friday of each month … [and] Art D'Lugoff opening his new club where folksingers have a special invitation." The Village Gate's opening act was Pete Seeger, followed by Earl Robinson.[13]

Opening a nightclub in the Village was not easy. D'Lugoff had to deal with local gangsters and crooked police, but managed to survive and flourish. The Village Gate and the nearby Folklore Center became centers of the folk revival, offering a welcoming space for new performers and their fans. When Dave Van Ronk rehearsed with Paul Clayton, Bob Yellin, and other musicians for a Folkways album of sailing songs, they gathered at the Gate in the afternoons. "Art D'Lugoff had just opened the club and was having trouble obtaining the necessary license to hire entertainment," Van Ronk recollected. "He was a Jew in an Italian neighborhood where liquor licenses had traditionally been acquired only by becoming someone's son-in-law, so everything he did in that place had to be done two or three times, because the other bar owners had the inspectors coming back again and again. … It being a new place, Art was more than happy to have some people in there, so he invited us to do our singing in the downstairs room and even supplied pitchers of beer to fend off dehydration." Their album, *Foc'sle Songs and Shanties,* produced by Kenneth Goldstein, appeared on the Folkways label in 1959.[14]

At the same time, the Beat poetry scene flowered in Greenwich Village cafes. "In the fifties, the original iconoclasts were the beat poets. It was very much a literary scene in the Village," Paul Colby, the owner of the Bitter End, remembered. Poets sometimes did readings accompanied by jazz. By the decade's end, hordes of weekend visitors were crowding into such nightspots on Bleecker Street as Cafe Borgia, the Figaro, the Rafio, the Flamingo, the Dragon's Den, the Cock and Bull, and Take 3 to enjoy readings. MacDougal Street had the Rienzi, the Reggio, the Continental, Cafe Wha?, the Gaslight, and Playhouse Cafe. Most of these did not feature folk

performers, but there was overlap between the Beat literary movement and the folk music revival, in New York as well as in San Francisco and Chicago. Folksingers David Amram and John Cohen, for instance, straddled both artistic trends, and the poetry of Allen Ginsberg and the novels of Jack Kerouac influenced the folk music of Bob Dylan.[15]

The emergence of the Beat and folk movements in Greenwich Village was in part a result of the area's coffee-house boom in the 1950s. Long a feature of Italian enclaves in American neighborhoods such as New York's Little Italy, Boston's North End, and San Francisco's North Beach, coffeehouses exploded in popularity in the postwar era. When the South Village was overwhelmingly Italian, coffeehouses sold espresso and pastries and functioned as social gathering places for area residents. The exodus of Italian Americans to the suburbs and the ascent of the literary and musical movements transformed the South Village in the late 1950s. Aware of the trends, entrepreneurs opened a number of coffeehouses in the Bleecker-MacDougal district to provide venues for poets and folksingers. To enhance the artistic milieu and attract a diverse clientele, cafe owners frequently hung the work of local painters on the walls. Beat poetry readings sometimes became theatrical as bards modulated their voices and made physical gestures to maintain an audience's attention. Allen Ginsberg in particular was a master at captivating audiences through his freewheeling delivery. A *Nation* reporter described the scene at a Beat reading in 1959: "With tom-toms beating behind them, the soft, intense voices of young men fascinated their audience, who applauded lustily and chanted, 'Yeah, man' after each rendition." In the effervescent environment of a coffeehouse, artists exchanged ideas across genres and performed on small stages in front

above: A spray-painted sign outside Cafe Wha?, May 1960. At the corner of MacDougal Street and Minetta Lane, Cafe Wha? was au courant with alternative artistic trends and featured entertainment that included Beat poets, jazz musicians, and folksingers. This sign playfully incorporates some of the hip jargon of the day in an appeal to potential customers.

left: Entrance to Cafe Wha?, January 1967. The nightclub's marquee announces a performance by The Fugs, a satirical folk-rock band known for their opposition to the Vietnam War and their candid and provocative lyrics.

DAVID WILKES

In the late 1940s, my parents, music lovers from the Bronx, used to send me to summer camp at Camp Woodland in upstate New York. The most moving experience of my youth was sitting around a campfire at night listening to a folk musician singing and playing his banjo. Subconsciously, I remembered his name, but it wasn't until a decade later, when I became enamored by the Weavers, that I put two and two together and remembered that this folksinger was Pete Seeger! That set my musical tastes for life. I bought loads of folk albums by all the labels and visited Greenwich Village basket houses—music venues that didn't pay the artist or charge an admission fee but passed a basket among the customers for them to drop in any monies they wanted to pay.

One of those coffeehouses was the Cock and Bull, owned by a New Yorker named Fred Weintraub with his partner Manny Roth, who also owned the Cafe Wha? on MacDougal Street. Fred later bought out Manny and changed the name of the place to the Bitter End, probably because it was the last stop on Bleecker Street before the long and dark walk east towards the Bowery. Actually, there was one more establishment, right next to the Bitter End, called the Dugout—a dive that mostly served the down and out, but which later became a hip spot for the singers and patrons of the Bitter End ... especially since the Bitter End didn't serve alcohol ... just ice cream, cake, coffee and teas.

As I hung around the Village and frequented all the clubs, I met a woman who worked for Fred Weintraub named Bea Marks. She told me to drop by the club at any time. Since I already got in free, it didn't seem like that great an offer, but late one night while I was walking past the club, Bea was on the phone near the door, saw me, and offered me a job as the Door Man! I took it and started my path in the music business in the front door of the most famous folk club in the nation. Night after night I would see the new stars, such as Peter, Paul and Mary, Tom Paxton, and the Tarriers (with Eric Weissberg, my old bunkmate at Camp Woodland), in addition to the hot new stand-up comedians, such as Bill Cosby, Joan Rivers, and Woody Allen, and the old folk standard bearers Pete Seeger, Josh White, Theo Bikel, Ed McCurdy, and Oscar Brand.

In short order, I became the manager of the Bitter End and established friendships with many artists. Stars emerged, such as Richie Havens, John Denver, and José Feliciano. The club was packed every night. We turned the house with three shows nightly. Movie stars and the world's media hovered over us. It was magical, made possible by the unique social, political, and artistic atmosphere of Greenwich Village in the 1950s and '60s.

– – –

David Wilkes has been an integral figure in New York's folk scene for six decades, as manager of the Bitter End; a music publisher of popular songs; an executive producer of many recordings; a manager or co-manager of artists, such as Jerry Jeff Walker, Emmylou Harris, Richie Havens, Tom Paxton, and Josh White Jr.; and Vice President of A&R for Vanguard Records, a folk label that helped launch the careers of many folk luminaries of the 1950s and 1960s. He is still active as a manager, agent, and publisher of folk artists, a consultant to the Canadian folk music industry, and the U.S. representative to their popular folk group, Sultans of String.

above: Entrance of the Gaslight Cafe, June 1959. Owner John Mitchell opened the Gaslight Poetry Cafe on MacDougal Street in 1958, initially presenting Beat poetry readings and subsequently offering folk music. The subterranean establishment, formerly a coal cellar, quickly became a premier venue in the neighborhood for folksingers.

of engaged crowds. The Beats' experimentation with text, image, and sound influenced folk musicians and aspiring theatermakers in Off-Off-Broadway productions to take risks in their own performances.[16]

Some venues, such as the Gaslight Poetry Cafe at 116 MacDougal Street, featured both poetry readings and folk music. Of the numerous folk houses in Greenwich Village in 1960, the Gaslight was particularly prominent. "It was a club I wanted to play, needed to," Bob Dylan remembered about his first days in the Village in 1961. Formerly a coal cellar, the Gaslight was musty and filthy, furnished mostly with round oak tables and barely illuminated by Tiffany-style lamps hanging overhead. Without air conditioning, the room often became stifling in the summer. According to fire codes, the maximum capacity was 110 people, but sometimes 130 squeezed in for a hootenanny. Founded in 1958 by John Mitchell, the coffeehouse featured readings in 1959 by poets like Allen Ginsberg, Gregory Corso, and Ted Joans, and subsequently showcased flamenco, comedy, and folk music. At the outset, the Gaslight was a "basket house," where performers circulated a basket to solicit contributions after sets. Some early regular folksingers were Roy Berkeley, Len Chandler, and Tom Paxton. All blossoming songwriters, they helped the squalid basement gain a reputation for excellent entertainment.[17]

The Gaslight Cafe's entertainment director was Beat poet Hugh Romney. A countercultural figure, Romney was comedic and irreverent. Blues and gospel singer Reverend Gary Davis presided over Romney's marriage to Bonnie Beecher in 1965 at the Gaslight in a ceremony attended by Bob Dylan, Tom Paxton, and Dave Van Ronk. Romney, later called Wavy Gravy when he adopted his hippie-clown persona, recollected ongoing conflict at the Gaslight between John Mitchell and municipal authorities. The tension made Mitchell wary and suspicious. "When Tom Paxton first showed up from Fort Dix, John Mitchell of the Gaslight was positive he was a cop," Romney recalled. "So everybody was nice to Tom until it was time to get stoned; then it was 'Well, we have an appointment.'"[18]

Mitchell experienced a series of legal problems at the Gaslight and often clashed with city officials. In June 1960, the fire department closed down his establishment for violating health regulations. He reopened in September after installing sprinklers but, along with other Village club owners, he ran into additional problems due to the police department's strict enforcement of the city's antiquated cabaret law. During the 1961 Washington Square folk music controversy, Mitchell, still fighting the city over code violations, sold the club to Clarence Hood, who managed it along with his son Sam through the 1960s.[19]

Dave Van Ronk's jug band performs at the Gaslight Cafe, November 8, 1963. Thanks in part to regular performances by the proficient Van Ronk (second from right), the dimly lit club gained a reputation for excellence.

GERDE'S FOLK CITY
AND THE BITTER END

In 1952 William Gerdes sold his South Village restaurant on West 3rd Street to Calabrian immigrant Mike Porco, his brother John, and their cousin Joe Bastone. For around four years, business was brisk at Gerde's Restaurant. The business depended largely on local factory workers, who came for the good Italian food, affordable drinks, and relaxed conversation. Mike Porco was widely regarded as a personable owner, and Gerde's Restaurant became popular in the community.[20]

A turning point occurred in 1956, when city officials ordered the closing and demolition of Gerde's to accommodate the construction of high-rise buildings that were part of Robert Moses's Washington Square Southeast Title I project. Fortunately for Mike Porco, he was able to relocate his restaurant to the corner of West 4th and Mercer Streets, but he lost nearly all customers as a result of the demolition of the area's factories and tenements. The Washington Square Southeast project irrevocably transformed the character of the neighborhood.[21]

The new Gerde's Restaurant worked to adjust to the changing environment in the late 1950s. The Porcos engaged their customers with jokes and banter. The restaurant was

Mike Porco (center) with Folk City kitchen staff, May 1961. Photograph by Irwin Gooen.

approximately 2,000 square feet and included a bar and a dining room, separated by a partition. To increase business, Porco hired a piano player and tried a singing trio, but neither did well. "I knew I would have to try something different," he recollected.[22]

In 1960 Tom Prendergast, who worked in advertising, walked into Izzy Young's Folklore Center and convinced him to consider transforming Gerde's into a folk music club. Young recognized the need for a major venue, and the two walked a few blocks to Gerde's to discuss the proposition with Mike Porco. Porco recalled the conversation between him and Prendergast and Young at the bar:

> They ordered a bottle of beer and I see them looking and looking. They finally asked me, 'Do you have entertainment here?' I said, 'Yes, certain days I do.' 'Oh,' they say, 'do you have a cabaret license?' 'Yes. I have every license which is necessary.' He says, 'Tell me, would you like to put folk music here?' So I said, 'Tell me what is that.' So he says, 'Those people who play guitar.' I said, 'Well, a lot of people play guitar. But the type of music you talk about don't ring no bells with me.' So he says, 'Have you heard of Pete Seeger?' I said, 'Yes.' He said, 'Have you heard of Burl Ives?' I said, 'Yes.' He said, 'Well, those are all folksingers.' 'Oh,' I said, 'those are people who sing songs, who try to deliver messages through their songs.' He said, 'You've got it! I would like to offer you something. Do you have microphones?' I said, 'No; if I have a piano player, you can hear him. I don't want anything too loud.' He said, 'Well, you've got to have microphones. I'll tell you what I want to do. If you want to get together, we'll give you an offer. We will take care of the music. We'll bring in some

The Kossoy Sisters and Billy Faier, 1957–60. Billy Faier was an expert banjo player, and the Kossoy Sisters—Irene on guitar and Ellen with the banjo—were practitioners of old-time music. All three were born and raised in New York City, and they became "citybillies": musicians who transmitted traditional rural songs to urban audiences in ways that were respectful and faithful to indigenous styles. Photograph by Ray Sullivan.

above: Marquee at Gerde's Folk City, December 1961. Located at 11 West 4th Street and owned by Mike Porco, Gerde's was a focal point of the folk music revival in New York. Photograph by Fred W. McDarrah.

Following: Gerde's Folk City, early 1960s.

lights. I guarantee we'll bring some people in here. This way you can do more business at the bar.' I said, 'Yeah, but how are you going to pay the entertainers?' He said, 'We're gonna charge at the door. Whatever we charge at the door, we'll keep. Whatever food or drinks you sell, you keep.' I said, 'I have friends who come in at night. How am I going to charge them at the door?' 'If you have a few friends,' he said, 'just give me the signal, we'll let them come in.'[23]

It was a simple deal. Prendergast and Young would pay for publicity and the singers and would keep the gate at the door. Porco would sell food and drinks and keep the returns. They reached an agreement and shook hands. There was nothing in writing. Izzy Young, a whirl of energy and a fountain of ideas, was a lousy businessman. About the arrangement with Porco, he later reflected, "He couldn't lose. We couldn't win."[24]

Porco, Young, and Prendergast called the club "The Fifth Peg," after the fifth tuning peg of a banjo. They officially opened it on January 26, 1960, featuring Brother John Sellers and Ed McCurdy. Opening night was memorable, and the Fifth Peg was filled beyond capacity. Some wanted to hear the music, while others were simply curious. In the following weeks, Young booked some of the finest musicians on the folk music circuit, including Cynthia Gooding, Tommy Makem and the Clancy Brothers, Memphis Slim, Billy Faier, the Tarriers, Brownie McGhee and Sonny Terry, Carolyn Hester, Cisco Houston, and

Theo Bikel. *New York Times* critic Robert Shelton came to shows regularly, and the club earned a place on the radar of musicians' managers, such as Harold Leventhal. Crowds thinned out after those opening weeks, but the Fifth Peg acquired a reputation for first-class folk music.[25]

In some ways, the Fifth Peg was a sociological experiment, bringing together folkies, generally middle-class and liberal in background, with Italian workers, mostly culturally conservative. By and large, the scene was lively, and the crowds mixed well, but sometimes there were incidents as customers encroached upon each other's territory. Fights occasionally broke out as workers at the bar disturbed shows that were taking place on stage in the adjacent room, or because a folksinger's ballad interrupted a conversation among workers. Ramblin' Jack Elliott recalled an incident when his friend Harry Jackson, a cowboy singer, performed in front of a drunken audience. As Elliott remembered, chatter increased during a song, prompting Jackson to blurt: "Well … ar … ar … ah … I ah … shuck … you know … I mean … doggone it … what I mean is … a fella gets up to sing a song, he's got something to say and it's good. A lot of you are just drinkin' and talkin' and it's kinda hard to hear, and a fella wants to sing and ah … doggone it, *shut up!*" The crowd became silent. Jackson continued. A couple of songs later the crowd started talking again. Elliott described it as one of the finest moments in the club's history.[26]

Despite the artistic success of the Fifth Peg, Young barely made money even on a good night, and the tension between him and Porco increased. Admission was a modest $1.50, and Monday nights were free, making the club an unsustainable business proposition. It seemed to Young that Porco was trying to push him out and find another booking manager. In late April, Porco asked Young and Prendergast to take a leave of absence from the club and "see what happens." At this juncture, Young did not even have enough money to pay artists, so the end of the Fifth Peg was imminent. The business relationship between Young and Porco terminated when Young asked Porco for a portion of the bar receipts. Young became angry with the club's new booking manager Charlie Rothschild and the emcee, folksinger Logan English, concluding that they took the reins from him. On May 12, 1960, Young took out an ad in the *Village Voice* that stated: "I FEEL BAD. Everything I do turns out to be successful—artistically only. Now THE FIFTH PEG is added to the list." On June 1, 1960, another ad appeared in the *Voice* announcing the first official performance at what was now known as "Gerde's Folk City," featuring Carolyn Hester and Logan English as emcee.[27]

Thanks in large part to the management skills of owner Mike Porco and booking agent Charlie Rothschild, Gerde's Folk City became the preeminent folk music venue in the nation. Porco lacked knowledge about folk music and seemed an

opposite: Gerde's Folk City, January 1961. Photograph by Irwin Gooen.

below: Logan English, October 1957. Originally from Kentucky, English was the emcee at Gerdes Folk City. On June 1, 1960, the club's opening night, he performed with folksinger and songwriter Carolyn Hester. Photograph by Aaron Rennert.

below: Richie Havens at Gerde's Folk City, 1965. Photograph by Joe Alper.

unlikely impresario, but he demonstrated business savvy and continually landed top talent and promising newcomers. Folksinger Oscar Brand reflected, "He kept calling on people who were damn good. I don't know how Mike Porco managed to show such good taste. Better than anybody I know." Rothschild worked tirelessly and was particularly close to critic Robert Shelton. Shelton often recommended acts to Rothschild and indicated that he would review them in his column. Aware of Shelton's influence, Rothschild urged Porco to book the acts.[28]

Crowds descended on Folk City throughout the day. In the afternoon, Gerde's Folk City functioned as an Italian restaurant, serving New York University students and factory workers from the area. The concerts started at 9 or 9:30 at night. When a popular performer took the stage, Porco filled all the tables. Customers paid the admission and the two-drink minimum, and the bar was full as well. "But Mike would always say he never made any money," Rothschild remembered.[29]

Monday night hootenannies at Folk City were often the highlight of the week. The events helped launch the careers of folksingers, who sang and played for free in exchange for publicity. Consequently, overhead was basically nothing. Established performers sometimes tried new songs; newcomers hoped to get attention. Porco chose Monday for these events because it was usually a slow night. Admission was free, but there was generally a minimum drink order or the request for a dollar toward a drink. The hootenanny format was straightforward. Singers arrived early and signed up to perform or picked a number that would determine their placement in the lineup. They might have a drink or social-ize with others while they waited. Folksinger Richie Havens recalled, "A lot of people would sign up on a list. It was really well-run. Everyone would go to the basement, so there wouldn't be a lot of singers standing around the bar. We'd all hang out in the basement and they'd come down and call us when they wanted us to go up and play. We'd have fun waiting down there for our turn."[30]

In a November 1960 feature in *The New York Times*, Robert Shelton paid tribute to Gerde's and the expanding folk music scene in the city. "Folk music is leaving the imprint of its big country boots on the night life of New York in unpar-alleled fashion, from the grimiest Greenwich Village espresso joint to the crooked-finger elegance of the Waldorf Astoria," he observed. "A tour of the night spots featuring folk music can be an amusing, confusing, but rewarding journey. There is a standardless jumble of performing styles and performers' purposes. … But beneath it all, there is a deep core of creativ-ity that represents one of the biggest contemporary booms in a popular art form." He pointed out that the Village Gate "will begin next month a monthly series of Sunday afternoon show-cases called 'Washington Square Indoors' at which the frozen-out banjo pickers from the park will have a winter refuge." Shelton cited a few outstanding performers in Village venues, praising in particular the performances of Dave Van Ronk at the Gaslight. Describing Gerde's Folk City, Shelton noted that since its debut earlier in the year, it "has offered about 40 per-formers, including some of the best to be heard in town."[31]

- - -

A few blocks from Gerde's Folk City was Manny Roth's club, the Cock and Bull, located at 147 Bleecker Street, close to the Village Gate. It was a modest venue that featured theatrical productions and poetry readings as well as folk music. Dustin Hoffman performed there in a minor Off-Broadway produc-tion, and Beat poet Hugh Romney read his work. Roth, also owner of Cafe Wha? on the corner of MacDougal Street and Minetta Lane, often presented blues guitarist and singer-songwriter Mark Spoelstra. Spoelstra, a Missouri native, con-tributed to *Broadside* magazine and recorded for Folkways, among other labels.[32]

Roth never developed a strong attachment to the Cock and Bull, and he sold it on June 6, 1961, to Fred Weintraub, a successful businessman originally from the Bronx. Weintraub aimed to capitalize on the folk music revival boom and estab-lish himself in the entertainment business. He enjoyed the spirit of Greenwich Village and liked to spend his leisure time in the neighborhood. "I get nervous anytime I'm above 14th Street," Weintraub quipped.[33]

Weintraub renamed the venue the Bitter End, as it was the last club on Bleecker Street, and began major renova-tion work. To begin, he removed plaster from the walls to

This ca. 1961 flier announces performances by Logan English, from Kentucky, and Ramblin' Jack Elliott, from Brooklyn, both of whom gained prominence in New York. English was emcee at Gerde's Folk City in the early 1960s, helping to organize concerts and often performing himself, while Elliott fashioned himself as the greatest disciple of Woody Guthrie. Photographed by John Halpern.

RECOLLECTIONS

DOMINIC CHIANESE

As master of ceremonies at Gerde's Folk City, I met hundreds of performers. They all tuned their instruments in the cellar. After a brief interview, I brought them to the tiny stage that held only one microphone. But it was a stage that held the attention of audiences. Mike Porco's bar and restaurant was an important showcase for American and international performers. The performers looked to the left, the center, and the right of the room, and could expect a rapt audience. Music was paramount. Drinking and eating were important, but the most important things were what people were singing about. The finest musicians, instrumentalists, songwriters, and singers came to Gerde's. I personally had the privilege of introducing Arlo Guthrie, Dave Bromberg, José Feliciano, Sonny Terry, Brownie McGhee, John Lee Hooker, Tom Paxton, Oscar Brand, Paul Butterfield, Tommy Makem and the Clancy Brothers, Jack Hardy, Buffy Sainte-Marie, Jean Ritchie, Ian & Sylvia, Happy and Artie Traum, Dave Van Ronk, Suzanne Vega, Barbara Dane, Odetta, and so many others.

Everyone learned from everyone else. I could feel it in the conversations, and at the end of the night when Mike and John would lock up, I went home singing the songs we heard that night. Michael Moriarty, the actor, once told me: "You grow as an artist when you present yourself to an audience like the ones at Folk City." Michael was right. Truth in singing and storytelling was the key. You can't learn that kind of communication in college courses. You learn from a discerning audience. You have to love them and gain their respect and the audience will tell you if you are doing it right.

I watched John Lee Hooker's stance when he sat down and started to play. His rhythm was his own, and he owned the room. José Feliciano, though blind, controlled his audience the moment he strummed his first chord. Oscar Brand would bring his recording equipment, and with the artist's permission, he would record for his radio show. Dave Bromberg was a master at the guitar and was writing new songs every week. Ed McCurdy was the first one to tell me, personally, that the Italian folk songs I knew were worthy to be heard. I needed that kind of encouragement.

Poetry, songs of Patriotism, songs of War, songs of Protest were all welcome. Folk City was a Town Hall meeting with music, in a sense. One time someone protested as I announced I was going to sing a song from Chile called "Mi Caballo Blanco." This gentleman yelled out: "Sing an American Song!" He got angry when I said that it was an American song—from South America. Some people thought Gerde's was anti-American. Wrong. Gerde's was the essence of what America is all about. Music is emotional, no question about it, but it says more than words sometimes. The main thing was the performance, and no performance is great without great audiences.

— — —

Dominic Chianese began his professional acting and singing career in 1952. He has performed in numerous Broadway and Off-Broadway productions and in regional theaters throughout the nation. His film career started with his role as "Johnny Ola" in The Godfather Part II *(1974) and culminated with "Uncle Junior" in 1999 on the television series* The Sopranos.

The Bitter End, ca. 1961. Owned by Fred Weintraub, this venue opened in 1961 at 147 Bleecker Street and featured folk music and comedy. Numerous acts, including Pete Seeger and the Tarriers, recorded live albums at the Bitter End, helping to catapult the club to national prominence.

reveal a striking red brick wall underneath. Weintraub liked the look, and the wall became an iconic backdrop for the club's folksingers and comedians on stage. He decorated the other walls with lithographs by Max Ernst. For seating, Weintraub installed church pews in a semi-circle around the stage, creating a small concert hall. The pews had ledges to hold sodas and ice cream drinks. "Unlike most churches, however, we didn't serve wine—or beer, or hard liquor, for that matter," Weintraub explained. "As a result, there were no loud, drunken hecklers to interfere with the acts or in the audience; performers thought I was even more brilliant for mandating that absolutely no food or drink be served while acts were on stage." There was no cover charge for the shows, which started at 8 p.m. Staff circulated a basket to help pay performers.[34]

The most popular act to emerge at the Bitter End was the trio Peter, Paul and Mary. The group, consisting of Peter Yarrow, Noel Paul Stookey, and Mary Travers, was the creation of manager Albert Grossman. Mindful of the mass appeal of the Kingston Trio, Grossman conceived of the idea of forming his own group to tap into the nationwide craze for folk music, but he wanted two men and one woman in the trio to strike a gender balance. Grossman began with Peter Yarrow, a native New Yorker and Cornell University graduate. He had heard Yarrow perform at the Cafe Wha? in 1960

and decided to manage him. Grossman advised Yarrow to find other singers to form a group, insisting that it would increase his visibility and get him additional work. Grossman and Yarrow were in Izzy Young's Folklore Center one day looking at the pictures of singers on the wall. "Who's that?" Yarrow asked Young. "That's Mary Travers," Young replied. "She'd be good if you could get her to work." Raised in Greenwich Village, Travers had appeared on four Folkways albums with Pete Seeger. Yarrow called Travers, and the two met to discuss the idea and to sing songs. They agreed to form a group and to find a third member. Grossman unsuccessfully tried to recruit Logan English and Dave Van Ronk. ("David would have been a total bomb," his wife Terri Thal observed.) They eventually found Noel Stookey, at the suggestion of Travers. Stookey, a stand-up comedian, was the emcee and an occasional singer at the Gaslight, known for his impersonation of a flush toilet, imitation of Hitler at the Nuremberg Rally in a high falsetto voice, and parody of Little Richard. The trio rehearsed for many months in Travers's apartment. Their personalities and looks complemented each other well. Yarrow was charismatic and earnest; Stookey was hilarious and sweet; and Travers had a mournful, sweet voice and was statuesque and beautiful, with flowing blond hair. Stookey used his middle name "Paul," and the trio called themselves Peter, Paul and Mary.[35]

Performing at the Bitter End for a few weeks at the end of 1961, Peter, Paul and Mary gained notice but did not receive

Bob Dylan performs at the Bitter End, January 1961. Arriving in New York in 1961 from Minnesota, Dylan quickly navigated the Greenwich Village folk music circuit and began playing the premier clubs in the neighborhood.

instant praise. The club took out an ad in *The New York Times* and urged readers, "You better see this trio before you have to pay fancy uptown prices at the Blue Angel." The crowds increased in size the second week but did not fill the club to capacity. The Bitter End paid for another ad in *The Times*. "If you really want to see this incredible new act, I recommend you make reservations during the week. We are going to expand the premises to accommodate more of you." The third week was the turning point. The trio's performances helped earn them a contract with Warner Bros. Records, based in Los Angeles. They signed the deal in January 1962 and released their debut album, *Peter, Paul and Mary,* in May. The cover featured the group on stage at the Bitter End in front of the club's signature brick wall. The wildly successful album included their renditions of "If I Had a Hammer" by Pete Seeger and Lee Hays and "Where Have All the Flowers Gone?" by Seeger. The album sold more than two million copies and launched the trio to national stardom. Yarrow frequently expressed indebtedness to the club. "Playing the Bitter End was like playing the Palace," he remarked.[36]

Peter, Paul and Mary helped elevate the Bitter End to a nationally known folk music venue. Artists, agents, and producers increasingly wanted to make live records there. The list of "live from the Bitter End" albums was extensive. It included recordings by Fred Neil, the Chad Mitchell Trio, Pete Seeger, the Tarriers, Curtis Mayfield, Eric Andersen, Arlo Guthrie, Len Chandler, Tom Paxton, and many others. The only other venues with more recording credits were the Village Gate and Carnegie Hall.[37]

The radio program *Theodore Bikel at Home*, taped in front of a live audience at the Bitter End and broadcast on WBAI, brought additional luster to the club. Bikel's program blended folk music, poetry readings, and casual commentary and, reflecting the broad popularity of the folk music revival, attracted an audience of both bohemians and professionals. Joan Barthel wrote in *The New York Times* that the assortment of patrons was enough "to make a sociologist's head spin." She observed, "Even for Greenwich Village, where the colorful is commonplace, Bleecker Street is exceptional." Bikel, also a leading man in Broadway productions and Hollywood movies, welcomed the Bitter End as a home for his nationally syndicated show. "Anyone who was anyone on folk wanted to be on his show," Weintraub explained, "and guests such as blues greats John Lee Hooker, Sonny Terry, and Brownie McGhee introduced a different kind of music to the congregation on Bleecker Street—as well as living rooms in greater New York, Chicago, San Francisco, and Los Angeles." Bikel presented the Tarriers and Judy Henske, among other folksingers and blues musicians.[38]

The Bitter End held a hootenanny night every Tuesday, similar to Gerde's Folk City's Monday night event. "Hoot night"

Created by manager Albert Grossman, the trio Peter, Paul and Mary released their debut album in 1962 to remarkable success. Featuring the iconic red brick wall of the Bitter End in the background, the album sold more than two million copies and immediately catapulted the group to stardom.

at the Bleecker Street venue was the equivalent of ama-teur night, but club managers did not allow every aspiring artist on stage. An avalanche of musicians and comedians wanted to perform, eager to win the attention of agents and recording executives, so the club screened each act briefly in advance. "There were comics who were not funny, sing-ers who couldn't hold a note, and musicians who couldn't play their instruments," Bitter End manager and booking agent Paul Colby recalled. (Colby became owner of the club in 1974.) Audiences were typically supportive, aware that the sets were in effect auditions. Comedian Murray Roman or folksingers Logan English, Ed McCurdy, or Bob Gibson often acted as the moderator. For a time, songwriter Dick Reicheg hosted hootenanny night at the club. He recalled a story about auditioning a young guitar player with a "ter-rible haircut." "He came in with a guitar and he had glasses and he looked like a nerd," Reicheg remembered. "He took out the guitar, and my reaction, before he played, was 'This is not going to be so good.' He picked up the guitar in the dressing room and he started to play unbelievably great." It was David Bromberg, on the verge of breaking into the Village scene.[39]

below: The Greenbriar Boys, 1957-60. At this point, the influential northern bluegrass trio comprised Paul Presopino on mandolin, John Herald on guitar, and Bob Yellin on banjo. Photograph by Aaron Rennert.

FRIENDS OF OLD TIME MUSIC, 1961–1965

Greenwich Village performance spaces not only supported new talent, but also provided a platform for traditional country, bluegrass, and blues musicians from rural regions of the nation. Friends of Old Time Music (FOTM), an organization started by Ralph Rinzler of the Greenbriar Boys, John Cohen of the New Lost City Ramblers, and Izzy Young of the Folklore Center, presented a series of 14 concerts in the neighborhood from 1961 to 1965. Other folklorists and musicians, including Mike Seeger, Alan Lomax, Jean Ritchie, and Sam Charters, were instrumental in coordinating the FOTM series, which introduced New Yorkers to obscure and forgotten performers including Clarence Ashley, Doc Watson, Mississippi John Hurt, Maybelle Carter, Fred McDowell, Dock Boggs, Roscoe Holcomb, Jesse Fuller, and the Stanley Brothers. Dedicated New York folkies were already familiar with several of them through Alan Lomax's 1947 Brunswick albums, *Mountain Frolic* and *Listen to Our Story*; Harry Smith's 1952 Folkways compilation, *Anthology of American Folk Music*; and John Cohen's 1960 Folkways record, *Mountain Music of Kentucky*, created from his 1959 field recording trip in eastern Kentucky. But these Southern musicians had never performed live in New York or, like Dock Boggs and Mississippi John Hurt, had not recorded in the city since the 1920s. Held at P.S. 41 on the corner of 11th Street and Sixth Avenue, and on New York University and New School campuses, the concerts played a critical role in the folk music revival process by transmitting the nation's traditional music to urban "folk" audiences. FOTM concerts were in effect a rebuttal to trends that dominated the commercial boom of the folk music revival. FOTM folksingers seemed to be authentic and noncommercial, in sharp contrast to popular slick bands such as the Kingston Trio, the Chad Mitchell Trio, the Highwaymen, the Limeliters, and the Brothers Four.[40]

Rinzler, Cohen, and Young combined their extensive musical, administrative, and organizational skills as FOTM directors. Rinzler, a native of Passaic, New Jersey, and a graduate of Swarthmore College, played bluegrass music in the style of Bill Monroe of the Blue Grass Boys, based in New York City. Cohen, originally from Queens, performed Southern mountain music in the New Lost City Ramblers. He was also a gifted photographer known for his images of Abstract Expressionist painters, Beat poets and novelists, and pop artists. The Greenbriar Boys and the Ramblers were the quintessential citybilly bands, committed to bringing rural musical traditions to the modern urban milieu. Young produced dozens of concerts in his MacDougal Street shop and in rented halls throughout the city; musicians he presented included

STRING BAND INSTRUMENTALS

THE NEW LOST CITY RAMBLERS

MIKE SEEGER
TRACY SCHWARZ
JOHN COHEN

FOLKWAYS RECORD FA 2492

Though originally from New York City and Long Island, members of the New Lost City Ramblers strove to evoke rural culture. A rustic barn serves as the backdrop for the photograph on the cover sleeve of the band's 1964 Folkways album *String Band Instrumentals*.

Ramblin' Jack Elliott, Reverend Gary Davis, and Peggy Seeger.
All three FOTM founders were concerned that New Yorkers
lacked knowledge of the basis of the folk music revival and
that polished commercial bands ransacked the work of traditional musicians for personal aggrandizement. In a thinly
veiled gibe at the Kingston Trio, they complained in a *Sing
Out!* article about FOTM's purpose, "So much is being made
from folk music while almost nothing is being put back into
it. There have been millions for exploitation and profit and
scarcely a penny for tribute."[41]

Cohen and Rinzler hatched the idea for FOTM after a
concert presented by Young's Folklore Center on December
23, 1960, at 13 Astor Place that featured the New Lost City
Ramblers and Elizabeth "Libba" Cotten. It was the New York
City debut for blues singer and guitarist Cotten, age 67.
Cotten, originally from North Carolina and known for her signature song "Freight Train," was the star of the show. Both
Cohen, from his vantage point on stage, and Rinzler, in the
audience, were happy that she had the opportunity to gain
recognition in New York City after years of obscurity. They
talked about continuing to bring traditional artists to the
city to give them similar chances. The two enlisted Young to
help out and invited folksinger Jean Ritchie and folk dance
advocate Margot Mayo to join the nonprofit FOTM board. The
Folklore Center became the FOTM center of operations, distributing fliers, sending out mailings, and selling tickets. All
FOTM workers were volunteers, and proceeds from ticket

above: Roscoe Holcomb
(left) and John Cohen at
the Berkeley Folk Festival,
Berkeley, California, 1962.
Photograph by John Cohen.

opposite: Flier for a Friends
of Old Time Music concert,
February 1961.

sales and occasional donations went solely toward payment for the performers and concert expenses.[42]

The first FOTM concert, on February 11, 1961, at P.S. 41 in the Village, featured Kentucky singer and banjoist Roscoe Holcomb, who was relatively unknown in New York but legendary in Hazard County, Appalachia. A coal miner and a farmer for most of his life, Holcomb sang in a falsetto, influenced by the hymn-singing vocal tradition of the Old Regular Baptist churches of the region. He performed hymns, blues ballads, and old-timey music, and also played the harmonica, fiddle, and guitar. Cohen described him as the epitome of the Appalachian "high lonesome sound." To ensure an audience at the event, FOTM planners put the New Lost City Ramblers, the Greenbriar Boys, and Jean Ritchie on the bill. The Ramblers began with a short set, and then Cohen introduced Holcomb, whom he had "discovered" on his trip to Kentucky in 1959. Cohen told the crowd about Holcomb, extolling his authenticity:

> And now it's my great privilege—and I guess all of our great privilege—to meet Roscoe Holcomb ... He's a construction worker, he lives down in Kentucky near Hazard, in a little town called Daisy. I met him several years ago when I was down there collecting songs and trying to find out what the music was about, see where it came from. And now I guess we're giving you and ourselves a chance to hear what it really sounds like. So here's my friend, Roscoe Holcomb.

Holcomb took the stage and transfixed the audience with a pulsating rendition of "East Virginia Blues." The crowd erupted into applause, and the FOTM series started off with a bang.[43]

The next FOTM concert, on March 25, 1961, featured a quintet from the Blue Ridge Mountains of Tennessee and North Carolina and earned a glowing review in *The New York Times* from Robert Shelton. Led by clawhammer banjoist and guitarist Clarence "Tom" Ashley, the group performed an array of ballads, hoedowns, blues, spirituals, and instrumental breakdowns. Ashley and his guitarist Doc Watson, both "rediscovered" by Rinzler in 1960 at the Old Time Fiddlers' Convention in Union Grove, North Carolina, stood out. Shelton commented, "The leader of the group is an easy-voiced singer with a weaving, word-swallowing style, a low pressure banjo delivery, and a whimsical stage manner." He described Watson as a "pleasant singer and sure-fingered guitarist who, as accompanist, was the workhorse of the evening." Shelton returned to the idea of authenticity, grappling with an issue that preoccupied New Yorkers and making it clear that audiences craved something more than the contrivances of mass

The Friends of Old Time Music present

ROSCOE HOLCOMB
Traditional singer of Kentucky
JEAN RITCHIE
the
GREENBRIAR BOYS
the
NEW LOST CITY RAMBLERS

FEB.11,1961
P.S.41
8:30 P.M. at 11th st. & 6th Ave.
Tickets $1.50 at Folklore Center
110 Mac Dougal St. GR7-5987
a non-profit organization

culture. "Unlike the slick, technically flashy Bluegrass bands that roam the South today, Mr. Ashley's group is as down-to-earth as the open collars and galluses they wore," he commented. Shelton ended with a hearty endorsement of the FOTM. "The Friends of Old Time Music represents a refreshing interest in real folk music, without any personal or commercial axes to grind. The group deserves all the support and recognition it can muster," he concluded.[44]

Though FOTM folksingers embodied the notion of authenticity during the commercial boom of the revival, many of them had relationships with record companies and were hardly unfamiliar with business trends. Classifications of northern urban "adulterated" music and Southern rural "pristine" ballads were in fact deeply problematic. For example, Dock Boggs, old-time singer and banjoist, and Mississippi John Hurt, country blues singer and guitarist, had recorded in New York—Boggs for Brunswick in 1927 and Hurt for Okeh in 1928. Both performed at the Newport Folk Festival in July 1963 prior to their appearance together at a FOTM concert in New York on December 13, 1963. FOTM folksingers Clarence Ashley and Maybelle Carter, of the Carter Family, had also recorded for major companies in the late 1920s. But the Great Depression had limited the operations of New York record companies and thus hit Southern rural

Izzy Young (left) introduces blind blues singer and guitarist Reverend Gary Davis at a Folk Festival at Town Hall, March 8, 1958. Photograph by Ray Sullivan.

above: The New Lost City Ramblers at a Folksingers Guild Concert at P.S. 41, February 28, 1959. The New Lost City Ramblers, consisting of (from left) Tom Paley, John Cohen, and Mike Seeger, were a Northern trio that performed Southern traditional music. They learned songs in part by listening to old 78-rpm "hillbilly" albums originally recorded in the 1920s and 1930s. Photograph by Ray Sullivan.

following: Prior to his appearance at a Friends of Old Time Music concert in New York in December 1963, Mississippi John Hurt plays at the Newport Folk Festival in Newport, Rhode Island, July 1963. Dave Van Ronk (left) and Brownie McGhee (third from left) share the stage. Photograph by David Gahr.

musicians particularly hard, forcing many of them back into agricultural jobs and obscurity until their rediscovery during the peak years of the revival.

The FOTM series not only captivated New York audiences and reinvigorated the careers of many Southern rural musicians, but also provided a model for similar festivals throughout the nation. In 1961 the New Lost City Ramblers worked with Mike Fleischer of the University of Chicago's Folklore Society to launch the University of Chicago Folk Festival, with the idea of introducing Midwestern urban audiences to traditional folk music. In a review of the festival for *The New York Times*, Robert Shelton observed, "The key words were taproots, tradition, authenticity, and non-commercial." In 1964 FOTM's Ralph Rinzler became director of field programs at the Newport Folk Foundation and helped establish a partnership between the Rhode Island festival and the final four FOTM concerts. The formats of the FOTM, Chicago, and Newport concerts were critical in informing crowds about the music. Rinzler, Seeger, or other folklorists, such as Alan Lomax and Sam Charters, presented the acts and discussed the cultural significance of the songs and the performance styles of the artists. Program notes filled a similar role. Educational workshops afforded musicians opportunities to talk about their instrumental techniques. As co-founder of the annual Smithsonian Folklife Festival, launched in 1967 in Washington, D.C., Ralph Rinzler incorporated these elements, expanding the ethos of the folk music revival onto a national stage.[46]

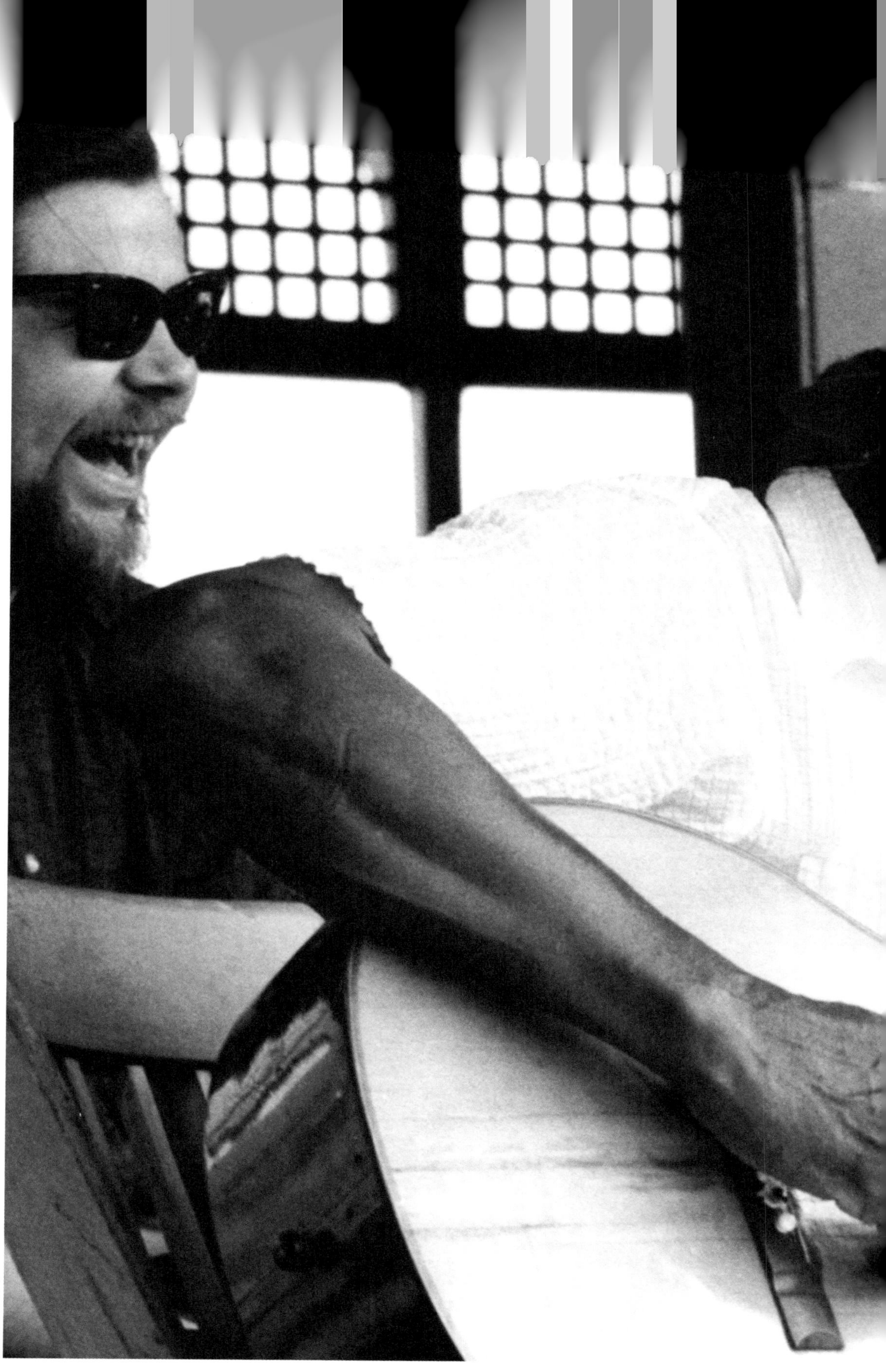

SATURATION AND BACKLASH

The popularity of the folk music revival in the Village peaked in 1963–1964, reflecting the trend nationwide. The major clubs, including the Village Gate, the Gaslight, Gerde's Folk City, and the Bitter End, continued to showcase established performers as well as hopeful prospects. They were breeding grounds for new talent. Other smaller but notable clubs at this time included the Commons, Cafe Wha?, the Cafe Bizarre, and the Night Owl. Basket houses continued to proliferate during this period. They were small, with capacities of less than 40 people, and were located throughout the coffeehouse district. "In 1963–64 there was a whole scene which revolved around Bleecker, MacDougal, and 3rd streets," Greenwich Village native John Sebastian remembered. "It was all those coffeehouses where you could play for the passing of a basket. It was in these coffeehouses where I first established myself as a solo."[47]

Other significant venues, such as the Cafe au Go Go at 152 Bleecker Street, opened in this period. At first club owner Howard Solomon featured folksingers, comedy acts, and jazz groups. The array of performers in the first two years included Muddy Waters with Otis Spann, Lord Burgess, the Au Go Go Singers, Bob Gibson, Ian & Sylvia, John Lee Hooker, the Paul Butterfield Blues Band, John Hammond Jr., Jim and Jean, and the Blues Project. Solomon scheduled a *Blues Bag* series, recorded by Verve Records, with recently rediscovered older bluesmen such as Son House, Bukka White, and Skip James, who performed along with Eric Andersen, Big Joe Williams, and John Lee Hooker. The Cafe au Go Go became a site of controversy in 1964 when undercover police detectives arrested comedian Lenny Bruce for his use of obscene words during his routines. The police also apprehended club owner Solomon. The trial attracted national attention and triggered contentious debates about the meaning of obscenity. Luminaries from the entertainment and literary world—including Woody Allen, Bob Dylan, Allen Ginsberg, Norman Mailer, and James Baldwin—weighed in with support for Bruce. Nevertheless, the three-judge panel found Bruce and Solomon guilty of obscenity. Ultimately, Bruce died during the appeals process, and Solomon's conviction was overturned.[48]

While the clubs continued to present noteworthy musicians and comedians, some observers complained that the Village in general was becoming increasingly tawdry, in part due to the saturation of coffeehouses in the MacDougal-Bleecker district. Native American singer-songwriter Roland Mousaa recalled, "At one time I counted 37 coffeehouses in the Village. It was so jam-packed, it would take an hour to get from Folk City to the Bitter End." Folk artist Charlie Chin added, "There were lots of fly-by-night coffeehouses. They'd be open for a month or two and then they'd close." Dave Van

above top: Flier for the "Blues Bag" concert series organized by Cafe au Go Go owner Howard Solomon in November 1965. The series featured eminent blues musicians like Muddy Waters and John Lee Hooker. Verve Folkways recorded the sessions and released the album *Live at The Cafe Au Go Go* in 1966.

above bottom: Cafe au Go Go, shown here on the front of its ca. 1966 menu, opened at 152 Bleecker Street in 1964 as the folk music revival crested in popularity. Similar to other venues in the area at the time, the club attracted large crowds of tourists and featured an array of entertainment that included folk music, comedy, and jazz.

JOHN COHEN

In September 1958, Izzy Young's Folklore Center presented a concert by Mike Seeger, Tom Paley, and myself at Carnegie Chapter Hall. After the show, many of the young urban
folksingers in attendance clambered onstage to sample our
instruments. At a time when banjos and guitars were dominant on the folk scene, Mike's autoharp, mandolin, and
fiddle were the source of great fascination. The next day
at Moe Asch's Folkways Records we made our first recording
together, released as The New Lost City Ramblers. Though
it sold only about 400 copies in its first year, it generated a fresh perspective on what folk music could be. Partly as a critique of the expanding commercial scene, dominated by the likes of the Kingston Trio, The Limeliters,
Brothers Four, and Peter, Paul and Mary, who were raking
in lots of money by performing slicked up versions of traditional folk songs, the Ramblers offered another idea:
perform the music in the form it was originally played and
evoke the performance styles heard on old hillbilly records and Library of Congress field recordings.

Few people performed in this manner at the time. All of
us in the Ramblers drew inspiration from Harry Smith's
Anthology of American Folk Music, issued by Folkways in
1952, and other recordings of early country music from
the '20s and '30s. Our objective was not to revel in or
duplicate the past; we just loved to play this music. We
visited "traditional" musicians in their homes in Appalachia and valued them as people and as sources. Mike was
particularly dedicated to introducing bluegrass music to
urban audiences.

Following our breakthrough performance at the first Newport Folk Festival in 1959, we did concerts, led workshops, and advised folksong clubs nationwide. The Ramblers provided a model to other young "folk" musicians.
As we toured around the country, old-time string bands
sprouted up—initially at colleges and festivals. They,
too, caught the spirit of the music. We inadvertently

created an underground network and earned the label "Cru-
saders for Old Time Music." That which had begun as an
act of love became a movement.

John Cohen © 2014

— — —

*Born in 1932 in Sunnyside, Queens, John Cohen is a founding
member of the New Lost City Ramblers as well as a noted
musicologist, filmmaker, and photographer. His 17 documentary
films about traditional music include* The High Lonesome
Sound *(1962), a portrait of the songs of churchgoers,
miners, and farmers of eastern Kentucky. His photographs,
in the collections of the Museum of Modern Art (MOMA), the
Metropolitan Museum of Art, and the Victoria and Albert
Museum, chronicle crucial artistic figures in 1950s and
1960s New York, including Abstract Expressionist painters,
Beat Generation novelists and poets, and Bob Dylan amid the
boom of the folk music revival.*

above: A sign outside the Cafe Au Go Go in November 1965 advertises performances by, among others, John Hammond, the Paul Butterfield Blues Band, Richie Havens, Eric Andersen, Al Cooper, and the Lovin' Spoonful. Photograph by Don Paulsen.

Ronk remembered, "Around 1963 they put sawhorses up between Bleecker and 3rd on MacDougal Street on weekends. Cars simply couldn't get through. It was a pedestrian lane. There were that many people crowded on a block."[49]

The boisterous scene attracted the attention of racy magazines. In 1963, *Dude,* a men's magazine "Devoted To Pleasure," published Nicholas Breckenridge's article "Village '63." "New York's Greenwich Village has been condemned by visitors from all over the country as Not Being the Way It Used To Be more loudly and consistently than any other community in the United States, but this charge has no basic truth at all," he began. "Life there moves in cycles." Breckenridge observed, as in the past, "the Village is still a mecca for young kids out of college or art school who want to find themselves and wear sneakers or beards or no brassieres, and talk with like-minded people over beer or coffee." At the same time, Art D'Lugoff's article, "Greenwich Village at Night," treated *Cavalier*'s male readers to a tour of the neighborhood: "This year and next year, and long after, more entertainment will come out of Greenwich Village than from anywhere else in the nation for the simple reason that more good and great talent has a chance to begin in the Village."[50]

The issue of the Village's changing character became the focus of the 1963 local political campaign for Democratic district leader between Carmine De Sapio from the neighborhood

Tamawa Club and his opponent from the VID, lawyer Ed Koch. De Sapio, a hero of the Italian South Village, concentrated his campaign on the disorderly atmosphere on MacDougal Street. The neighborhood was changing from primarily residential to a mix of residential and commercial uses. Amid the Beat literary and folk music movements, not just coffeehouses but jewelry shops, gift shops, strip clubs, pizza stands, and bars sprouted on MacDougal and Bleecker Streets. The district took on a garish quality reminiscent of Coney Island in the 1920s. Many shops were decorated with gaudy banners, and barkers loudly solicited passersby for business. In a front-page article in *The New York Times*, Edith Evans Asbury described unruly crowds of "teenagers looking for trouble, soldiers and sailors on the prowl, interracial couples, panhandlers, motorcyclists, sex deviates, and exhibitionists of various kinds." Area residents, mostly Italians, complained about the noise and traffic. At a community planning board meeting, James O'Neill of the Tamawa Club presented a petition with 4,000 signatures that protested coffeehouses without licenses, the disregard for zoning laws, and the lack of police presence and action. De Sapio asserted that the VID had neglected the grievances of its constituents since it won power in 1961. VID supporters retorted that the problems had started while De Sapio was district leader.[51]

Racial incidents in the South Village further complicated the MacDougal Street concerns. Interracial strife had plagued the community since the late 1950s, especially around the time of the 1961 folksingers' protests in Washington Square Park. African Americans went to the Village in large numbers, particularly when black entertainers, such as Bill Cosby and Dick Gregory, performed in area coffeehouses. On numerous occasions, fights broke out between South Village youngsters and visitors to the neighborhood. But the conflicts on MacDougal Street were not always due to racism. African-American folksinger Len Chandler reflected on the violence:

> Of course a lot of the hostility still lands on the Negro. But you can't say it's a result of anti-Negro feeling alone. There are Negroes, men and women, who've worked around here for years and not had any trouble. But the Negro just coming on to the street—he's such an easy symbol to the neighborhood of this new wave of outsiders. Strike at him, and you strike at a very tangible part of the crowd pressure being put on the neighborhood. Naturally. He's the easiest to pick out![52]

The unruly behavior of MacDougal weekend crowds represented a stark contrast to the ways of South Villagers. One Italian-American owner of a business on MacDougal Street cited coffeehouses as the source of the disorder. He

above: The Cedar Tavern on University Place between 8th and 9th Streets, seen here in 1959, was a favorite haunt of the Abstract Expressionists. Photograph by John Cohen.

complained, "These Goddamn places with their barkers out front and their girls strutting up and down have changed everything. They draw the motorcycles, and the hoods, and the troublemakers. They've helped ruin Washington Square, too. Now my wife can't walk down the street on a week-end—her own neighborhood mind you—without getting insulted by some bastard who don't even live around here." His resentment typified the views of local residents. Some longtime Villagers left the neighborhood as a result of the carnival atmosphere. Sal Petrillo, owner of Frank's Pizzeria on Bleecker Street, moved his family out in 1960 but indicated a desire to return. "The street noise keeps me from doing it," he remarked. "I've got children and on hot summer nights I know they won't be able to get to sleep."[53]

Ed Koch addressed the "MacDougal Street Mess" by focusing not on racial tension but on quality-of-life issues. One month before the 1963 primary, the community planning board held a hearing on the topic at the Grosvenor Hotel on Fifth Avenue. Approximately 300 Villagers attended, and 35 people spoke, presenting a range of views. Several local politicians—including Amos Basel, Liberal Party candidate for councilman-at-large; Stanley Shapiro, community affairs chairman of the First Assembly District Republican Club; and former Assemblyman Nicholas Rossi—discussed the racial problem. Ed Koch, however, avoided the thorny topic of race and outlined a plan to confront the "anti-social behavior" of

below: Unidentified man with Carmine De Sapio and Anthony Dapolito, ca. 1960. Former Tammany Hall boss and Greenwich Village Democratic District Leader Carmine De Sapio (center) made an issue of the "Mess on MacDougal Street" as he tried to regain his position in a 1963 campaign against his rivals from the Village Independent Democrats. Photograph by Harry J. Fields.

visitors to the area. Koch proposed a series of steps to reduce noise and traffic, increase police presence, and regulate commercial establishments. Most importantly, he advocated the formation of a neighborhood council to protect the interests of the community. With the exception of coffeehouse owners, who called for the reform of city licensing laws, most audience members agreed with Koch's plan.[54]

Victorious in the 1963 primary against De Sapio, Koch plunged back into the strife surrounding the coffeehouses of the South Village. The area remained boisterous on weekend nights, and Italian residents continued to register complaints with authorities. In July 1963, Koch arranged a meeting with residents, businessmen, and civic leaders to discuss the problems. Despite his work with Save the Village and Save the Pushcarts, Koch was still largely persona non grata in the South Village due to his campaigns against Councilman William Passannante and De Sapio. The mood inside the hall was confrontational, but the residents warmed up to their district leader as the meeting proceeded. Some figures at the forum expressed concerns that a crackdown on the cafes would harm artists who performed at the venues. Beat poet Allen Ginsberg remarked, "If you make a law banning all coffeehouses, then you will close down a lot of valuable artistic enterprises." Koch explained that it was not his intention to close coffeehouses, but to limit the noise and traffic that disturbed the tenants. He went on to establish the MacDougal Street Area Neighborhood Association (MANA) and named a steering committee of 18 people chaired by Village attorney Emanuel "Wally" Popolizio. Most members of the group were

Crowds at MacDougal and 3rd Street 1966. The Greenwich Village coffeehouse district began to witness a surge of visitors in the early 1960s, particularly on weekends. The popularity of the neighborhood created overcrowded conditions and congestion in the Washington Square area and led to numerous complaints from longtime residents about noise and disorder. Photograph by Robert Otter.

residents; landlords, New York University officials, and coffee-house owners were also represented.[55]

As a result of MANA's initiatives, the city reduced park-ing on MacDougal Street at night, enforced noise and zoning regulations, and added police to patrol the area on weekends. By 1966 the locale was no longer an arena of rowdy fanfare, though it remained a popular tourist destination. While Koch partially credited the work of MANA, he attributed this devel-opment largely to the shift of the carnival scene to St. Mark's Place in the East Village. At the center of the maelstrom, Koch faced criticism from different fronts. On one hand, some Italians, such as John D'Apolito, owner of Tony's restaurant on Bleecker Street, accused him of ethnic pandering. On the other hand, some members of the VID disapproved of his work against loyal coffeehouse operators. Many proprietors of artistic enterprises, such as the Village Gate's Art D'Lugoff and Caffe Cino's Joe Cino, were furious at Koch, but Koch's practical decision to reach out to Italians and expand his base served him very well in his successful bid for New York City Council in 1967.[56]

The Washington Square Park folksinging ban of 1961 and the MacDougal Street controversy from 1963-65 illustrated the dramatic effect of the folk music revival in Greenwich Village. The artistic trend triggered heated political and cultural dis-putes in the Village. But the political wing of the New York folk music community had interests beyond the famed lower Manhattan neighborhood. They were directing their efforts to the civil rights and pacifist movements. Music and politics intersected at both the local and national levels.

The political folk song belongs to all
of us—and maybe if more of us exercised
our rights in using it and developing
it, we would be helping to make America
a better place to live.

Irwin Silber, *Sing Out!* editor
May 1958[1]

POLITICAL ACTIVISM AND THE FOLK MUSIC REVIVAL

The capacity crowd at Carnegie Hall was enthusiastic, and for good reason. On September 21, 1963, the Midtown venue staged its annual hootenanny with 15 acts representing a range of traditional and contemporary folk music. Theo Bikel and Izzy Young were the evening's charismatic emcees as bluegrass groups and ragtime jug bands delighted the mostly young audience. The Charles River Valley Boys and Dave Van Ronk's Ragtime Jug Stompers elicited hearty applause. Folksinger and educator Tony Saletan led everyone in a sing-along, fostering a communal feel. Not surprisingly, topical songwriters were a formidable presence; after all, the leftist *Sing Out!* magazine sponsored the program. Mark Spoelstra, a conscientious objector, poignantly sang about pacifism, while Peter La Farge called attention to the plight of Native Americans. Phil Ochs demonstrated his acerbic humor and earnest humanism in pointed material about current events. Len Chandler sang provocative civil rights songs. The Southern Freedom struggle was on the minds of many in the summer of 1963. Moving renditions of "We Shall Overcome" had stirred crowds at the Newport Folk Festival in July and the March on Washington in August. The Carnegie hootenanny, if overly ambitious in the number of acts, was a "sprightly show of representative city currents," concluded music critic Robert Shelton in his *New York Times* review. Above all, it reinforced the connection between the folk music revival in New York and political activism.[2]

New Yorkers embraced the folk music revival for different reasons. For some Midtown entrepreneurs, it represented an opportunity to profit from a craze. To many college students and young adults, anguished by feelings of alienation in a conformist society, it signified a rebellion, a chance to interact with kindred spirits in a lively community. For ambitious musicians, it meant the opportunity to fulfill artistic dreams in recording studios. To others, disenchanted with insipid mass culture, the revival represented a quest for authenticity, a search for America's roots in the music of Appalachia, the Piedmont, and the Mississippi Delta.[3] To still others, it was a protest song movement, a vehicle to advance their progressive ideas on race and peace."

In the broader public imagination, the postwar folk music revival in the early 1960s was fundamentally political, inextricably linked to the civil rights, pacifist, antiwar, and antinuclear movements. Even though most balladeers seldom, if ever, sang protest songs, folk music developed an association with politics due in large part to media coverage. Images of activists singing for racial equality in places like Washington, D.C. and Selma, Alabama, became iconic and ubiquitous. "We Shall Overcome" was not simply the anthem of the civil rights movement, but the prevailing symbol of the Southern Freedom struggle itself, and "Blowin' in the Wind" became a standard at civil rights rallies and antiwar events. During the Kennedy and Johnson eras, New York folk music community activists formed alliances that transcended the metropolitan area and extended to other cities, the rural South, and college campuses nationwide.

In New York, as support for racial justice intensified at the end of the Eisenhower administration, an informal network of magazines, newspapers, coffeehouses, record labels, and singer-songwriters promoted the cause to great success. They often worked with allies in the South, notably Guy Carawan at the Highlander Folk School in Tennessee. Participants in the civil rights movement sang in meetings, marches, demonstrations, picket lines, even jails. Some New York figures, including Folkways Records executive Moe Asch, music critic Robert Shelton, *Sing Out!* editor Irwin Silber, and *Broadside* editors Sis Cunningham and Gordon Friesen, deepened the folk music revival's relationship with civil rights. Singer-songwriters also participated in the civil rights movement with many New York folk musicians traveling to the South to perform in churches, workshops, and Freedom Schools. Other performers, such as Mahalia Jackson and the SNCC Freedom Singers, were based outside of New York but sometimes performed in the city, usually at fundraisers to educate audiences about the civil rights cause.[4]

Meanwhile, during the Kennedy era, Cold War tension increased after the Bay of Pigs invasion, the Berlin Crisis, the Russian resumption of nuclear testing, and the creation of a massive fallout shelter program; in response, the expanding political wing of the New York folk music community fueled movements against America's military-industrial complex. Similar to the revival's civil rights coalition and involving many of the same individuals, a constellation of magazines, coffeehouses, record labels, and singer-songwriters protested political and economic policies that supported the Cold War. They participated in rallies, vigils, and marches; held benefit

The Carnegie Hall hootenanny of 1963 featured 15 acts, a mix of folk groups and singers representing traditional and contemporary musical styles. Topical songwriters, such as the political activists Phil Ochs, Mark Spoelstra, and Len Chandler, were prevalent at the concert, which was held at a moment when the civil rights movement captivated the nation.

above: The SNCC Freedom Singers perform in Harlem in support of the voting rights march in Selma, Alabama, March 1965. Established after the campaign to desegregate Albany, Georgia, in 1962, the SNCC Freedom Singers toured the nation to educate Americans about the Southern Freedom struggle and to raise money for the movement. Photograph by Diana Davies.

following: We Shall Overcome: An encore ensemble at the Newport Folk Festival (from left: Peter Yarrow, Mary Travers, Paul Stookey, Joan Baez, Bob Dylan, Bernice Reagon, Cordell Reagon, Charles Neblett, Rutha Harris, Pete Seeger), Newport, Rhode Island, July 1963. Photograph by David Gahr.

concerts; and battled against the residual effects of the Red Scare. After the American involvement in Vietnam escalated in 1964 following the Gulf of Tonkin Resolution, a growing number of singers championed an antiwar movement as the folk-rock genre developed.[5]

FOLK MUSIC AND CIVIL RIGHTS

Though typically viewed as the struggle against Southern Jim Crow, with origins in the 1954 Supreme Court *Brown v. Board of Education* decision, the civil rights movement in fact was a nationwide effort that emerged in the 1940s during the second Great Migration of African Americans from the South to Northern cities. Centered in New York City, the movement had a broad agenda. Black activists and their Left-liberal white allies fought to end discrimination in housing, the workplace, schools, and public transportation. They called for government to ensure full employment, and universal health care, and they battled against police brutality, discriminatory banking policies, and racist textbooks. From their base in New York, they worked to integrate national institutions, such as the military, major league baseball, and YMCAs. Religious, labor, and legal radicals and reformers provided leadership, bolstered by grassroots activists in communities such as Harlem and Bedford-Stuyvesant.[6]

During this era, New York folk music activists focused less on racial matters than on class issues, though they stressed their integral connection. Activist musicians, producers, and entrepreneurs, including Lead Belly, Josh White, Paul Robeson, John Hammond, Alan Lomax, and Moe Asch, nurtured the cause of racial equality through record albums, benefit concerts, radio broadcasts, and political campaigns. Of particular note was the album by Josh White and the Carolinians called *Chain Gang*, featuring tenor Bayard Rustin who later became a leading civil rights activist. Produced by John Hammond for Columbia Records in 1940, it marked a breakthrough as the first album explicitly about civil rights. Although highly controversial at the time, it was embraced by both the black press, including the *Amsterdam News*, and a white liberal audience.[7]

As the civil rights movement became nationally prominent and gained widespread media attention during the Montgomery Bus Boycott of 1955-56, the role of songs in the struggle and the relationship between music and social activism changed dramatically. Freedom songs, based on familiar gospel music, buoyed the boycott's participants; traditional African-American music, grounded in the church, fostered solidarity and signified resistance to oppression. The Montgomery Gospel Trio, formed in 1954 and comprised of Mary Ethel Dozier, Minnie Hendricks, and Gladys Burnette Carter, sang at church meetings during the boycott and inspired members of the black community to soldier on. Their songs were rooted in spiritual and gospel traditions and developed deep resonance during the boycott. The spiritual "Keep Your Hand on the Plow (Hold On)," for instance, stirred feelings of resolve and firmness. The Montgomery Bus Boycott not only catapulted Reverend Martin Luther King Jr. to national prominence but also incorporated music into the civil rights movement.[8]

While the Montgomery Boycott represented a pivotal event, the work of Guy Carawan, musical director at Highlander Folk School in Monteagle, Tennessee, in the late 1950s and early 1960s, transformed the Southern Freedom struggle into a singing movement. As much as any folksinger committed to racial justice, Carawan fused music and activism. In classes, workshops, conferences, and other forums, Carawan taught activists freedom songs. He worked in particular with the Student Nonviolent Coordinating Committee (SNCC), introducing it to "We Shall Overcome." Though other songs such as "Keep Your Eyes on the Prize," "We Shall Not Be Moved," and "This Little Light of Mine" were influential, "We Shall Overcome" unquestionably became the unofficial anthem of the civil rights movement.[9]

While an undergraduate at Occidental College in the late 1940s, Carawan, a California native, met Bill Oliver, a member of the Los Angeles branch of People's Songs.

above: Produced by John Hammond at Columbia Records in 1940, *Chain Gang* by Josh White and the Carolinians was an early civil rights album that conveyed the sorrow of a Southern chain gang. Played on white radio stations and sold in stores in the South, the record caused controversy. The album shown here, released by Elektra in 1958, contains several songs from the earlier effort.

above: Guy Carawan, pictured here in New York City in December 1958, became director of the Highlander Folk School's influential music program in 1959. Photograph by David Gahr.

Following: (From left) Ralph Rinzler, Guy Carawan, Jimmy Collier, unknown man, and Reverend Frederick Douglass Kirkpatrick sing during the Poor People's Campaign in Washington, D.C., 1968. Photograph by Diana Davies.

Through the Oliver family, Carawan developed relationships with other People's Songsters, including Vern Partlow and Frank Hamilton, and studied the music of Lead Belly, Woody Guthrie, and Pete Seeger. Carawan started a folk music duo with Hamilton as he was finishing a master's degree in sociology at UCLA. While on a trip to Los Angeles, Seeger taught them banjo techniques and invited them to visit him in Beacon, a town located near New York City. Carawan accepted the offer and in 1953 went to New York and stayed with the Seegers. Despite the blacklisting of the Weavers, or perhaps because of it, his interest in folk music intensified, inspired in part by his father's North Carolina-Appalachian background. He journeyed to the city on weekends and played Sunday afternoons in Washington Square, where he met Mary Travers, Erik Darling, and other talented musicians.[10]

At Seeger's urging, Carawan visited the South in 1953 to expand his folk music education and to learn ways to blend vernacular songs and progressive politics. A stop at the Highlander School in Tennessee was the highlight of his "Southern pilgrimage." Founded in 1932 by Presbyterian minister Myles Horton, trade union organizer Don West, and Methodist minister Jerry Dombrowski, Highlander was an adult education and leadership training center. Both Horton and Dombrowski were graduates of Union Theological Seminary in New York City. In conjunction with other institutions in the region, including Commonwealth College, the John C. Campbell Folk School, and Pine Mountain Settlement, Highlander collaborated with churches, unions, farmers, community groups, and civil rights organizations to challenge social hierarchies and reduce class and racial inequality. The co-founders modeled Highlander on Danish folk schools that espoused socialism and cooperative agricultural practices and encouraged respect and interaction between teachers and students. Highlander's strategy involved organizing workshops for activists ("students") to help them assess problems in communities, develop solutions, coordinate tactics, and establish goals. Eschewing paternalistic pedagogical approaches, the staff used consultants, films, music, drama, audio recordings, and other material to enrich the knowledge of students and provide them with possible road maps to achieve their objectives. Staff and students discussed ways to empower historically oppressed groups with little education and few resources. Teachers worked with students to build coalitions in their communities and beyond, challenging them to find common ground even with groups with disparate aims. Above all, the instructors stressed the importance of developing activist organizations that merged into the fabric of a community.[11]

In 1958, after years of expanding his musical repertoire, Carawan's career as a folksinger began to blossom in New York as he recorded his first album for Folkways and

developed a relationship with producer Moe Asch. Recorded by Mel Kaiser at Cue Studios, *Songs with Guy Carawan* made a respectable debut and illustrated Carawan's interest in world folk music. Impressed by his eclecticism, Asch signed Carawan to an exclusive contract with Folkways, and in 1959 Carawan recorded two more albums at Cue: *Guy Carawan Sings Something Old, New, Borrowed and Blue* and *This Little Light of Mine*. Both incorporated a range of styles, featuring Woody Guthrie songs and African-American blues and ballads. In liner notes for *Guy Carawan Sings*, Alan Lomax remarked that many folk revival singers, though competent in instrumental technique, frequently lacked awareness of the original emotional content and singing style of the songs. But Carawan was different. "Guy looks the part he sings," commented Lomax, "that is frontier America come alive again, direct, unpretentious, genuine, and full of unrestrained feeling."[12]

The Carawan-Asch relationship strengthened the connection between political activism and folk music in New York City and represented yet another rural-urban bond that fueled the genre's revival. In 1959, at the urging of Pete Seeger, Carawan returned to Highlander to work as a volunteer for the summer. Impressed by Carawan's commitment to social justice and his artistic talent, Myles Horton offered him the position of musical director. Carawan accepted and filled the void created by the death of Myles's wife, Zilphia, in 1956, reintroducing music

above: (Left to right) Martin Luther King Jr., Pete Seeger, Charis Horton, Rosa Parks, and Ralph Abernathy outside the Highlander Library for the school's 25th anniversary, 1957. A focal point of social justice movements since its founding in 1932, the Highlander Folk School in Tennessee functioned as a training ground for civil rights activists and helped transform the Southern Freedom struggle into a singing movement.

into the school's curriculum. In a note to Asch, he enthused, "There is such great potential here for developing a program around folk music and to make the integration movement in the South into a singing movement."[13]

Carawan corresponded regularly with Asch, informing him of his initiatives and challenges. While there was consensus among civil rights organizations about the value of music in the movement, the choice of particular songs was a source of debate. Black college students, often middle-class and urban in background, at first largely disavowed traditional rural music and instead preferred formal hymns in a westernized performance style, such as "The More We Get Together, The Happier We'll Be" and "Onward, Christian Soldiers." Carawan explained, "At colleges like Fisk in Nashville, many of the students initially reacted with embarrassment to new freedom songs that were sung with hand clapping and in a rural free-swinging style." Many Negro spirituals had origins in slavery and to some observers reflected attitudes of deference, subservience, and hope for eternal salvation, hardly appropriate at a time when determined resistance to segregation was necessary.[14]

Carawan realized that as a white man in the black freedom struggle he had to avoid a didactic tone, but also needed to express his views with a sense of conviction. Interracial relationships in the movement were invariably complicated, often mutually beneficial and essential to success, but also fraught with underlying tension that was rarely communicated until the rise of the Black Power movement. As much as any institution involved in the civil rights movement, Highlander was effective at creating an egalitarian atmosphere. Shaped by the communal ideas of the folk music revival, Carawan fit right in. He did not view himself as a

below: Billboard with photo of Martin Luther King Jr. in a classroom at Highlander Folk School, 1965. Against the backdrop of the Cold War, the reactionary opponents of civil rights attempted to tarnish Highlander as a "communist training school" and labeled those associated with it, especially Martin Luther King Jr., as subversive. Photograph by William Lovelace.

performer out to refine his skills, but rather as a song leader intent on finding material that groups of people liked to sing. Carawan was conscious of cadence, rhythm, and tempo, the way that voices sounded together, the sensibility of a group, and the feelings generated from the collective act of singing. Aiming to make music together in a manner similar to the black church, he gravitated to songs that expressed moral righteousness and were rooted in black traditions of spirituals and Christianity, though he was aware that the legacy of slavery and segregation hardened in people's minds the inferiority of African-American culture. In summary, he helped create the genre of freedom songs. It was not inevitable or spontaneous but a fluid process, the result of diligence, boldness, negotiation, and experimentation. "There were some definite cultural resistances to it," Carawan reflected.[15]

A 1959 NAACP meeting in Charleston, South Carolina, illustrated different approaches to the use of music in the civil rights movement. In a letter to Moe Asch, Carawan observed that the NAACP song sheet included "very uninspirational stuff—parodies and limericks to songs like Sweet Adeline, Old Mill Stream, etc. There were no songs of negro background." Carawan's sheet consisted of several "white" folk songs that failed to move the audience, including Dick Blakeslee's "Passing Through" and Guthrie's "This Land Is Your Land." There seemed to be a gulf between the songs and audience, though the lyrics were progressive and the melodies catchy. However, Carawan also introduced songs that stirred meeting participants, including "We Shall Not Be Moved," "Oh Freedom," and "We Shall Overcome."[16]

Characteristic of many songs in the revival, "We Shall Overcome" had disputed authorship and a complex history. The song evolved in different eras, modified by practitioners to suit their needs at the moment. Most folklorists agree that the song was initially a gospel song entitled "I'll Overcome" or "I'll Be All Right" and copyrighted by African-American reverend and composer Charles Tindley in 1901. During the Southern textile strikes of the late 1920s, the labor movement transformed it into the collective "We Will Overcome." Although published in several union songbooks in the next two decades, it remained relatively obscure. Zilphia Horton, one of Highlander's teachers, heard black workers sing it in 1947. She slowed the tempo, incorporated additional verses, and used it in the center's cultural programs. In 1948 she published "We Will Overcome" in *People's Songs* and commented, "Its strong emotional appeal and simple dignity never fails to hit people. It sort of stops them cold silent." In the late 1940s, Horton taught Pete Seeger the song at Highlander; Seeger tweaked the title and added verses. "I changed it to 'We shall,'" Seeger recollected. "Toshi kids me that it was my Harvard grammar, but I think I liked a more open sound; 'We will' has alliteration to it, but 'We shall' opens the mouth wider; the 'i' in 'will' is

not an easy vowel to sing well." Highlander students taught the song to folksinger Frank Hamilton, who, in turn, imparted it to Carawan. From 1959 to 1961, Carawan reintroduced it to black labor and civil rights activists in workshops, conferences, jails, and other forums. In 1963 Seeger, Carawan, Hamilton, and Zilphia Horton, represented by Highlander founder Myles, copyrighted the amended song, and the royalties went to Highlander to support cultural and educational initiatives in African-American communities in the South. The hymn immediately resonated and rose to prominence as the dominant protest song of the civil rights movement. As they sang, audiences usually linked arms and swayed back and forth. SNCC field secretary Reginald Robinson reflected, "The tone of our 'We Shall Overcome' is quite different from the way it was in union days. We put more soul into it, a sort of rocking quality, to stir one's inner feeling. You really have to experience it in action to understand the kind of power it has for us. When you get through singing it you could walk over a bed of hot coals, and you wouldn't feel it."[17]

The relationship between Carawan and Asch deepened but was often turbulent, largely due to Asch's prickly personality. Energized by the possibilities to propel the movement as Highlander musical director, Carawan shared many ideas for projects with Asch, including recording the songs, folk tales, and rituals of the black community on Johns Island, one of the South Carolina Sea Islands. Asch eventually responded, but he did not address Carawan's request for a portable tape recorder. Instead, he criticized Carawan for using a small "n"

previous: Pete Seeger performs for Freedom School students, local African-American residents, and volunteers at the community center established by Freedom Summer participants at Palmers Crossing in Hattiesburg, Mississippi, as part of Freedom Summer, August 4, 1964. Photograph by Herbert Randall.

above: Performance at the Highlander Folk School, Tennessee, 1978-82.

and "j" in referring to "negroes" and "jews" in his letters. "I believe that you must give dignity and understanding to ALL people," commented Asch. "The small 'n' is the Southern approach of minimizing peoples."[18]

Despite Asch's sanctimonious tone, he was unequivocal in his support of civil rights. He had released several volumes of *Negro Folk Music of Alabama* by folklorist Harold Courlander and an *Anthology of Negro Poetry* by black poet and critic Arna Bontemps. Many of his recording artists, including Pete Seeger and a few singers from the *Broadside* circle, were especially active in the movement. Asch also distinguished himself as a champion of African-American culture. He had recorded Lead Belly from 1941 to 1947, for instance, and released records of African-American bluesmen. Asch was supportive of folklorist Frederic Ramsey's initiative to build the Folkways jazz catalog, giving him autonomy to choose musicians for sessions, shape records, and write liner notes for 78-rpm albums. By the time the civil rights movement gained national attention, Asch had already assembled an unmatched record of African-American cultural production.[19]

Keen on documenting the movement, Carawan and Asch found unparalleled opportunities with the sit-ins of 1960. Against the backdrop of the Nashville sit-ins in April, Carawan attended the first organizational meeting of the SNCC in Raleigh. Approximately 200 student leaders were present; many were Highlander alumni. Carawan brought his collection of freedom songs, introducing many of the participants to "We Shall Overcome." The following week he arrived in Nashville to witness the campaign to desegregate lunch counters in the city's downtown business district using the practices of nonviolent direct action and civil disobedience. The jails teemed with students, many singing rhythm and blues songs while they were imprisoned.[20]

Toward the end of his two months in Nashville, Carawan had the idea to document some of the music of the sit-ins on a record for Folkways and to intersperse the songs with dramatic recreations of the momentous events. Participants included many of the prominent figures of the movement from SNCC and the Southern Christian Leadership Conference (SCLC)—Reverend C. T. Vivian, the vice president of the Nashville Christian Leadership Council, and student leaders John Lewis, Diane Nash, Marion Barry, James Bevel, Bernard Lafayette, and Candie Anderson. Some of them wrote the scripts for the episodes, titled "the lunch counter incident," "jail sequence," "court room scene," and "scene on Mayor's steps." The group recorded the album in a Nashville studio, and, though some of the spoken word was mannered and affected, it captured the intensity of the events. The album opened with a poignant version of "We Shall Overcome," described in the notes as "an old spiritual with new words—the theme song of the Nashville sit-ins." The Nashville Quartet

below: Founded by activist and *Sing Out!* magazine editor Irwin Silber, Oak Press in New York published numerous political songbooks. The pictured songbook was compiled by Guy and Candie Carawan and issued in 1963. It included approximately 40 songs, as well as commentary by activists such as Julius Lester, James Bevel, and John Lewis.

performed "You Better Leave Segregation Alone," "Moving On," and "Your Dog Loves My Dog." Carawan brought the tape to New York City and edited it with Mel Kaiser at Cue Studios, and Asch released the album later that summer. Titled *The Nashville Sit-in Story*, it marked a breakthrough as the first documentary recording of the Southern Freedom struggle to be made commercially available.[21]

Buoyed by the achievement, Carawan worked to distribute the album, but he was limited in his efforts due to quarrels with Asch and other Folkways representatives. Carawan sold the documentary album at concerts and other civil rights events. Septima Clark, an educator and prominent civil rights activist, used the record in her citizenship and literacy workshops, especially in combination with other Folkways albums such as Langston Hughes's *The Glory of Negro History*. Carawan also envisioned selling the record at Baptist churches and black college bookstores and newspapers, but the Folkways office was often negligent in replenishing his stock. Asch was particularly bothered that Carawan retained the copyright to the album, commenting to him that it "necessarily limits the dissemination of the material from all viewpoints." Carawan retorted that while Folkways was a known entity in Northern liberal circles, it had little reach in the South. Moreover, the album was comparatively expensive. While Asch typically gave his artists discounts when they purchased their own albums, he did not extend the same offer to SNCC and SCLC.[22]

The New York folk music community increasingly embraced the civil rights movement, in good measure due to the efforts of Carawan and Asch. In a *Sing Out!* editorial in the summer of 1960, Irwin Silber praised Carawan. "Somewhere in the South today there is a tall, good-looking, clear-eyed young man with a banjo—and a mission," he mused. "At this moment, he may be standing on a platform at a prayer meeting in a Negro church, head thrown back, leading an audience in an old hymn of hope and determination, singing along with a new generation in the Negro South." Folksinger Tom Paxton, who was serving in the army and stationed close to New York City in Fort Dix, New Jersey, often performed on the weekends in Village clubs and drew inspiration from the battlegrounds in the South. He recalled, "The Civil Rights Movement was gaining strength at that time, and songs from the sit-ins and the jails were coming North, songs with the immediacy and snap of a police dog or a fire hose … They had choruses that could raise the courage of those who sang them."[23]

Carawan worked to broadcast the struggle in places near and far. In February 1961, he organized a concert at Carnegie Hall to commemorate the first anniversary of the sit-ins. The event was a fundraiser to benefit Highlander's training program for civil rights activists, and the lineup was an eclectic blend of religious and secular musicians reminiscent of John

The Nashville Sit-In Story, released by Folkways in 1960, was the first commercial documentary recording of the civil rights movement, consisting of freedom songs and reenactments of events of the Tennessee desegregation campaign. It marked the initial collaboration between Guy Carawan of Highlander and Moe Asch of Folkways and strengthened the link between the New York folk music community and the Southern Freedom struggle.

LEN CHANDLER

As Wavy Gravy said, "If you remember the '60s, you weren't there." Well, I guess I wasn't there, because I remember them, oh so clearly.

I got to New York by winning a scholarship contest in Ohio for advanced instrumentalists. On the oboe, I played "The Winter's Past" by Wayne Barlow, which is based on the folk songs "The Wayfaring Stranger" and "Black Is the Colour (Of My True Love's Hair)." I won because I had an ally who arranged to have the contestants play behind a screen that would conceal the fact that black was the color of this true son's skin.

In New York, I met Dave Van Ronk at Izzy Young's Folklore Center. Dave was the first person I ever saw finger pick. He introduced me to the Washington Square Park folk scene. Every Sunday it was filled with folk singers. I remember learning to play on borrowed guitars in the park until someone said "buy your own damned guitar." I said OK, and bought his for 40 bucks.

While I was immersing myself in folk songs from players on the square, I was also being inundated by images and information about the unfolding events in the South.

Upon attending a freedom song conference in Atlanta, I met Cordell Reagon of The Freedom Singers who took me to Nashville, where I was arrested three times in one week, learned and wrote new songs in prison, and became involved in direct action in the movement. This changed my life forever.

There were events in the North, too.

Tom Paxton wrote a song about discrimination at the Woolworth department store lunch counter in New York. I joined him on the picket line to sing it. That was my first demonstration in the city.

Dylan was the only person I talked with about current
political events. Sometimes we talked two or three times a
day. Can't recall the content of any of those conversations.
Well, I guess I really was there.

— — —

In Greenwich Village, I remember the tall black man walking
down Bleecker Street
How he fell like a rotten poplar in a windstorm
After that police-style baton broke over his head
Big mouth me dancing in the street
Pointing my finger yelling ... He did it! He did it!
Tourist screaming as the blood spread
Neighborhood pre-mafia racing for the car on the corner
Trunk opening, baseball bats coming out
Now they're racing for me
I'm darting past Fred Weintraub in the doorway of the
Bitter End
I'm screaming "Lock the door"
and breaking for the back.
I'm running through the courtyard and disappearing in the
maze of tunnels
and storage area I'd checked before
Fred got 10 stitches in his head for trying to negotiate
at the door
Perhaps he saved my life.

— — —

No, I never wrote a song about that.
Just songs about stuff like that.
That was a part of my America.

Len Chandler © 2014

— — —

*Len Chandler was an oboe player in high school in Ohio, a folk
singer during the heady days of the folk music revival in New
York, and a topical songwriter during the emotional peak of
the civil rights movement. He sang his songs in New York City
at Carnegie Hall, Town Hall, and Lincoln Center, among other
venues; at major events, such as the March on Washington in
1963 and the Selma to Montgomery marches in 1965; and in every
major folk music club in the nation. A prolific songwriter for
the KRLA radio program* The Credibility Gap, *Len co-founded
the Los Angeles Songwriters Showcase in the 1970s with John
Braheny to promote new talent.*

Hammond's 1939 "From Spirituals to Swing" concert in the same venue. The Montgomery Gospel Trio and the Nashville Quartet made their New York debuts, and other performers included bluesmen Memphis Slim and Willie Dixon, Reverend Fred Shuttlesworth from Birmingham, and Pete Seeger, with Carawan himself rounding out the bill.[24]

On the morning of the planned return to Alabama and Tennessee, Asch asked Carawan to bring the Montgomery Gospel Trio and the Nashville Quartet to Cue Studios to record an album. The result of the impromptu session was *We Shall Overcome: Songs of the "Freedom Riders" and the "Sit-Ins,"* released by Folkways in 1962. Though the students were exhausted after an exhilarating week, the album was technically polished, containing a mix of spirituals, gospels, and freedom songs, such as "Hold On," "We Shall Not be Moved," "Oh, Freedom," and, of course, the already popular title song. Carawan's liner notes, accompanied by pictures from Nashville, provided a description of student activism in the movement since the formation of SNCC in 1960. Critics of the album, such as Robert Shelton, observed that the music in a professional studio lacked the fervor that it had in an actual meeting or a demonstration with crowds of people joining in. It nevertheless marked a contribution to the budding genre of freedom songs, introducing many New Yorkers to the soundtrack of the civil rights movement in a context other than a newscast.[25]

No New York folksinger was as prominent in the civil rights movement as Harry Belafonte, a fervent advocate of the cause as a confidant of Martin Luther King Jr., a major fundraiser for organizations such as SNCC, a supporter of voter registration drives, and an organizer of rallies, including the 1963 March on Washington. Propelled to international stardom by his *Calypso* album of 1956, Belafonte was an outspoken activist who used his celebrity to recruit other singers, as well as Hollywood actors, to the civil rights cause. Aware of King's relatively meager salary, Belafonte provided financial assistance to the family. He recalled, "I knew what Martin earned as a preacher: about $6,000 to $7,000 a year. Even in 1963, that wasn't a lot of scratch. Maybe he couldn't afford help, but how could Coretta cope with four children alone?" He subsequently supported the family with a housekeeper, secretary, and personal driver. He also bailed King out of jail in Birmingham in 1963, wiring $50,000—some of it his own, most of it raised—to Alabama for bail bonds. To aid the 1963 Greenwood voter registration campaign, he raised $70,000 at events in New York, Chicago, and Montreal, and delivered the funds personally to SNCC activists in Mississippi, accompanied by actor and friend Sidney Poitier. Belafonte became inextricably associated with the cause. "Folk songs were anthems of the dispossessed, rallying cries for justice, and when white audiences listened to this black singer bring

above: *We Shall Overcome: Songs of the "Freedom Riders" and the "Sit-Ins"* (Folkways, 1964)

following: Harry Belafonte speaks in New York City at an equal rights rally marking the sixth anniversary of the Supreme Court's decision in *Brown v. Board of Education of Topeka,* 1960. Belafonte, a singer, songwriter, and actor, was also a social activist prominent in the civil rights movement who worked closely with Martin Luther King Jr. to raise funds for the cause.

left: (From left) Charlton Heston, Harry Belafonte, and Burt Lancaster at the March on Washington for Jobs and Freedom, August 28, 1963. Photograph by Roosevelt H. Carter.

opposite: *Sing Out!*, Vol. 15, No. 1, March 1965, featuring Lead Belly on the cover.

opposite below: *Sing Out!*, Vol. 18, No. 1, July 1965. The cover of this issue features an image of demonstrators in Selma, Alabama, singing in front of the Dallas County courthouse. Included inside is "A Folksinger's Report" of the Selma-Montgomery March written by Len Chandler.

them to life, they were doing more than enjoying the tunes, or the way I sang them, or even the sex appeal I brought to the mix," Belafonte reflected. "If you liked Harry Belafonte, you were making a political statement, and that felt good, the way it felt good to listen to Paul Robeson, and hear what he had to say."[26]

The New York folk music community's support for the Southern Freedom struggle in the early 1960s intensified as Robert Shelton concentrated his analysis in *The New York Times* on the role of songs in the movement. Shelton was sympathetic to the cause and gave activists a mainstream media outlet. On August 20, 1962, in a lengthy feature on the front page of the *Times*, Shelton characterized folk songs as a "vital force" and a "weapon" in the battle. "The music rings with the bombast of election songs, the sanctity of marching tunes for a holy crusade and the spirit-building of fraternity anthems," he commented. Shelton described the emergence of freedom songs, explaining that many of them were adaptations of old spirituals. "Keep Your Hand on the Plow," for example, evolved into "Keep Your Eyes on the Prize." Because the melodies were familiar, the new versions were easy to embrace. Shelton stressed the empowering effect of songs on African Americans. In a meeting of the NAACP Hart County Chapter in Georgia, local leader Vernon E. Jordan Jr. observed, "The people were cold with fear. Music did what prayer and speeches could not do in breaking the ice." Shelton concluded by observing that freedom songs not only were common in

demonstrations, meetings, jails, vigils, sit-ins, and freedom rides in the South, but also more and more had "echoes in the North"—in, for instance, topical songs by such folksingers as Bob Dylan.[27]

Indeed, the political wing of the New York folk music community continually affirmed the dignity of African Americans in an array of outlets, including *Sing Out!*, which published union songs, peace songs, traditional ballads, children's songs, blues, gospel, and, in greater frequency by the end of the decade, songs of civil rights. The magazine also produced an African-American history and folk song issue each year, and promoted the careers of black musicians such as Paul Robeson, Hope Foye, Leon Bibb, Laura Duncan, and Osborne Smith. In forceful editorials and articles, the magazine also denounced the commercial exploitation of black culture by the entertainment industry.[28]

Articles, editorials, reviews, and songs about civil rights filled the pages of *Sing Out!* during the Southern Freedom struggle. The black spirituals, of course, were old, while freedom songs were modified versions of gospels or new topical songs written about current events. *Sing Out!* often included background information about the music to provide historical context or even instructions about the appropriate ways to sing the spirituals. "Sing it slowly with the strength and dignity it merits," advised the magazine about "Break Bread Together," a spiritual about solidarity and thanksgiving sung by Laura Duncan. *Sing Out!* leaned toward publishing spirituals that were conducive to group singing, such as "Walk In Jerusalem Just Like John" and "Go Tell It on the Mountain." Many songs adapted and revised by Guy Carawan appeared in the magazine, including "Sinner Man" and "Let My Little Light Shine (This Little Light)." Some freedom songs were original, such as "Walk on Alabama" about the Montgomery Bus Boycott by University of Michigan undergraduate Bill McAdoo, and "State of Arkansas" about the integration of Central High School in Little Rock by California teacher Dave Arkin.[29]

Though committed to civil rights and other progressive political issues, *Sing Out!* published relatively few current topical songwriters in a period that witnessed a surge of them. The marriage of political activism and folk music was especially prevalent on college campuses during the Kennedy era. As jazz and folk critic Nat Hentoff observed, "Find a campus that breeds Freedom Riders, anti-Birch demonstrators, and anti-bomb societies, and you'll find a folk group." But there was still a dearth of outlets for young performers. From California, folksinger and political activist Malvina Reynolds observed the gap. In a letter to *Sing Out!* in 1960, she explained, "Pete Seeger and I have been discussing, cross continent, a project that we'd like to put before the readers of *Sing Out!* for advice, comment, and discussion. I am proposing the publication of a song book or journal of top-ical songs, to be called *Broadside*. This would begin to round up, and make available all over the country, the songs that are arising out of the peace, labor, civil rights movements in dif-ferent areas." But neither Reynolds nor Seeger had the time to edit such a magazine.[30]

Broadside, co-founded in 1962 by Agnes "Sis" Cunningham and her husband Gordon Friesen, filled the gap by publishing the topical songs of an emerging generation of songwriters, including Bob Dylan, Phil Ochs, Tom Paxton, Len Chandler, Peter La Farge, Eric Andersen, and many oth-ers. It was a time when folksingers increasingly wrote their own material and did not simply interpret traditional bal-lads. Cunningham and Friesen, both veterans of the Almanac Singers and People's Songs, maintained their radical politi-cal and artistic commitments and enthusiastically support-ed young songwriters, though they themselves struggled fi-nancially and lived in public housing on the Upper West Side. Initially, *Broadside* was a mimeographed magazine run on a shoestring. Pete and Toshi Seeger occasionally offered finan-cial assistance, and Moe Asch helped by paying for advertis-ing. But despite the modest appearance, *Broadside* trans-formed the folk music revival, promoting the careers of edgy singers that commercial publications were ignoring. Gil Turner, songwriter, member of the New World Singers, and politi-cal activist, was another crucial figure in the early years of the magazine. He was emcee at Gerde's Folk City and brought many performers from the Village venue to Cunningham and Friesen's apartment, where they sang into a tape record-er. Cunningham transcribed the songs and, with Friesen and Turner, decided which to publish. Artists also mailed them their taped songs, and *Broadside* became *the* national outlet for topical songwriters.[31]

Broadside published numerous songs about civil rights as the movement reached its emotional and legislative peak from 1962 to 1965. In contrast to freedom gospel songs that were instruments of mass organization and rooted in the church, *Broadside*'s topical songs, typically written by Northern folk-singers, blended narrative and commentary about political and social events. They generally were not conducive to group singing, as songwriters aimed to dramatize injustice with pow-erful lyrics and indignation. One example was Len Chandler's "I'm Going to Get My Baby out of Jail" (1964) about the fear and anxiety of relatives of people arrested for civil disobedi-ence. In "Birmingham Sunday" Richard Fariña memorialized the deaths of four black schoolchildren killed in the bomb-ing of a Birmingham church. In 1962 Phil Ochs contributed "Freedom Riders" to celebrate the courage of activists who rode interstate buses into the segregated South in mixed ra-cial groups and "The Ballad of Oxford, Mississippi" after hearing civil rights leader James Farmer speak at Ohio State

above: *Broadside* magazine founder Sis Cunningham at a concert held in her New York apartment, mid-1960s.

opposite: Elaine White (left) and Janis Ian perform at a *Broadside* Hootenanny at Sis Cunningham and Gordon Friesen's New York City apartment, 1965. Photograph by Diana Davies.

University. In 1962 and 1963, Bob Dylan recorded 14 songs for *Broadside*, using the pseudonym "Blind Boy Grunt" to avoid contractual issues with Columbia Records. Many of the songs addressed civil rights, including "The Death of Emmett Till" about the murder of the African-American teenager and trial of his killers in 1955, "Oxford Town" about the enrollment of African-American student James Meredith in the University of Mississippi, and "Only a Pawn in Their Game" about the murder of Medgar Evers.[32]

As the number of topical songs increased in *Broadside* and, to some extent, in *Sing Out!*, Guy Carawan continued his mission to chronicle the Southern Freedom struggle for New York record companies. In 1962 he produced recordings of interviews and church meetings that he had collected from the 1961–62 voter registration and desegregation campaign in Albany, Georgia. Led by Albany State College students, the movement was largely unsuccessful due to the resistance of Albany Police Chief Laurie Pritchett, the lack of coordination between SNCC and the city's local NAACP chapter, and the failure to apply adequate pressure on the city's economic interests. But SNCC leaders learned lessons and subsequently modified their approach, and the campaign yielded an abundance of beautiful singing.[33]

Carawan approached Folkways with a plethora of footage, but SNCC objected, upset by Asch's handling of the documentary album *The Sit-In Story: The Story of the Lunch Room*

Sit-Ins (1961). Carawan then contacted Alan Lomax to edit and produce the material. Lomax accepted the assignment with enthusiasm. Employing his skills as a radio show producer and working in Maynard Solomon's Vanguard recording studios, Lomax mixed narration, preaching, and choral and individual singing into the acclaimed *Freedom in the Air: A Documentary on Albany, Georgia, 1961–1962.*[34]

The Albany campaign was also significant as the impetus for the formation of the SNCC Freedom Singers, an a cappella quartet. The group initially consisted of Bernice Johnson, her future husband Cornell Reagon, Charles Nesblett, and Rutha Mae Harris. Expelled from Albany State College for her arrest in a local demonstration, Johnson had a booming voice and a charismatic presence that captured the attention of Pete Seeger. The two performed at a 1962 SNCC benefit in Atlanta, and Johnson and the Seegers became close. (Johnson named her first daughter after Toshi.) Pete arranged for her to record an album for Asch called *Folk Songs: The South*. Toshi managed the SNCC Freedom Singers and used her contacts in New York and on college campuses nationwide to organize concerts for them, helping the group raise money and spread awareness of the civil rights movement. Commenting on the quartet's performance in a 1963 benefit at Carnegie Hall, Robert Shelton wrote, "The Freedom Singers are the ablest performing group to come out of what is perhaps the most

previous: SNCC Freedom Voices at *Broadside* magazine Concert, September 1964. Photograph by Diana Davies.

above: (From left) Gil Turner, Thom Parrott, Pete Seeger, unknown, unknown, unknown, Peter La Farge, and Eric Andersen perform at a Hootenanny for *Broadside* magazine, New York City, 1965. Photograph by Diana Davies.

opposite: The Freedom Singers at Carnegie Hall (Bernice Johnson Reagon, Charles Neblette, Cordell Reagon, Mahalia Jackson, Rutha Harris), 1963. Photograph by Joe Alper.

spontaneous and widespread singing movement in the world today. Their message was delivered in stirring fashion, musically and morally."[35]

As the Southern Freedom struggle intensified, New York folksingers increasingly traveled to the South and participated in various civil rights initiatives, such as voter registration campaigns and Freedom Schools—free classes provided to African Americans, designed to foster political participation as well as provide education. In the spring of 1963, for example, Joan Baez performed at Miles College during the Birmingham desegregation campaign. In the summer of 1963, Pete Seeger, Bob Dylan, and Theo Bikel went to Greenwood, Mississippi, to support a voter registration drive in the Delta. They sang in a festival sponsored by SNCC that was attended by approximately 300 people.[36]

The Greenwood voter registration struggle was the basis of Guy Carawan's last Folkways civil rights album, which was released at the time of the movement itself. A sharecropping town in the heart of rural Le Flore County, Greenwood was the site of protests and violence in the early 1960s. In Le Flore County, blacks outnumbered whites three to two, and the local Klan, equating equitable voter registration with loss of power, fired guns at SNCC workers in their cars and their homes and greeted white "nigger lovers" from the North with bullets and beatings. Klan members threatened economic retaliation against African Americans who attempted to register to vote. On March 24, 1963, they burned down the local SNCC office.

On March 26, an activist was shot as he entered his home, and on March 27, Greenwood police used attack dogs to repel protesters from the courthouse, providing photojournalists with dramatic images that made the front pages of newspapers nationwide. Carawan arrived in April to record the accounts of SNCC leaders and local congregations singing. Prominent activists, including Dick Gregory, Fannie Lou Hamer, and the NAACP's Medgar Evers, descended on Greenwood to participate in the campaign. At a mass meeting, Carawan recorded all three delivering speeches. On June 12, Evers was assassinated by a member of the White Citizens' Council, triggering a national mourning and reckoning. *The Story of Greenwood, Mississippi*, produced by Carawan for SNCC, was released by Folkways in 1965. Narrated by SNCC co-founder Bob Moses, the album captured the saga of Greenwood, featuring accounts by SNCC workers, hymns, prayers, freedom songs, and speeches at mass meetings by Dick Gregory, Fannie Lou Hamer, and, hauntingly, Medgar Evers.[37]

- - -

The Mississippi Freedom Summer of 1964 represented the climax of Village folksingers' participation in Southern racial justice initiatives. Following the passage in June of the historic Civil Rights Act of 1964, a wave of songwriters made their way from New York to Mississippi to support voter registration and other civil rights activities. Musicians who visited Mississippi included Pete Seeger, Phil Ochs, Peter La Farge, Julius Lester, Judy Collins, Bob Cohen, and Carolyn Hester. They worked closely with black activists, played many engagements, donated banjos and guitars, and received a powerful education about race relations in the Deep South.[38]

But already interracial relationships between folksingers and activists were tense, evident in the sometimes uneasy moments when white musicians attempted to lead black audiences in song. Pete Seeger's performance in an Albany church in October 1962 resulted in, by his own admission, an awful failure. In a packed room, a teenage girl led the congregation in traditional spirituals. Between songs, congregants spoke about physical beatings and verbal harassment at the courthouse during the recent desegregation campaign, and a spirit of righteousness and defiance became palpable. Then the pastor introduced Seeger, who carried his banjo to the pulpit. Unaware that the instrument had connotations of derogatory minstrel shows, he picked away. The audience was quiet and restrained during "If I Had a Hammer," but singer and crowd were out of both rhythm and tune on the union hymn "Hold On." In the next ballad, a lengthy old English tune, the gulf widened. "If this is white folks' music, I don't think much of it," a congregation member murmured. Seeger, self-critical, recalled, "I sang with a deadpan expression purposely not to detract from the words, and this only made the melody seem more boring to them." Though the crowd joined

above: Recorded and produced by Guy Carawan and released by Folkways in 1965, *The Story of Greenwood, Mississippi* documented the Mississippi voter registration campaign of 1963. Carawan incorporated hymns, prayers, songs, and homilies into the album, which also included a moving speech by activist Medgar Evers delivered just weeks before he was assassinated.

opposite: Bob Dylan plays guitar outside the SNCC office in Greenwood, Mississippi, 1963. In the early 1960s, New York folksingers increasingly participated in the civil rights movement, strengthening the association of music with activism. In the summer of 1963, Bob Dylan and other musicians, such as Pete Seeger and Theo Bikel, went to Greenwood, Mississippi to assist in a voter registration campaign.

him on "We Shall Overcome," it was a difficult night for Seeger, who took pride in his ability to engage audiences.[39]

These and related challenges did not simply stem from racial difference. Carawan had success in these situations, though he too encountered obstacles on occasion, especially when he tried to teach labor songs to African-American audiences. The issues were also cultural and stylistic. The Southern Freedom struggle became a singing movement because the music stemmed from the community—from the church in particular. Freedom songs resonated as they incorporated traditional African-American forms of leader-and-response singing and the frequent repetition of lyrics. There were no performers on a stage separate from an audience, but rather song leaders facilitating a group from the pulpit, on the street, in a workshop, or in jail. Participation in the movement meant singing music. This focus differed from the Old Left approach of using song as a propaganda weapon to instruct the untutored and mobilize the oppressed—such methods did not work in this environment.[40]

Friction between black activists and white liberal allies in the civil rights movement increased in the mid-1960s, coinciding with the rise of the Black Power movement, a broad ideology that stressed the importance of black cultural heritage, racial identity, and self-determination. Black Power advocates, including members of the Nation of Islam, emphasized active self-defense rather than nonviolent resistance and focused on issues that concerned African Americans in

above: Stokely Carmichael speaks at the University of California's Greek Theater, 1966. Activist Carmichael was a leading figure in the rise of Black Power in the 1960s. The ideology's emphasis on self-determination for people in America of African descent alienated many white liberals from the civil rights movement.

opposite: Marchers crowd the streets in a Peace March and Rally, New York City, April 27, 1968. Photograph by Diana Davies.

Northern urban ghettoes, including poverty, discrimination, and segregation. Though similar in more ways to the Southern integration movement than the national media recognized, Black Power was indeed distinct. The black nationalist focus on self-sufficiency reshaped civil rights organizations such as SNCC. Following the Selma Voting Rights Campaign and the Watts Riots of 1965, SNCC became militant as Stokely Carmichael took a leadership position. The organization eventually expelled whites. A SNCC position paper indicated, "If we are to proceed toward liberation, we must cut ourselves off from the white people." SNCC leaders advised whites to organize and eliminate racism in their own communities.[41]

The 1965 Selma march caused tension among folksingers. While Pete Seeger noted the creativity of demonstrators in developing new songs, SNCC Freedom Singer Bernice Reagon saw a disproportionate focus on celebrity singers when the marchers reached Montgomery. "The music and speeches stood out as different from the music of the March just completed and the earlier Selma campaign. The Selma Freedom Choir did not sing. Music was provided for the marchers by professional entertainers like Harry Belafonte, Joan Baez. and Peter, Paul and Mary," she observed. As SNCC's strategy changed, the use of folk music in the movement decreased.[42]

Under the direction of Stokely Carmichael, SNCC alienated many longtime white liberal allies from the New York folk

d–Telegram.

previous: Marchers carry a banner reading "We March with Selma," March 15, 1965. Some 15,000 individuals marched in Harlem in support of voting rights in Alabama. Photograph by Stanley Wolfson.

left: "Incident at 133rd Street and Seventh Avenue last night as Harlem was torn by disorder for second time," 1964. Photograph by Dick De Marsico.

music community. Theo Bikel, for example, had been active in the movement for many years, hosting SNCC meetings in his Village apartment, participating in marches and rallies in Alabama and Mississippi, serving time in jail in Birmingham, and endorsing voter registration campaigns. He was especially hurt when SNCC issued a newsletter that contained anti-Semitic caricatures, and he resigned from the SNCC in a lengthy letter that was published in newspapers nationwide. On another occasion, Carmichael confronted manager and promoter Harold Leventhal about the publicity for his singers, including Seeger and Baez, in the South. Leventhal, an organizer of many civil rights fundraisers in New York, including a 1961 birthday benefit concert for Martin Luther King Jr. in Carnegie Hall, retorted that they helped raise a good deal of money for the cause. Carmichael became upset and "anti-Semitic, anti-white charges crackled in the room," recalled Leventhal.[43]

Still, many New York folksingers continued to support civil rights, but as racial riots tore apart Northern cities from 1964 to 1968, circumstances changed and pessimism and disillusionment set in. The Harlem Riot of 1964, in particular, demonstrated the racial division in New York, exposing not only the strained relations between African-American communities and the police department, but also the broader issues of black poverty and unemployment. At the same time, the Vietnam War increasingly absorbed the energy of folksingers.

FOLK MUSIC AND THE PACIFIST AND ANTINUCLEAR MOVEMENTS

Movements against Cold War policy flourished in New York concurrently with civil rights efforts, though they received less media coverage. Radical pacifism and antinuclear activism were particularly significant. Forged in World War II conscientious objector communities and oriented around the tactic of nonviolent direct action, radical pacifism gained momentum in the middle of the 1950s after a time of isolation and decline during the McCarthy era. Movement leaders, particularly David Dellinger, Reverend A. J. Muste, and Bayard Rustin, disavowed the Old Left's focus on labor and elevated militarism to the top of their agenda. In 1957 their campaign against nuclear proliferation intensified with the establishment of the Committee for Non-Violent Action (CNVA) and the Committee for a Sane Nuclear Policy (SANE). CNVA advanced pacifism largely through direct action campaigns. Led by Norman Cousins, editor of *Saturday Review*, SANE was less confrontational, seeking to win the support of the middle class. Focused on raising public awareness about the health risks of nuclear fallout from tests conducted above ground, SANE had 130 chapters and 25,000 members nationwide within a year

Josh White testifies before the House Un-American Activities Committee (HUAC), accompanied by his wife, 1950.

of its founding in 1957. Since 1957 Greenwich Village's branch of SANE had lobbied local and national politicians with petitions calling for global disarmament. The Village also had a chapter of Women Strike for Peace, spawned by a 1961 protest in Washington by women against nuclear testing. Women Strike for Peace endorsed a platform that stressed an end to nuclear testing, world disarmament under United Nations safeguards, and the general strengthening of the United Nations. In 1961 the Greenwich Village Peace Center opened on West 3rd Street to coordinate pacifist activities. The center sponsored a film and speaker series, circulated a newsletter, and organized conferences and classes on nonviolence. The board of directors included Julian Beck and Judith Malina from the Living Theatre, Mary Perot Nichols of the *Village Voice*, and Ted Wilentz of the Eighth Street Bookstore. The *Voice* itself became an organ of pacifism, often featuring Jules Feiffer's cartoons that reflected the anxieties of the nuclear age and explicitly condemned the atomic bomb.[44]

In this era, Pete Seeger remained active in movements against American Cold War policy, singing in rallies and benefits and recording peace songs. In 1957 a federal grand jury indicted him on 10 counts of contempt of Congress for refusing to answer questions two years earlier before HUAC about his political beliefs and affiliations. In a jury trial in New York in 1961, Seeger contested his indictment and, in front of 500 spectators, his defense attorney, Paul Ross, denounced HUAC's prosecution of Seeger. "In no instance in this committee's investigation was the matter of national security, espionage, sabotage, or the advocating of the violent overthrow of the government involved," contended Ross. Government lawyer Irving Younger countered that the issue concerned Seeger's refusal to cooperate. Judge Thomas Murphy excluded 102 of Ross's questions, portending trouble for Seeger. It did not take the jury long to deliberate; after 80 minutes it returned with a guilty verdict.[45]

Before the sentencing, the Seegers participated in the annual New York Easter peace march sponsored by SANE. Despite the cold and rainy weather, approximately 3,500 people participated, invigorated by the Ban the Bomb movement. Some demonstrators played guitars, mandolins, and banjos, and sang peace songs. Others carried signs that called for global disarmament. At the culmination of the march in the United Nations Plaza, the crowd called for Seeger to speak. "Pete's been through hard times recently. For fighting HUAC, the government wants to lock him away! Let's give him our support," people yelled. Though loath to talk about himself in public, Seeger climbed on top of a truck with his guitar. Uncomfortable with the adulation and upset by the conviction, he led the group in a rendition of "Roll On," about the dangers of nuclear warfare, and urged everyone to redouble their commitment to disarmament. Seeger later found out

The signs in the photograph read:
14 ANNIVERSARY OF HIROSHIMA DAY WE SPEAK FOR LIFE, **US...USSR HALT TESTS**, **HALT BOMB TESTS**, **FALLOUT KILLS!**, **ANNIVERSARY HIROSHIMA DAY speak for life!**

West Side Committee for a Sane Nuclear Policy members walk to commemorate the 14th anniversary of the dropping of the first atomic bomb on Hiroshima, August 9, 1959. Small in number but vocal and determined, pacifists in New York campaigned vigorously against the proliferation of nuclear weapons during the Eisenhower and Kennedy eras. During this period, many New York folksingers, such as Pete Seeger and Phil Ochs, protested against the expansion of the military-industrial complex and American Cold War policy in general.

that the sponsors of the SANE program did not want him to sing, lest their organization be tarnished by association with a convicted felon.[46]

Seeger returned to court for sentencing, toting his banjo. He told the judge that he had not "sung anything in any way subversive to my country." After denying Seeger's request to sing "Wasn't That a Time," Judge Murphy sentenced him to ten one-year terms in federal prison to be served simultaneously, for a total of one year. Seeger was radiant, though speechless. "It's a hard thing to explain," he recalled. "But when you're following what you think is the right course, it may not be fun, but you feel a certain satisfaction in doing it."[47]

While he appealed the decision, Seeger balanced a busy performance and recording schedule with respite and relaxation, as he revitalized himself. A family vacation in the fall of 1961 and a tour with Jack Elliot in England lifted his spirits.

In January 1962, as part of an event associated with the paci-
fist group General Strike for Peace and organized by the Living
Theatre, he and Gil Turner sang in a march down Fifth Avenue
from Grand Army Plaza on 59th Street to Washington Square
Park, strumming tunes such as "You Can Dig Your Grave in
Your Own Back Yard." Later in the week, he performed at a
peace benefit at the Village Gate, sharing the bill with Bob
Dylan. Seeger sang "We Shall Overcome" and Dylan sang
"Blowin' in the Wind." On May 18, 1962, an appeals court ruled
that Seeger's indictment was flawed and overturned his con-
viction. Though acquitted on a technicality, Seeger was relieved. "Hooray for all of us and for Tom Jefferson," he told
Sing Out!.[48]

Despite the repeal of Seeger's conviction, many successful albums, glowing features in national magazines, and capacity audiences at concerts, in 1963 ABC-TV barred Seeger, as
well as the Weavers, from appearing on its *Hootenanny* show,
triggering another firestorm in the New York folk music community. Amid the peak of the folk revival craze, ABC unveiled
the program in a primetime slot on Saturday night, featuring
mostly slick, packaged performers, including the Limeliters,
the Chad Mitchell Trio, and the Journeymen, who were appealing to a mass audience. The variety show also provided a
platform for traditional bands such as the Carter Family and
the Foggy Mountain Boys. Produced by Richard Lewine and
hosted by Jack Linkletter, *Hootenanny* was filmed on college

Pete Seeger (right) and his
lawyer, Paul Ross, in the
courtroom, April 4, 1961.
Seeger's battle against HUAC
continued into the 1960s. Seeger
was convicted of contempt of
Congress and sentenced to one
year in prison, but his conviction
was overturned in 1962.

campuses and offered musicians national exposure as well as generous paychecks. At first Seeger was optimistic about the chance to appear on the show, though he resented the title of the program and the general exploitation of the term "hootenanny" by producers of mass culture. Fred Weintraub, the program's chief adviser and owner of the Bitter End, told him, "We're going to get you on this show somehow. Can't do it in the first shows, but I'm going to get you on somehow." However, Seeger's manager Harold Leventhal heard through attorney William Kunstler that the network had no intention of inviting him due to "pressure from advertising agencies, sponsors, and stations." Leventhal related the story to *Village Voice* columnist and free speech champion Nat Hentoff, who confirmed the broadcaster's true intent and denounced ABC in a scathing piece titled "That Ole McCarthy Hoot!"[49]

Some 50 artists formed a *Hootenanny* boycott committee, sparking lively debates in the folk music community. Even before the show aired, Joan Baez indicated that she would boycott it if ABC blacklisted Seeger. (CBS's *Dinner with the President* had also banned both Seeger and the Weavers in 1962.) Following Baez's lead, Carolyn Hester, Bob Dylan, Tom Paxton, Barbara Dane, Logan English, Dave Van Ronk, Tommy Makem, the Kingston Trio, Peter, Paul and Mary, and other folk musicians boycotted the program. Theo Bikel appeared on the show, disappointing many liberals, as did the Clancy Brothers. At a meeting about the boycott at the Village Gate, musicians, producers, managers, and others held a spirited discussion. Izzy Young, a boycott supporter, conceded, "It would be a terrible thing to cut folk music off TV when it took so long to get on." Upon hearing the news about the formation of the Folksingers Committee to End the Blacklist, ABC executive producer Richard Lewine announced that there was no blacklist. "Pete Seeger just can't hold an audience," he explained. The remark prompted an incredulous Dave Van Ronk to retort, "At that the entire entertainment business, left, right and center, broke into howls of laughter."[50]

Seeger himself had mixed feelings. On one hand, in his *Sing Out!* column he lambasted ABC, the Ashley talent agency, and the sponsor Procter & Gamble for manufacturing "claptrap" to appeal to a mass audience. "When will the TV producers learn that some of the best music in our country is made by unlettered farmers, miners, housewives?" Seeger wondered. On the other hand, he encouraged many performers to appear, including Judy Collins and his brother Mike of the New Lost City Ramblers. Seeger reasoned, "The fact they've blacklisted me attracts more attention to the folk-song movement." Feeling pressure, the network made a slight concession to Seeger, indicating a slot was available for him on the condition that he sign a loyalty oath. "Dear ABC," Seeger replied, "I just finished a seven-year court battle to prove the principle that such oaths are unconstitutional, and I

Magazine published to accompany ABC-TV's *Hootenanny* television show, 1964. ABC-TV featured the show at primetime on Saturday nights from 1963 to 1964. The network banned Pete Seeger from the program, prompting protests from many New York folksingers.

was acquitted and vindicated." The issue became moot when ABC dropped *Hootenanny* from its lineup in the fall of 1964. *Sing Out!*'s Irwin Silber was delighted, wishing good riddance to "Madison Avenue's Answer to Folk Music."[51]

Silber battled American militarism and the residue of McCarthyism during the height of the Cold War in multiple ways, in particular by publishing peace songs, articles, and editorials in *Sing Out!*. During the Kennedy era, pacifist songs proliferated in the quarterly magazine. Not surprisingly, many of them, such as "The Flowers of Peace" and "One Man's Hands," were written by Pete Seeger. From Great Britain, his sister Peggy Seeger contributed "Come Fill Up Your Glasses" in 1961, and her lover Ewan MacColl published "Five Fingers" in 1962. Selections that conveyed the effects of war on children were particularly poignant. Turkish poet Nazim Hikmet's verse "I Come and Stand at Every Door (Dead Little Girl of Hiroshima)" about a plea for peace from a little girl 10 years after she perished in Hiroshima was adapted into a song by Pete Seeger.[52]

Broadside, even more than *Sing Out!,* published peace songs by contemporary artists, strengthening the relationship between the revival and pacifism. The compositions reflected national anxiety about the nuclear arms race in general and the atomic bomb in particular. Songwriters, for example, wrote about nuclear fallout, the yellow-and-black fallout shelter sign, the Atomic Energy Commission, Strontium 90, and the civil disobedience tactic of "going limp" while being arrested. Some songs addressed the bravado as well as the naivete of young soldiers going off to war, such as "The Times I've Had," written by Mark Spoelstra and performed by the Broadside Singers, Phil Ochs, and Pete Seeger. In 1964 Seeger submitted "The Willing Conscript," a satirical song by Tom Paxton about army basic training exercises that included the practice of bayoneting a dummy. Dylan's "John Brown," published in 1963 but never released on an official studio album, was a deeply unsettling portrait of a proud mother sending her son to fight in a foreign war, only to see him return blinded and wounded, a broken man.[53]

Of all of Dylan's pacifist and antiwar songs published in *Broadside,* none was as influential as "Blowin' in the Wind." And because of the song's general and adaptable messages about peace, war, and freedom, it became a standard in the civil rights movement and countercultural events. Indeed, in contrast to Dylan's topical songs about particular individuals, events, and places, "Blowin' in the Wind" had universal qualities that contributed to its status as an iconic symbol of the 1960s. Dylan wrote the song in April 1962, adapting the melody from the old Negro spiritual "No More Auction Block," and brought it to Gil Turner, who was emcee at Gerde's. Upon hearing it backstage, Turner was astonished. "Jesus Christ," he exclaimed, "I've never heard anything like that in my entire

Pete Seeger arrives at Federal Court with his guitar, April 4, 1961. Photograph by Walter Albertin.

life! That's the most incredible song!" Turner went upstairs and played it with his group, the New World Singers, for the Gerde's crowd. The New World Singers recorded the song for *Broadside*, which published it in May 1962, and the next month Turner published it in *Sing Out!*. Dylan recorded it for Columbia in July, and in May 1963 Columbia released it on *The Freewheelin' Bob Dylan*. Peter, Paul and Mary's version of "Blowin' in the Wind," released by Warner Bros. in June, sold more than 250,000 copies in its first week and eventually reached #2 on the *Billboard* charts. In *Sing Out!*, Dylan reflected on the song:

> There ain't too much I can say about this song except that the answer is blowing in the wind. It ain't in no book or movie or T.V. show or discussion group. Man, it's in the wind—and it's blowing in the wind. Too many of these hip people are telling me where the answer is but oh I won't believe that. I still say it's in the wind and just like a restless piece of paper it's got to come down some time … But the only trouble is that no one picks up the answer when down so not too many people get to see and know it … and then it flies away again … I still say that some of the biggest criminals are those that turn their heads away when they see wrong and know it's wrong. I'm only 21 years old and I know that there's been too many wars … You people over 21 should know better … cause after all, you're older and smarter.[54]

IT'S A HARD THING TO EXPLAIN… BUT WHEN YOU'RE FOLLOWING WHAT YOU THINK IS THE RIGHT COURSE…YOU FEEL A CERTAIN SATISFACTION IN DOING IT.

While Dylan's music emerged in the New York milieu, many *Broadside* peace songs came from Britain, demonstrating the transatlantic nature of protests against nuclear armament and illustrating the extensive reach of the city's activist networks. From the United Kingdom, the Glasgow Song Guild contributed "Ding Dong Dollar" about the American Polaris submarine nuclear base west of Scotland. Glasgow schoolteacher and songwriter Morris Blythman, the organizer of the group, convinced Moe Asch to record an album of their material, and in 1962, Folkways released *Ding Dong Dollar: Anti-Polaris and Scottish Republican Songs*, produced by Pete Seeger.[55]

Broadside and Folkways developed a close relationship at this time, creating a treasure trove of compositions that comprised a vast record of 1960s political activism. From 1963 to 1964, Folkways released three volumes of *Broadside Ballads*, featuring the budding generation of topical songwriters, including Bob Dylan, Phil Ochs, Peter Le Farge, Mike Spoelstra, Gil Turner, Tom Paxton, and Len Chandler. While there was an organic connection between the albums in terms of content and style, each was unique in structure. Volume

I was recorded in the cramped Upper West Side apartment of Cunningham and Friesen and offered a sense of intimacy and spontaneity; Volume II featured Pete Seeger singing 14 *Broadside* compositions and liner notes that honored young artists and the importance of controversial songs; Volume III showcased numerous singer-songwriters, accompanied by the Broadside Singers. The musicians on these albums agreed to use their royalties to sustain the publication of the magazine, still a modest but nevertheless costly endeavor.[56]

More than any other folksinger, Phil Ochs flourished in *Broadside*, publishing an unmatched 73 songs in the magazine and writing numerous editorials. He arrived in New York from Ohio in 1962 and quickly became part of the *Broadside* circle. Ochs studied the material of fellow topical songwriters intensely and developed spirited relationships and rivalries with them, particularly with Dylan. He also had a passion for current events and devoured newspapers and magazines, especially *The New York Times* and *Newsweek*. The prevalence of contemporary content in his songs earned him the nickname the "singing journalist." While some commentators chided his lyrics for their lack of literary grace, others appreciated his direct style and willingness to engage controversial topics. He was a vociferous critic of the American military-industrial complex, regularly denouncing Cold War policy in his songs and condemning the government for meddling in the affairs of nations all over the world. He wrote about the Vietnam War before the Gulf of Tonkin Resolution in 1964 and performed at numerous benefits for peace in venues such as the Village Gate. Though a regular presence at marches and demonstrations, he believed above all in the power of a song to inspire people. "One good song with a message can bring a point more deeply to more people than a thousand rallies," he remarked in 1963. Among his many notable peace songs, "I Ain't Marching Anymore" stood out and became a signature piece in concerts. Written in 1964, the song's verses each take on the voice of an American soldier serving in every American war, beginning with the War of 1812, and asking if the price of victory is worth the cost of lives.[57]

The Gulf of Tonkin Resolution and the deployment of the first American ground troops to Vietnam in 1965 led to a shift from pacifism and antinuclear activism to the antiwar movement. While there was considerable continuity in activists' criticism of American militarism throughout the 1960s, there were also differences—not only in style, as folk rock developed in the middle of the decade, but also in content. Atomic bombs and fallout shelters mattered less than Vietnam. And though topical songwriters like Phil Ochs and Joan Baez vehemently opposed the Vietnam War from the beginning, many folk music fans were initially ambivalent or unsure about the war. The tension was evident at two consecutive "Sing-In For Peace" concerts at Carnegie Hall on September 24, 1965,

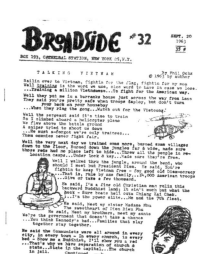

above: Phil Ochs on MacDougal Street in Greenwich Village, January 1965. Photograph by Fred W. McDarrah.

opposite: Phil Ochs published dozens of his topical songs in *Broadside* magazine, including "Talking Vietnam" in issue #32, September 1963. Long before the antiwar movement became conspicuous in the mid-1960s, Ochs drew attention to the nation's increasing political involvement in southeast Asia.

organized by a group of folk activists that included Irwin Silber, Pete Seeger, Harold Leventhal, Jac Holzman, Barbara Dane, and Izzy Young. The concerts featured 60 black and white performers, and, though the event received minimal press coverage due to a newspaper strike, it represented a watershed. The capacity crowd of 5,000 reflected a variety of sentiments about the war. The *Christian Science Monitor* observed, "The audience was a mixed group. This reporter talked to a number of them, and at least half of those interviewed said they were at the performance strictly for entertainment. Some were even strongly against the peace movement." Other audience members and many of the artists, including Theo Bikel, Bernice Reagon, Pete Seeger, Mimi and Richard Fariña, and Fannie Lou Hamer and the Mississippi Freedom Singers, embraced antiwar ideas. After the second concert ended at 4 a.m., many of the performers walked down to the Village Gate and sang together until the early morning. They also talked about the connection between civil rights and antiwar efforts. Fannie Lou Hammer proclaimed, "Until we straighten out the mess in this country, we should stop messing around in other places." Irwin Silber beamed, "The essence of the creative union between folksong and social value had been recaptured."[58]

Joan Baez at a demonstration against the Vietnam War in Trafalgar Square, London, May 29, 1965.

One former protest singer was conspicuously absent from the event: Bob Dylan. In an incisive essay in the inaugural issue of the *East Village Other*, Izzy Young decried Dylan's transformation from a topical songwriter optimistic about the potential for progress to an introspective artist, weary of the world, whose songs were increasingly surreal, personal, abstract, and alienated. Young reflected, "Where he has obscured his words he has intensified his voice. His voice now tells the true story of Bob Dylan. He screams from the bottomless pit and it is truly heart-rending. But it is like sharing something dirty. It is no longer in the open arena of life's possibilities and we mourn for it."[59]

The only thing I can compare him with
is blotting paper. He soaked everything
up. He had this immense curiosity; he
was totally blank, and ready to suck up
everything that was within his range.

Irish singer Liam Clancy, on Bob Dylan's
early days in New York[1]

BOB
DYLAN
IS TALKIN'
NEW
YORK

Bob Dylan, 1965. Dylan was at the height of his career in 1965, releasing *Bringing It All Back Home* and *Highway 61 Revisited,* two icons of the era and acclaimed classics in American music.

AT the dawn of the 1960s, most folksingers still fashioned themselves as interpreters of traditional ballads, not original lyricists. So Bob Dylan's decision to write his own songs was significant. The idea did not come to him in a flash. Rather, it was a deliberate process, an accumulation of experiences, the result of conversations, contingencies, and ironies in his life.[2]

But a particular incident in 1961, the year he arrived in New York, gave him clarity. It unfolded at Camilla Adams's apartment on Fifth Avenue near Washington Square Park. Adams was a regular at Gerde's Folk City, where she had met Dylan. She was friends with Cisco Houston, formerly a performer with the Almanac Singers and a recording artist for Moe Asch's Folkways Records. Ill with terminal stomach cancer, Houston was poised to go to his sister's home in California. In April Adams held a party for him in her spacious residence and invited Dylan, who brought along Delores Dixon of the New World Singers.[3]

Various luminaries from the New York folk music community were present, and most treated Dylan with indifference, if they recognized him at all. This was not a surprise. He had been in the city only a few months and was still mostly playing Village basket houses. "They could tell that I wasn't from the North Carolina mountains nor was I a very commercial, cosmopolitan singer either," Dylan recalled. But Pete Seeger greeted him. For much of the night, Seeger, just convicted for contempt of Congress, conversed with Harold Leventhal, manager of the Weavers. In the crowded rooms, Dylan noticed Moe Asch and Irwin Silber, as well as many musicians, including Theo Bikel, Lee Hayes, Erik Darling, Sonny Terry, Brownie McGhee, and Logan English. They represented a range of styles and genres that characterized the revival

in New York, from eastern European music to the Piedmont blues, from labor songs to jazz-folk, and more.[4]

Amid the cigarette smoke and glasses of whiskey, Dylan glimpsed choreographer and dancer Judith Dunn, independent filmmaker Ken Jacobs, and Bread and Puppet Theatre founder and director Peter Schumann. Each exemplified the spirit of artistic experimentation that pervaded Greenwich Village, expanding the boundaries of methods in performance and visual arts. In his sheepskin jacket, peaked cap, khaki pants, and motorcycle boots, Dylan, age 19, clearly was enjoying himself. "Delores and I didn't feel out of place," he later recalled.[5]

After a long night, it was time to leave, but on his way out Dylan caught sight of Mike Seeger of the New Lost City Ramblers, the trio of citybillies that also included John Cohen and Tom Paley. The Ramblers, formed in 1958, were instrumental in reinvigorating Southern mountain and bluegrass music during the revival in New York. Through their study of Library of Congress field recordings and old 78s, the Ramblers replicated Southern folk styles, introducing many New Yorkers to Appalachian string-band music. They viewed themselves as caretakers of old-time music and aimed for an authentic sound, not a polished version for a major label and mass audience. They recorded for Asch's Folkways and played the Village coffeehouse circuit and Washington Square on Sunday afternoons. In the process, they helped trigger debates about the meaning of authenticity during the folk music revival.[6]

Mike Seeger (center) and Ralph Rinzler (right) in Washington Square, 1957-60. Mike Seeger of the old-time trio the New Lost City Ramblers and Ralph Rinzler of the bluegrass group the Greenbriar Boys, both from the North, devoted themselves to performing Southern folk music in a traditional manner. Photograph by Ray Sullivan.

Dylan stopped in his tracks. He loved the Ramblers, whom he first heard at a school on East 10th Street, and he especially admired the virtuoso Seeger, adept on the banjo, fiddle, mandolin, autoharp, guitar, and harmonica. Seeger's knowledge of folk music was encyclopedic. By Dylan's account, Seeger "played on all the various planes, the full index of the old-time styles, played in all the genres and had the idioms mastered—Delta blues, ragtime, minstrel songs, buck-and-wing, dance reels, play party, hymns, and gospel—being there and seeing him up close, something hit me. It's not as if he just played everything well, he played these songs as good as it was possible to play them." Dylan understood the value of learning and memorizing melodies and lyrics, but he recognized that what apparently came instinctively to Seeger would be arduous for him. As he spied Mike Seeger in conversation with Moe Asch, he realized that he had to recalibrate his thinking and become open to different creative possibilities.[7]

"The thought occurred to me that maybe I'd have to write my own folk songs," Dylan concluded. Then he said good-bye to Cisco Houston and made his way with Delores Dixon out of the building toward Sixth Avenue, hands in pockets on a cold Village night.[8]

BOB DYLAN'S NEW YORK, 1961

The year 1961 witnessed momentous political and cultural shifts in Greenwich Village. Heated debates about the governance of the city played out there, changing the course of New York City politics. In an era when the principles and practices of modern urban planning and bossism shaped New York life, Villagers voiced their resentment toward powerful individuals who were dismissive of community opinion. Neighborhood residents questioned the notion of a "professional" like master planner Robert Moses or Tammany boss Carmine De Sapio dictating policy from above, and they maintained that efficient urban redevelopment and municipal politics depended on citizen involvement at the local level. While these trends occurred in other brownstone neighborhoods in Manhattan and Brooklyn, they reached a critical point in Greenwich Village in 1961. In what was hailed as a victory for the causes of popular democracy and clean government, James Lanigan of the VID vanquished De Sapio of the Tamawa Club in the primary for District Leader. As a result of the pressure of the Save the West Village movement led by Jane Jacobs against the backdrop of a contentious mayoral primary race, Mayor Robert Wagner withdrew his plan to redevelop a 14-block area in the neighborhood. And the Right to Sing movement, headed by Howard Moody and Izzy Young, launched a series of protests that compelled Mayor Robert Wagner to repeal the ban against folksinging in Washington Square that had been

(Left to right) Thomas Deegan, president of the World's Fair Executive Committee; Mayor Robert F. Wagner; and Robert Moses, organizer of the 1964 New York World's Fair and the city's master builder of the mid-20th century, 1963.

instituted by Parks Commissioner Newbold Morris. These developments not only restructured Democratic Party politics and urban planning and redefined the use of the public space, but they also helped spark an increase in civic participation in New York. They were landmarks of community mobilization against entrenched powers in the city, reinforcing the reputation of the Village as a hotbed of activism. "You people in the Village have developed to a fine art the public presentation of the problems of your community," declared Mayor Wagner in a speech to neighborhood residents in 1961. "And that is as it should be. That is what helps make the Village a brilliant example of a community and a neighborhood with a real community and neighborhood spirit."[9]

In the cultural realm, Village artists were similarly skeptical of the idea of professionalism. Neighborhood theatermakers and filmmakers disavowed the established methods of Broadway and Hollywood. In a wide variety of media, Village artists demolished hierarchies, leveling differences between highbrow and lowbrow entertainment, between the serious and the playful. They borrowed copiously from a range of sources, from classical art to popular culture, finding value not only in the sublime but also in camp. Eclectic in outlook, they developed pastiches from literary, musical, and theatrical texts.[10]

below: Artist Show, October 1955. The Washington Square Outdoor Art Show afforded local painters the opportunity to show and sell their work and tourists the chance to have their portraits done. Photograph by Albert Abbott.

above: Inaugurated in 1932, the biannual Washington Square Outdoor Art Show, seen here in October 1955, exhibited and sold the work of local artists. The event became a popular tourist attraction and a Village tradition, reinforcing the link between the neighborhood and the arts. Photograph by Albert Abbott.

The neighborhood's artistic accomplishments of 1961 were impressive. In that year, *Village Voice* cinema critic Jonas Mekas not only made his first major film, *Guns of the Trees*, a portrait of Beat culture, but he also established the New American Cinema Group, an organization devoted to devising new methods of financing, exhibiting, and distributing the work of independent filmmakers. The Living Theatre founded by Julian Beck and Judith Malina returned to 14th Street from a European tour with the Grand Prix from the Théâtre des Nations festival in Paris. (The Becks also founded the General Strike for Peace, a pacifist group that called for "work stoppages" to pressure the military-industrial complex to abolish nuclear weapons.) At the Caffe Cino on Cornelia Street, Doric Wilson presented his play *And He Made a Her*, an ironic comedy about conservative angels bickering in the Garden of Eden after the creation of Eve.

This was do-it-yourself artistic culture, small in scale. Bring your guitar down to Washington Square on Sunday afternoon and practice fingerpicking. Write a song and publish it in *Broadside*. Compose a poem and read it at the Gaslight Cafe. Produce a play and stage it at Cafe Manzini. Start a fanzine and circulate it at the Folklore Center. Create a "happening" and perform it at Judson Memorial Church. Direct a film and screen it at the Bleecker Street Cinema. Choreograph a dance and stage it at the Living Theatre. Overhead was minimal; artists did not have to gain the approval of donors for funding,

opposite: Bob Dylan at Gerde's
Folk City, April 11, 1961.
Photograph by Irwin Gooen.

so they had license to be bold in their methods and content. The milieu fostered experimentation. It was a rejection of pre-packaged entertainment. The Village scene promoted participation in the arts; mass culture, by contrast, encouraged consumption of products.

These were heady times in New York City and Greenwich Village in particular. The city was the worldwide capital of commerce, finance, media, art, culture, fashion, and entertainment, and the Village was probably the most famous neighborhood in the nation, a locus of grassroots activism and artistic creativity. It was a time of flux, a period that presented those with ambition, talent, and the knack for self-invention with opportunities to achieve greatness.

This was Bob Dylan's New York; this was his Greenwich Village. With guitar in hand, Dylan arrived in the neighborhood in 1961, eager to become the next Woody Guthrie. With the exception of perhaps F. Scott Fitzgerald's fictional Gatsby, no one else possessed Dylan's capacity for personal reinvention. Just as James Gatz transformed into Jay Gatsby, Robert Zimmerman became Bob Dylan, and he emerged as a transformative figure of the folk music revival. And here was the irony: in a movement that valued authenticity above all, Dylan was at his core a series of shifting personas.

- - -

In 1961, as the middle class continued to leave New York City for the suburbs in droves, young artists like Bob Dylan from Minnesota streamed into the city to realize their dreams. Though raised in the small mining town of Hibbing and just 19 years old, Dylan was hardly a greenhorn. A University of Minnesota dropout and a habitué of Minneapolis's bohemian Dinkytown district, he had a seriousness of purpose that belied an outward shyness and a fluid identity. His decision to shun college and pursue art countered prevailing trends. And though he knew no one in the great metropolis, it mattered little. "I had a heightened sense of awareness, was set in my ways, impractical and a visionary to boot. My mind was strong like a trap and I didn't need any guarantee of validity," he recalled about his world view upon arrival in New York.[11]

Ostensibly, Dylan, still legally Robert Zimmerman, came to New York to meet Woody Guthrie, his idol. Dylan's bible was Guthrie's autobiography, *Bound for Glory* (1943), a blend of fact and fiction about the Oklahoma troubadour's travels across the United States with migrant workers uprooted by the Dust Bowl during the Great Depression. Taking his cue from John Steinbeck in *The Grapes of Wrath* (1939), Guthrie empathized with Okies, Arkies, and Texans devastated by the severe drought and the loss of their farms, and he documented their hardship in the California agricultural sector. He also learned many of their folk songs.[12]

Bound for Glory startled and inspired Dylan, an impressionable college student uninterested in traditional

above: *Bound for Glory* (1943), Woody Guthrie's partly fictionalized autobiography, became a source of inspiration for the impressionable Bob Dylan, who read the work as a teenager in Minneapolis. In 1956 Folkways released a Guthrie album of the same name, shown here, about Americans hit hard by the Great Depression. Millard Lampell of the Almanac Singers described it as a record of songs "filled with the determination of a people to damn well endure."

education. Guthrie was multifaceted and rootless; he defied categorization. He was at once a singer and a poet, a worker and an organizer, a traveler and a writer, a vagabond and a refugee. Guthrie was a rugged individualist, a playful balladeer, and a sensitive humanist. He championed the downtrodden, the disinherited, and the displaced, celebrated the dignity of their labor, and spoke out for them when injustice occurred, whether perpetuated by unscrupulous bankers or exploitative bosses. In Guthrie, Dylan found his muse and spiritual forebear. "He's the greatest holiest godliest one in the world," Dylan exclaimed.[13]

In 1960 he began to channel Guthrie's persona in Dinkytown coffeehouses and folk music venues such as the Ten O'Clock Scholar and the Bastille. His obsession was evident in his affected dialect, set lists, and flatpicking technique. On the change in Dylan, Bastille owner Harvey Abrams later commented, "For the next two years he patterned his life after what he'd read. Bob started doing everything the way Guthrie did. For many months thereafter, everything Bob sang sounded like Guthrie. ... He would sit and listen to a record, then repeat it. It was phenomenal. Even his speech patterns began to change. That Oklahoma twang ... came into his voice."[14]

In his first year in New York, Dylan visited an ailing Guthrie in Greystone Park Psychiatric Hospital in New Jersey and in the home of folk enthusiasts Robert and Sidsel Gleason in East Orange. Ravaged by Huntington's chorea, Guthrie suffered immensely. His hands trembled, his shoulders shook, and he was barely able to utter words. The Gleasons held Sunday gatherings for him and invited friends to provide company. Ramblin' Jack Elliott often attended, as did Cisco Houston, who was unwell himself. Dylan saw Guthrie numerous times and usually just sat in the room, watching, listening, and occasionally playing a tune. Elliott remembered, "Bob probably felt he could get through more than I could, but I knew Woody so well that we would talk to each other without words. But it was the same with Bob. He told me he had the 'feeling' of talking with Woody that went beyond words. I knew then what he meant." After his first Sunday visit, Dylan wrote "Song to Woody," paying homage to his idol, as well as to Cisco Houston, Sonny Terry, and Lead Belly, in a tune based on Guthrie's "1913 Massacre," about the deaths of striking copper miners and their families in Calumet, Michigan.[15]

Dylan came to New York not only to commune with Woody Guthrie, but also to plunge into the New York folk world scene. "New York City," Dylan remarked, was "the city that would come to shape my destiny." He did not know it, but his timing was perfect. He threw himself into the creative ferment of the Greenwich Village coffeehouse district, where artists exchanged ideas about music, theater, literature, dance, and film. Eager to broaden his horizons beyond folk music, Dylan saw foreign films at an art movie house on 12th

BOB STARTED DOING EVERYTHING THE WAY GUTHRIE DID. FOR MANY MONTHS THEREAFTER, EVERYTHING BOB SANG SOUNDED LIKE GUTHRIE.

RECOLLECTIONS

TERRI THAL

No one became a folk music manager or music publisher or
started a record company to make money in the late 1950s or
early 1960s. People who entered the business did so because
they loved the music and were happy to be around it.

I became a manager in 1960. Dave Van Ronk, my then-husband,
was performing in a new coffeehouse in Pennsylvania that
clearly wouldn't be able to pay him. His manager advised
him to fulfill his contract. Dave completed the engagement,
got stiffed, and asked me to handle his business. I was
in graduate school at City College, studying political
science, and I thought managing would be interesting.

Dave and I first met Bob Dylan in 1961, and thought he was
a genius.

We all became good friends, and Bob spent a lot of time at our
apartment. He thought I was smart, but his real admiration
was for Dave. Dave taught him a lot about guitar, lectured
him on left-wing politics, and encouraged him to read
Bertolt Brecht, the Goliard poets, and Francois Villon, all
satirical critics of their societies. Bob's fascination
with these poets showed up later, in his songwriting.

His girlfriend Suze Rotolo introduced him to theater and
visual art. The four of us roamed the Village, eating
breakfast in mid-day and playing penny poker in my kitchen
in the evening.

One day Bob asked me, "Would you get me gigs?" I said, "I'll
try." I didn't even think of asking him to sign a management
contract; we were friends.

I took an audition tape to clubs in Springfield, Cambridge
and Boston, Massachusetts. No one booked him. I got him an
appearance at the Caffè Lena in Saratoga Springs. Whenever
owners Lena and Bill Spencer found themselves without a
performer, Lena would call me, and I would find someone to

go there. When I asked her to book Bob, she objected because
he was too new and unknown. "Every time you need an act at
the last minute, I find one for you," I said. "Now, I want
a favor."

Bob played there and bombed. The audience talked throughout
his performance. At the end of the weekend, Lena called
and told me never again to ask her to book Bob Dylan into
her club.

There are several stories about who convinced Mike Porco,
the owner of Gerde's Folk City, to book Bob in April 1961.
I had spent a lot of time nagging Mike to hire Bob, and when
Mike decided to do so, he called to tell me. If others were
doing the same, that's good.

A while after that, Bob told me, "Albert Grossman wants
to manage me." "How wonderful," I said. "He can do so much
more for you than I can." I meant it. Of course, it already
was a done deal. And that was that. Bob went on to fame and
glory, and I continued to manage Dave and other musicians
whom I thought were wonderful, including Maggie and Terre
Roche and the Holy Modal Rounders. With signed contracts.

Terri Thal ©2014

– – –

*Terri Thal managed a number of folksingers and groups,
including Dave Van Ronk, Bob Dylan, Tom Paxton, the Holy
Modal Rounders, and Maggie and Terre Roche. During the
civil rights and antiwar movements of the 1960s, she merged
her politics and her career by arranging concerts for
CORE, SNCC, and civil liberties organizations. Although
she stopped managing performers in 1971, she continues to
create programs with folksinger Mark Ross, the Storm King
School, and other educational institutions in New York,
connecting folk music with aspects of American culture.*

Street and plays at the Living Theatre on 14th Street. With Liam Clancy of the Clancy Brothers, he hung out at the White Horse Tavern on Hudson Street, enthralled by the Irish rebel ballads sung by men from the old country.[16]

Dylan became adept at navigating Village coffeehouses, playing at venues such as the Commons and Cafe Wha? and building a personal and artistic network in the process. His vulnerable look and scruffy appearance endeared him to many. In a folk music community that placed special value on instruction and apprenticeship, it did not take long for the needy and curious guitar and harmonica player to form a web of nurturing relationships. At Cafe Wha? Dylan gained insight into the eclectic nature of Village entertainment and often accompanied blues singer-songwriter Fred Neil on harmonica. On afternoons Neil, an emcee at the Wha?, organized potpourris of acts that featured poets, comedians, magicians, hypnotists, ventriloquists, and other performers. He accommodated performers and was invariably supportive, particularly of Dylan. In the evenings, the professionals took the stage. Comedians, including Woody Allen, Joan Rivers, and Lenny Bruce, did their routines. In the cramped basement room, Dylan played Guthrie songs on hootenanny nights and also performed with singer-songwriter Mark Spoelstra and blues singer Karen Dalton.[17]

But while the poorly lit club nourished the talent of the young Midwesterner, it lacked the prestige of other venues in the immediate area. At 116 MacDougal, across the street from Cafe Wha?, for example, was the Gaslight Poetry Cafe, a venue that boasted a reputation for excellent music due, in no small part, to its association with folksinger Dave Van Ronk, who would become a crucial mentor of Dylan's. A Brooklyn native, Van Ronk adopted Greenwich Village as his home in the 1950s. In Washington Square Park, he had learned finger-picking techniques from experts like Tom Paley, Barry Kornfeld, and Dick Rosmini. By 1960 he had distinguished himself as the leading young folksinger on the scene. With an alternately fine and rough voice and an extensive repertoire consisting of jazz standards, Dixieland tunes, and blues hymns, the tall, gruff Van Ronk was embraced by Gaslight audiences and was dubbed the "Mayor of MacDougal Street." In Minnesota Dylan had listened to Van Ronk and copied some of his recordings. From Van Ronk's repertoire, Dylan performed "Dink's Song," "House of the Rising Sun," "Poor Lazarus," and "See That My Grave is Kept Clean." The two first met at the Folklore Center, where Dylan played him "Nobody Knows You When You're Down and Out." Impressed, Van Ronk invited Dylan to sing a few songs in his set that evening at the Gaslight. Subsequently, Van Ronk and his wife, Terri Thal, helped Dylan and his girlfriend at the time, Suze Rotolo, originally from Queens, acclimate to the Village. Dylan and Rotolo, who lived together at 161 West 4th Street, frequently

Bob Dylan's personal and artistic network in Greenwich Village included Tommy Makem and the Clancy Brothers, who in 1966 released *Freedom's Sons* (Columbia, 1966) to commemorate the Easter Rising of 1916 against British rule of Ireland. Dylan described Liam Clancy as "the best ballad singer I ever heard in my life." Photographed by John Halpern.

visited the Van Ronks at their apartment at 180 Waverly Place to listen to records, talk politics, eat dinner, and play cards. Dylan recounted the privilege of playing alongside Van Ronk at the Gaslight. "He turned every folk song into a surreal melodrama, a theatrical piece—suspenseful, down to the last minute," reflected Dylan."[18]

Dylan's other folksinging guru in the Village was, not surprisingly, Ramblin' Jack Elliott, another Guthrie disciple. The son of a Jewish surgeon from Brooklyn, Elliott was born Elliott Charles Adnopoz on, by his own account, "a 15,000 acre ranch in the middle of Flatbush." Early in life, he acquired a love for cowboy movies and rodeos at Madison Square Garden and began to learn the guitar. While a student at Adelphi College, he heard Woody Guthrie's records, and, over the objections of his parents, dropped out of school to become a folksinger. He also started to call himself "Buck Elliott" and eventually "Jack Elliott" to sound more like a Westerner. In the late 1940s, Elliott met Guthrie in his home on Coney Island and became part of his family circle. His goal was to play "Woody Guthrie songs exactly the way that Woody did." Elliott was humorous, avuncular, and a great, though longwinded, storyteller—hence the nickname "Ramblin'." His voice was gritty and flat. After a stint in the United Kingdom from 1955 to 1959, Elliott returned to New York and added blues and Hank Williams songs to his catalog. His ability to mimic Guthrie was remarkable, and his understanding of vernacular songs of the American plains was profound. Many observers had no idea that he was actually a citybilly.

Dave Van Ronk and Terri Thal at the George Lorrie radio studio, June 22, 1959. Van Ronk and Thal, husband and wife, became crucial mentors to Bob Dylan. In a tribute to the couple in his memoir *Chronicles*, Dylan described Thal as "definitely not a minor character" and reflected that Van Ronk "came from the land of giants." Photograph by Aaron Rennert.

Elliott and Dylan instantly clicked. Elliott taught the younger man a number of songs and educated him about the cowboy-Western tradition. He regarded Dylan as a devotee and sometimes, when covering Dylan's songs, announced to the crowd, "Here's a song by my son, Bob Dylan." Dylan, in turn, embraced Elliott's carefree drifter style. But while Elliott fashioned himself in this manner in part to make people around him comfortable and talkative, Dylan played the role while concealing his extraordinary ambition, something that Ramblin' Jack lacked.[19]

To satisfy those ambitions, Dylan set his sights on playing Gerde's Folk City, the premier folk music venue in the nation. Mel Bailey, a regular customer at Gerde's, and his wife, Lillian, lobbied Gerde's owner, Mike Porco, to give Dylan a chance. Eve and Mac MacKenzie, two other patrons and parental figures to Dylan, also urged Porco to let Dylan play. If Porco booked Dylan, Eve MacKenzie promised, she would call everyone she knew to bring in business. Porco liked the idea. He supported new talent, not least because "the newer the cheaper" was his financial strategy. After Dylan did well in a show for the New York University folk club on April 5, 1961, Porco's interest increased. He signed Dylan for a two-week slot to open for the legendary Mississippi bluesman John Lee Hooker beginning April 11. Porco also arranged for Dylan to join the American Federation of Musicians, Local 802, and helped him get a live entertainment permit. Dylan was ecstatic; it was his first contract. "Because I was underaged, Mike signed for me as a guardian on my cabaret and union cards, so he became like a father to me—the Sicilian father that I never had," he recalled.[20]

Emboldened and determined, Dylan pursued a recording contract, setting his sights on Folkways, "the label that put out all the great records." But his attempt was unsuccessful. "I went up to Folkways," he recollected. "I says: 'Howdy. I've written some songs.' They wouldn't even look at them. I had always heard that Folkways was a good place. Irwin Silber didn't even talk to me and I never got to see Moe Asch." Vanguard and Elektra similarly snubbed him. Despite the setbacks, Dylan persisted. He played additional shows, returned to Minnesota briefly, and came back to New York ever more motivated to make it in the big city.[21]

Despite a professed abhorrence of schmoozing, Dylan excelled at a variant of it when he had to, even extending his reach beyond New York to the Boston/Cambridge scene. He possessed an uncanny ability to engage others, not in casual conversation, but rather in clever, witty, and often pointed banter. He typically won his audiences over during his performances, though some dismissed him as a Guthrie derivative. Onstage he usually wore a corduroy cap and was slightly and purposefully disheveled. He told corny stories between songs or sometimes just mumbled a few words. His voice

I WENT UP TO FOLKWAYS. I SAYS: 'HOWDY. I'VE WRITTEN SOME SONGS.' THEY WOULDN'T EVEN LOOK AT THEM.

following: Bob Dylan and Ramblin' Jack Elliott in Greenwich Village, July 1964. Brooklyn native Ramblin' Jack Elliott was Woody Guthrie's greatest devotee and a mentor to Dylan. Photograph by Douglas R. Gilbert.

had a nasal quality—thin, rusty, and grainy—suggesting at times Van Ronk, Elliott, or Guthrie, but unique and seemingly rural in origins. In the Village, as he played and hung out at the Gaslight, Folk City, the Commons, the Folklore Center, the Mills Hotel bar, Kettle of Fish, and the White Horse, he made friends with such successful musicians as John Herald of the Greenbriar Boys, blues singer John Hammond Jr. (son of the Columbia producer), and folksinger Len Chandler. In June 1961, he went to Boston and played Cambridge's Club 47, the area's outstanding music venue, where Joan Baez had started her career, acquainting himself with the club's talent coordinator Betsy Siggins and with blues singer Eric Von Schmidt and jugband performer Jim Kweskin.[22]

As the buzz around him increased, Dylan met music critic Robert Shelton at a Monday night hootenanny at Gerde's Folk City. In Shelton's words, "the encounter was unforgettable." Dylan did his quirky narrative song "Bear Mountain," inspired by a Father's Day boat cruise up the Hudson River that became a fiasco due to the sale of counterfeit tickets and overcrowding. After the set, an impressed Shelton told Dylan to alert him about his next show and that he would try to review it in *The New York Times*. "I sure will, I sure will," Dylan replied.[23]

Folk City's Mike Porco hired Dylan for two weeks, from September 25 to October 8, to play second act on a bill with the Greenbriar Boys. The bluegrass trio was a favorite with audiences at the club, their sets marked by whooping jams that showcased John Herald's nasal, boyish voice, Bob Yellin's dexterity on banjo, and Ralph Rinzler on mandolin. It was the proverbial hard act to follow, but Dylan rose to the occasion. On "I'm Gonna Get You, Sally Gal," he alternated between guitar and mouth harp, keeping a fast tempo. His version of "Dink's Song," about a woman deserted by her lover, was emotionally intense. "Here's a song outta my own head," Dylan proceeded, called "Talkin' New York." Though an original composition, the song drew from Woody Guthrie's unrecorded "Talking Subway Blues" and his outlaw ballad "Pretty Boy Floyd." In a talking blues style, with a wry and sardonic touch, Dylan recollected his arrival in New York, referring to the challenges of landing gigs and gaining notice in Greenwich Village coffeehouses.[24]

Backstage in the club's kitchen, Shelton interviewed Dylan. "I was born in Duluth, Minnesota, or maybe it was Superior, Wisconsin, right across the line," Dylan began, rattling off a series of untruths. "I started traveling with a carnival at the age of 13. I did odd jobs and sang with the carnival. I cleaned up ponies and ran steam shovels, in Minnesota, North Dakota, and then on south," he explained. "I had the strange feeling he was putting me on," Shelton recalled. About his performance manner, Dylan noted, "As to that bottleneck guitar, when I played a coffeehouse in Detroit I used a switchblade knife to get that sound. But when I pulled out the switchblade, six people in the audience walked out. They looked afraid. Now, I just use a kitchen knife so no one will walk out." Shelton stared in disbelief. "Listen," Dylan assured him, "I'm giving it to you straight. I wouldn't tell you anything that isn't true."[25]

Shelton's rave appeared in *The New York Times* on September 29, 1961, framed by a bold headline and a photograph of the performer with his hat, tie, and guitar. He started, "A bright new face in folk music is appearing at Gerde's Folk City. Although only 20 years old, Bob Dylan is one of the most distinctive stylists to play in a Manhattan cabaret in months." Shelton praised his proficiency on guitar, harmonica, and piano, and compared his voice to the "rude beauty of a Southern field hand musing in melody on his back porch." Dylan was at once comic and tragic, slow in delivery but intense, poetic and yet at times scarcely coherent. With a flourish, Shelton concluded:

> Mr. Dylan's highly personalized approach toward folk song is still evolving. He has been sopping up influences like a sponge. At times, the drama he

Bob Dylan at Folk City, October 3, 1961. From September 25 to October 8, 1961, Dylan played a series of shows at Gerde's Folk City, earning a rave review in *The New York Times* from music columnist Robert Shelton. Photograph by Irwin Gooen.

aims at is off-target melodrama and his stylization threatens to topple over as a mannered excess. But if not for every taste, his music-making has the mark of originality and inspiration, all the more notewor- thy for his youth. Mr. Dylan is vague about his ante- cedents and birthplace, but it matters less where he has been than where he is going, and that would seem to be straight up.[26]

The review caused a stir, not only catapulting Dylan to prominence in the city but also inspiring contempt among some folksingers and leading to a backlash against Shelton. Elliott, Van Ronk, and the Clancy brothers all applauded Shelton, remarking that Dylan richly deserved the tribute, but banjoists Eric Weissberg and Marshall Brickman, two fine instrumentalists, ridiculed Shelton for his inability to discern talent. Folksinger Logan English, struggling to make it himself, responded to Shelton's view with sarcasm. The Greenbriar Boys were annoyed that the critic relegated them to an afterthought in the review. Songwriter and arranger Fred Hellerman of the Weavers saw Shelton on the corner of a street and blurted, "He can't sing, and he can barely play, and he doesn't know much about music at all. I think you've gone off the deep end!" In contrast, folksingers Carolyn Hester and Richard Fariña, married at the time, were enthusiastic. They admired Dylan and touted his skills as a harmonica player. Hester invited Dylan to play on her upcoming recording ses- sion at Columbia. The range of opinions mirrored the diversity of the folk music revival in New York City, challenging the pop- ular notion of a homogenous community. Dylan himself was deeply appreciative. He told Shelton that "you're a very good writer, not just music, but a very good writer."[27]

Dylan's exposure increased steadily after the review, thanks partly to Izzy Young of the Folklore Center. Dylan often went to the MacDougal Street shop, which he described as the "citadel of Americana folk music." He spent hours in the back room listening to records, and the loquacious and inquisitive Young chronicled some of their encounters in his notebook, jotting down pages of Dylan's tall tales and scat- tered ramblings. "His questions were annoying, but I liked him because he was gracious to me and I tried to be considerate and forthcoming," Dylan remembered. Young was happy to introduce Dylan to other influential figures in the New York folk music community, including Oscar Brand. Dylan did his first radio broadcast in the city on Brand's Sunday WNYC show on October 29, 1961, in part to promote his first official solo concert, on November 4, organized by Young at Carnegie Chapter Hall. "He came on my radio show, and he said noth- ing but lies about his life," Brand recalled. Typical of the farci- cal exchange was Dylan's remembrance of traveling with the carnival and learning songs during his teenage years. "Where

Flier for Bob Dylan's first official solo concert on November 4, 1961, at Carnegie Chapter Hall. Organized by the Folklore Center's Izzy Young, the event was attended by only 53 people and went largely unnoticed.

THE FOLKLORE CENTER

Presents

BOB DYLAN

IN HIS FIRST NEW YORK CONCERT

SAT. NOV. 4, 1961   8:40pm

CARNEGIE CHAPTER HALL

154 WEST 57th STREET • NEW YORK CITY

All seats $2.00

Tickets available at: The Folklore Center
110 MacDougal Street
GR 7 - 5987   New York City 12, New York
or at door

CAROLYN HESTER

Vital to our Village folk community were at least four elements: 1) The welcoming attitude toward folk musicians among coffee shop owners who, up until then, only booked poetry readings. 2) The fact that New York University was near the center of the Village, adjacent to Washington Square and across the street from Gerde's Folk City. NYU students were our first audience, and word quickly spread to other campuses. 3) A "Gathering" was taking place; the arrival of folksingers, who, due to historic circumstances, were to be called "The Children of Woody and Pete." Besides yours truly, there were Dave Van Ronk, Bob Dylan, Tom Paxton, Judy Collins, Phil Ochs, Eric Andersen, Patrick Sky, Buffy Sainte-Marie, Joni Mitchell, Peter, Paul and Mary, Carly Simon, James Taylor, John Sebastian, and more. We joined Odetta, Oscar Brand, Jean Ritchie, and The Clancy Brothers. 4) The Village Voice put us on the map of Greenwich Village. My first "print" attention was an interview by Jack Goddard. If the Voice declared you worthy, then The New York Times MIGHT consider you!

One night in 1961, I was playing my last set for the night at Gerde's. A few die-hard folk fans and NYU students were still there. I decided it would be okay to end with a NON-folk song. "This song was taught to me by a rock star who, sadly, died in a plane crash in 1959. This song was taught to me by Buddy Holly." So I sang my folk version of "Lonesome Tears." As the audience applauded, I saw a young fellow jump up and drag his chair close to the stage. He leaned in close to me and said, "Say, that IS Buddy's song! Did you mean it, that he taught it to you? How'd that happen?" So I explained that Buddy and I had had the same manager, Norman Petty, and that was why I had an album out already. The next thing he says is, "So you really did know Buddy Holly!" "Yes," I said, "I actually was at his last recording session. It was here in New York at The Pythian Temple. It is spooky that he recorded 'It Doesn't Matter Anymore' that night." I started packing my guitar to leave and the young fellow said, "I'm glad to meet you, my name is Bob Dylan."

In August 1961, I signed to record with John Hammond at Columbia Records. Bob Dylan had hitchhiked up to Cambridge and opened for me at Club 47. While there he asked if there were any other gigs coming up where he could open. I explained that I was not going out on the road just now because I had to start a new album. "For my album sessions, I already have a guitar player, Bruce Langhorne, but you could come play harp for me if you want to," I told him.

"Here is my phone number, I'll be there," said Bob.

– – –

Carolyn Hester, folksinger and songwriter, was, according to Don Heckman of the Los Angeles Times, "one of the originals—one of the small but determined gang of ragtag, early-'60s folk-singers who cruised the coffeeshops and campuses, from Harvard Yard to Bleecker Street, convinced that their music could help change the world." Featured on the cover of the May 30, 1964 issue of The Saturday Evening Post, *Carolyn is remembered in many books, including Bob Dylan's memoir* Chronicles, *as a critical figure among a network of singers, producers, and journalists that brought folk music to a generation of America's youth. Her artistic relationships and influences span decades and include Buddy Holly, Ravi Shankar, and Nanci Griffith.*

did you get your carnival songs from?" Brand asked. "Uh, people in the carnival," Dylan replied. The concert itself, not in the Carnegie main hall but in the debut room, was a modest affair, small and unmemorable. Only 53 people attended, and Young, charging two dollars per ticket, lost money.[28]

During that pivotal fall, Dylan received a Columbia recording contract, a great milestone in his career, and, though some observers assumed Shelton's piece was the precipitating factor, John Hammond had discovered Dylan before Shelton did. He first heard Dylan in Carolyn Hester's apartment, playing harmonica and guitar and singing harmony on some of her songs for her debut album. He confirmed with Dylan that he was not recording for any label. The day after Shelton's review, Dylan accompanied Hester to her recording session at Columbia in Midtown. As Dylan was leaving the studio, Hammond asked him to come into the control booth to talk. He told Dylan that he wanted him to record for Columbia Records. The label was nationally prominent and strong in several genres, in contrast to the niche folk music companies Folkways, Elektra, and Vanguard. "It felt like my heart leapt up to the sky, to some intergalactic star," Dylan remembered. "My whole life was now about to be derailed."[29]

Hammond was a transformative figure in Dylan's life. As a producer and a talent scout, he championed jazz, spirituals, and blues, fueling the careers of such musicians as Billie Holiday, Teddy Wilson, Charlie Christian, and Cab Calloway. He practically singlehandedly revived the career of the late Delta bluesman Robert Johnson. Hammond gave Dylan a copy of the guitarist's epic *King of the Delta Blues,* prior to its issue on the Columbia label, and the album floored Dylan. Hammond and Dylan conversed about Johnson and other giants of the music industry, including Pete Seeger. Hammond had recently brought Seeger to Columbia and was irate at the government's conviction of him. "Hammond was no bullshitter," Dylan recalled. "He explained that he saw me as someone in the long line of a tradition, the tradition of blues, jazz and folk and not as some newfangled wunderkind on the cutting edge." Hammond put the contract in front of him, and Dylan signed straight away. "I trusted him," Dylan reflected. "Who wouldn't? There were maybe a thousand kings in the world and he was one of them."[30]

Hammond wasted no time producing Dylan's first album, titled simply *Bob Dylan*, recording it in just three sessions in November 1961 and releasing it on March 19, 1962. As he prepared for the tapings, Dylan immersed himself in the extensive record collection of Carla Rotolo, the sister of his girlfriend Suze and a personal assistant to Alan Lomax. Rotolo owned a substantial portion of the Folkways catalog as well as some Lomax field recordings. Only two songs on *Bob Dylan*, "Talkin' New York" and "Song to Woody," were original compositions. The rest were interpretations of traditional folk

In an homage to his advocate and sometimes critic Izzy Young, Bob Dylan wrote the song "Talking Folklore Center." Young sold the sheet music, shown here, for 25 cents. Dylan frequented Young's MacDougal Street store to browse and to listen to records in the back room.

songs and blues, such as "Baby, Let Me Follow You Down" and "House of the Risin' Sun." Though the album received positive reviews in the *Village Voice*, *Sing Out!*, and *Little Sandy Review*, it was by most accounts a disappointment. Hammond recalled, "His guitar playing, let us say charitably, was rudimentary, and his harmonica was barely passable, but he had a sound and a point of view and an idea." Dylan himself expressed embarrassment at the rushed effort, and the long delay between recording and release irritated him. The album did poorly in the marketplace: fewer than 5,000 copies were sold in the first few months, prompting some Columbia figures to deride Dylan as "Hammond's Folly." Dylan briefly considered quitting music, but Hammond and others in his Village circle encouraged him to persevere, reminding him that he was just 20 years old.[31]

THE POLITICS AND CULTURE OF BOB DYLAN

Like others in New York City's folk music revival in 1962 and 1963, Bob Dylan turned political and penned an array of topical songs on civil rights and pacifism. As he expanded his repertoire and musical skills, he formed numerous artistic and professional relationships with established figures in folk music, including Agnes "Sis" Cunningham, Gordon Friesen, Pete Seeger, Albert Grossman, and Joan Baez. All the while he studied his craft intensely, reading the published songbook collections of the Lomaxes, Frances James Child, and Cecil Sharp, and listening to Harry Smith's *Anthology of American Folk Music*. Dylan learned traditional ballads and reinvented them, continuing the folk process of transmission and dissemination. He also increasingly composed his own material and shed the faux Okie accent and hobo look. His reach began to extend throughout the nation and crossed the Atlantic, demonstrating the power of New York culture to shape trends in distant corners of the country and internationally. Dylan became a touchstone for the contentious disputes that preoccupied the New York folk music community, particularly the questions of song ownership and of authenticity.

During these years, Dylan joined the *Broadside* circle, publishing dozens of topical songs in the mimeographed magazine and serving as a contributing editor. Introduced to *Broadside* by Gil Turner, emcee at Gerde's Folk City and coeditor of the magazine, Dylan regularly attended the monthly meetings in the apartment of Sis Cunningham and Gordon Friesen, singing his latest material into their reel-to-reel recorder, to be transcribed and perhaps selected for publication. Cunningham remembered, "Dylan was quite shy and would often sing just a verse or two of a song and instruct his companion, Suze, to send us a copy of the lyrics the following day, which she would do." Friesen added, "Bob just seemed a kid, somehow, quite nervous when he wasn't singing and playing, doing a perpetual little dance with his boot toes, even seated. But there was a tremendous transformation when he started playing and singing." In the magazine's inaugural issue (February 1962), Dylan published "Talkin' John Birch Paranoid Blues," a satirical account of the anti-communist John Birch Society's frenzied search for subversive activity in the nation. His pace did not let up. For the next 18 months, he contributed to nearly every issue, if not as a singer or an editor, then as an essayist. *Broadside* was precisely the type of outlet that Dylan needed, encouraging him to experiment with his lyrics and develop a politically and socially conscious style. The monthly meetings also afforded him the opportunity to forge relationships with other emerging singer-songwriters, such as Phil Ochs, Tom Paxton, and Peter La Farge, and with luminaries from the New York folk music community, including Pete Seeger. Seeger quickly embraced Dylan, performing many of his songs in 1962 and referring to him as the finest new songwriter on the scene. Many of Dylan's songs appeared in *Broadside* before he recorded them for Columbia. The most famous was "Blowin' in the Wind," published in the magazine in May 1962 and released by Columbia on his second album, *The Freewheelin' Bob Dylan*, in May 1963. Some of his *Broadside* material was never officially released, though some appeared on obscure bootlegs.[32]

Dylan's *Broadside* songs strengthened his connections to the pacifist and antinuclear movements. Particularly arresting was "Masters of War," publicly premiered at a Gerde's Folk City hootenanny on January 21, 1963, printed in *Broadside* in February, and released on *Freewheelin'* in May. A scathing indictment of the constellation of political legislators, military leaders, and defense contractors who promoted a hawkish stance during the Cold War, "Masters of War" expressed the New Left foreign policy critique in stark terms. The Port Huron Statement, the Students for a Democratic Society's manifesto written in 1962, elucidated the ideology of the burgeoning New Left, identifying racial segregation and the nuclear arms race as the paramount problems in American society. Drawing partly from the writings of sociologist C. Wright Mills, the authors (primarily Tom Hayden) of the statement observed that "the enclosing fact of the Cold War, symbolized by the presence of the Bomb, brought awareness that we ourselves, and our friends, and millions of abstract 'others' we knew more directly because of our common peril, might die at any time." Peeling away the rhetoric of American statesmen, they added, "The proclaimed peaceful intentions of the United States contradicted its economic and military investments in the Cold War status quo." In "Masters of War," Dylan similarly took aim at war profiteers. To illustrate the point, *Broadside*

Dylan published "Masters of War" in *Broadside* magazine in February 1963, several months before Columbia Records released the song on the album *The Freewheelin' Bob Dylan* (1963). Accompanied by a Suze Rotolo drawing of a figure carving up the globe with a fork and a knife, the song represented a blistering denunciation of the expanding American military-industrial complex during the Cold War.

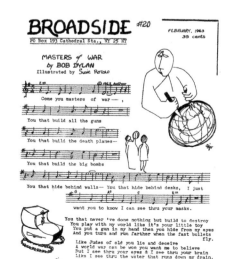

positioned Suze Rotolo's drawing of a ghastly figure carving up the globe with a fork and a knife adjacent to the song. Dylan's vitriolic lyrics accompanied the melody from the traditional English song "Nottamun Town," arranged by folksinger Jean Ritchie. By his own account, "'Masters of War' . . . is supposed to be a pacifistic song against war. It's not an antiwar song. It's speaking against what Eisenhower was calling a military-industrial complex as he was making his exit from the presidency. That spirit was in the air, and I picked it up."[33]

Dylan began to blossom as a songwriter in *Broadside* and became the object of several managers' interest. He signed a contract with Albert Grossman on August 22, 1962. The creator and manager of Peter, Paul and Mary, the Chicago-born Grossman, like Dylan, was a Midwestern transplant to New York. Also like Dylan, he fabricated his past, telling people that he earned a master's degree in economic theory from the University of Chicago when in fact he held a bachelor's in economics from Roosevelt University. Grossman was perceptive, shrewd, calculated, hard-nosed, and savvy—qualities that were crucial to success in the increasingly competitive New York music industry. At the inaugural Newport Folk Festival in 1959, he told Robert Shelton, "The American public is like Sleeping Beauty waiting to be kissed awake by the prince of folk music." In Greenwich Village, Grossman became a fixture at the Gaslight and Gerde's Folk City, scanning the scene for talent. Dylan remembered, "He looked like Sidney Greenstreet from *The Maltese Falcon*, had an enormous presence, dressed always in a conventional suit and tie, and he sat at a corner table. Usually when he talked, his voice was loud, like the booming of war drums. He didn't talk so much as growl." Dylan, until then informally managed by Terri Thal, understood the importance of an effective manager and joined forces with Grossman. "I welcomed the opportunity because Grossman had a stable of clients and was getting all of them work," he recalled. In Grossman he found a man protective of his artists and respectful of their peculiarities. Grossman shielded them from the tawdry aspects of show business and acted as a buffer between them and the media. He was impatient, easily annoyed, and cut down foes with bluster and brickbats. Robert Shelton contended that Dylan and Grossman absorbed the worst qualities of the other. Peter Yarrow added that Grossman represented a father figure to Dylan. "Bobby was imitating everyone at one stage, and he naturally began to imitate and learn a lot of Albert's tricks. I think Albert stimulated Bobby a great deal," Yarrow reflected.[34]

Grossman tried to persuade his new client to break his contract with John Hammond at Columbia and negotiate a better deal, arguing that the agreement was illegal because Dylan had signed it as a minor. Dylan refused but he did revise the terms with Hammond. "The mere mention of Grossman's name just about gave him apoplexy," Dylan recalled. "He

Sing Out!, Vol. 12, No. 4, October-November 1962. During the heyday of his career as a topical songwriter in 1962 and 1963, when he penned material in support of civil rights and pacifism, Bob Dylan became a favorite of the political wing of the New York folk music community, led by Sing Out! magazine. Some commentators even called him the "Spokesman of a Generation," a label that he emphatically rejected.

didn't like him, said he was as dirty as they come and was sorry Grossman was representing me, though he said he would still be supportive." Following the discord, Grossman convinced Columbia to replace Hammond with jazz producer Tom Wilson on Dylan's future albums.[35]

Hammond and Wilson both produced songs on *The Freewheelin' Bob Dylan*, a work that represented a quantum leap from the artist's debut effort and catapulted him to national and international fame. Dylan wrote 11 of the 13 tracks, an amalgam of topical songs on civil rights and pacifism, as well as love songs that reflected the uncertainty in his relationship with Suze Rotolo. Rotolo, the daughter of American Communist Party members, also helped shape Dylan's view of social strife. The couple adorned the album cover, strolling on Jones Street in the Village on a wintry afternoon. Against the backdrop of the activist movements of the era, the political material on *Freewheelin'* resonated deeply with young people nationwide. Dylan's ability to articulate their hopes, concerns, and anxieties earned him the nickname "Spokesman of a Generation"—a title that he famously rejected.[36]

Freewheelin' won Dylan plaudits from contemporaries and inspired numerous songwriters, such as Van Morrison and Leonard Cohen. Peter Yarrow of Peter, Paul and Mary, the trio that popularized "Blowin' in the Wind," remarked, "Bob Dylan is the most important songwriter in the country today. He has his finger on the pulse of America's youth." Joan Baez echoed, "Bob is expressing what all these kids want to say. He speaks for me." Pete Seeger and Dave Van Ronk both cited "A Hard Rain's A-Gonna Fall" in particular as a seminal work. Endlessly analyzed and frequently covered, like many of Dylan's songs, "A Hard Rain's A-Gonna Fall," which was based on the question-answer structure of the traditional Anglo-Scottish Child ballad No. 12, "Lord Randall," signified a paradigmatic shift in folk music, opening doors to fresh and imaginative lyrical possibilities. After the actual Cuban Missile Crisis, critics likened its surreal imagery of a post-apocalyptic landscape to the poetry of Arthur Rimbaud and Federico García Lorca, Picasso's "Guernica," and Goya's antiwar drawings. Seeger noted its timeless value, and, upon hearing Dylan perform the song for the first time at the Gaslight, Van Ronk recalled, "All I know is that afterward I had to get out of the club. I couldn't speak—to Bobby or anybody else for that matter. I remember being confused and fascinated that night because, on one hand, the song itself excited me, and on the other, I was acutely aware that it represented the beginning of an artistic revolution."[37]

The release of the album coincided with Dylan's deepest involvement in the civil rights movement. He was not an activist on the frontlines, though he participated in the 1963 Greenwood, Mississippi, voter registration drive with Theo Bikel and Pete Seeger. Dylan also played at a few fundraisers,

Bob Dylan reads the news, January 1962. His newspaper, titled *U.S. News & World Retort*, parodies the publication *U.S. News & World Report*. Photograph by John Cohen.

BOB IS EXPRESSING WHAT ALL THESE KIDS WANT TO SAY. HE SPEAKS FOR ME.

U.S.News
& World Retort
THE CALIFORNIA PELICAN
WAR
DECLARED
HOW TO AVOID THE DRAFT

such as a concert for the Congress of Racial Equality (CORE) at the City College of New York in 1962. The music of the SNCC Freedom Singers moved him, and he developed a friendship with Johnson, one of the group's key members. His performance of "We Shall Overcome" with other singers at the Newport Folk Festival in July 1963 became an enduring symbol of the entire folk music revival. On stage with Peter, Paul and Mary, Baez, the Freedom Singers, Seeger, and Bikel, Dylan, with his harmonica and guitar hanging from his neck, transformed, in the eyes of the crowd and the media, into a national star. In August 1963, he sang at the March on Washington, performing "When the Ship Comes In" and "Only a Pawn in Their Game." (Though the event represented the emotional climax of the Southern Freedom struggle, Dylan's performance underwhelmed the crowd.) More than his appearances on stage, his protest songs were his greatest contribution to the civil rights movement. "Blowin' in the Wind" and "The Times They Are a-Changin'" stirred the nation—and became significant cultural artifacts of the political tumult and social upheaval that characterized the 1960s.[38]

Around the time of the recording and release of *Freewheelin'*, Dylan also strengthened his personal and artistic relationship with Joan Baez. Regarded as the "Queen of Folk" by virtue of several successful Vanguard albums, Baez began to take Dylan on tours with her in 1963. He recalled seeing and hearing her for the first time: "She was wicked looking—shiny black hair that hung down over the curve of slender hips, drooping lashes, partly raised, no Raggedy Ann doll. The sight of her made me high. All that and then there was her voice." Baez introduced Dylan to crowds at her shows, covered his songs, and, to some extent, viewed him as a protégé. Her cachet unquestionably elevated his status. "Joan brought me up, man," Dylan reflected. "She recorded my songs and she was as important on that level as Peter, Paul and Mary." By his side, her commitment to pacifism and civil rights deepened. She also seemed to have a greater stage presence with him than as a solo act. The two developed an inconsistent friendship and an intermittent love affair. Cynics viewed their relationship as a case of mutual professional opportunism, but those closest to them understood the intensity of their connection.[39]

Paradoxically, while *Freewheelin'* revealed Dylan's talent as an original lyricist and attracted a legion of interpreters, such as Baez and Judy Collins, it also reinforced accusations that he was a plagiarist. Reports surfaced in *Newsweek* and in *Little Sandy Review* that Dylan stole "Blowin' in the Wind" lyrics from a New Jersey high school student. Though these charges were eventually proven false, they dogged him for years. Another song in question was "Don't Think Twice, It's All Right," about his strained relationship with Rotolo. Dylan based the composition on folksinger Paul Clayton's "Who's

Columbia issued *The Freewheelin' Bob Dylan* in 1963. The album cover shows Dylan and his girlfriend Suze Rotolo walking on snowy Jones Street in Greenwich Village. An activist in the civil rights organization Congress of Racial Equality (CORE) and the anti-nuclear group SANE, Rotolo helped shape Dylan's political views when they were a couple from 1961 to 1964.

Gonna Buy You Ribbons (When I'm Gone)," as evidenced by the clear melodic and harmonic similarities and some shared lyrics. Dylan and Clayton were friends and traveled across the country together in 1963. When Dylan did not acknowledge Clayton for the song, a legal battle ensued. Their respective publishing companies sued each other but resolved the matter out of court, and the friendship endured. "Don't Think Twice, It's All Right" came to be regarded as a tour de force, described by Paul Stookey as a "masterful statement" and by Dave Van Ronk as "self-pitying but brilliant."[40]

The plagiarism accusations triggered a review of Dylan's oeuvre. Critics found striking melodic similarities between his song "Farewell" and the traditional Anglo-Irish ballad "The Leaving of Liverpool," and between his "Ballad of Donald White" and the Canadian song "Peter Amberley." The number of Dylan detractors increased. Ian Tyson of Ian & Sylvia and Bob Yellin of the Greenbriar Boys were particularly vocal. Dylan became defensive about the issue. "What did I steal?" he asked. "Did I steal the word *the*, the word *a*, the word *so*? Everybody has to get their words from somewhere. Woody didn't write 10 original melodies, but nobody ever called him a thief."[41]

At times Dylan also violated unwritten rules between artists, as when he recorded Van Ronk's arrangement of "House of the Risin' Sun" on his first album without asking for permission in advance. From a legal standpoint there was no problem, as the song was in the public domain, but given the ballad's importance in Van Ronk's repertoire and the nature of the relationship between mentor and student, the act was an affront to Van Ronk. It was one thing for a revivalist to perform the material of another folksinger on stage or even record it for a niche label—after all, there was consensus that traditional songs were part of a common heritage. But it was another to record it for mass consumption on a major label like Columbia Records and potentially make a substantial profit. Van Ronk consequently stopped performing "House of the Risin' Sun" in public because people started accusing him of stealing it from Dylan. "Now that was very, very annoying," Van Ronk recalled. But the bitterness did not last, and Van Ronk had some vindication when the version by British rock group the Animals superseded Dylan's. Then, ironically, Dylan stopped playing it because people started accusing him of stealing it from the Animals.[42]

There were countless examples of song "theft" during the folk music revival, particularly in New York City, the home of the recording industry. To Dylan, increasingly considered a poet, lyrics eclipsed melody in significance. In his view, traditional melodies belonged to the collective folk music community. Their origins were uncertain to begin with, and thus the notion of song ownership was problematic. Dylan maintained that modern folksingers constructed songs

following: Joan Baez and Bob Dylan in Woodstock, New York, July 1963. In 1963 Dylan intensified his social and professional relationship with Baez, often called the "Queen of Folk." At this time, Baez, with greater national recognition than Dylan, helped him increase his visibility by taking him on tours with her and playing his songs. Photograph by David Gahr.

out of these cultural remnants, building on the work of their predecessors. The idea of adapting existing material was in fact an old one, as evidenced in the work of Mozart, Bach, Mahler, Shakespeare, Stravinsky, and Picasso, to name a few skillful thieves. As ethnomusicologist Charles Seeger reflected, "Conscious and unconscious appropriation, borrowing, adapting, plagiarizing and plain stealing ... always have been part and parcel of the process of artistic creation. The attempt to make sense out of copyright law reaches its limit in folk song. For here is the illustration par excellence of the Law of Plagiarism. The folk song is, by definition, and, as far as we can tell, by reality, entirely a product of plagiarism."[43]

The matter of song ownership related intimately to the question of authenticity, another critique of purists in regard to commercial trends in folk music in general and to the individuality of Dylan in particular. Authenticity was a slippery notion, and it evolved considerably during the folk music revival, especially as recording technology advanced. Encumbered by social and cultural baggage, the term frequently reflected the agenda of the user. But it was not simply an academic concept, debated by folklorists and ethnomusicologists; it mattered greatly in the community and to a large degree determined the response of audience to musician. "Authenticity" involved artistic purpose and personal style, stage performance and lyrical content, and even, in some cases, regional background and class and racial identity. At

above: Two months before the release of the semi-electric *Bringing It All Back Home* in March 1965, Dylan did a photo shoot with *Village Voice* photographer Fred McDarrah in Greenwich Village's Sheridan Square Park. Frustrated by media portraits of him as a "protest singer," Dylan increasingly wrote introspective, surreal, and personal lyrics, drawing from a range of artistic sources. Photograph by Fred W. McDarrah.

above: "Tom Dooley" songbook, 1958. More than any other song of the period, "Tom Dooley," recorded by the Kingston Trio in 1958, sparked mass interest in folk music and stimulated the nationwide revival. It sold more than three million copies as a single. The group faced criticism from folk music "purists," who were concerned that commercial interpretations of songs showed a lack of respect for traditional performance styles.

the outset of the folk music revival's boom period, to be an authentic performer above all meant to be genuine and sincere, and to be respectful of tradition and history. Authentic musicians were unadorned and earnest and rejected the trappings and trivialities associated with mass culture and Madison Avenue. Not surprisingly, groups such as the Kingston Trio, the Limeliters, and the Chad Mitchell Trio faced harsh criticism from purists for their slick appearance, commercial popularity, and polished arrangements.[44]

But Bob Dylan was a conundrum. To start, he was born Robert Zimmerman and was middle-class in background and Jewish. As a college student in Minneapolis, he began to efface his social identity, an act that he completed in New York with the legal change of his name in 1962. But it was not unusual for artists to change their names, as the case of Ramblin' Jack Elliott showed. Jewish actors often anglicized their names to avoid discrimination in Hollywood—Bernard Schwartz, for instance, became Tony Curtis. But folk music was not the movie business, and practitioners placed emphasis on transparency. Dylan's personal transformation went further than most. In casual conversations and media interviews, he claimed variously to be an Okie, an orphan from New Mexico, an Italian orphan, or a descendant of the Sioux Nation. Dylan talked about learning cowboy music from "real cowboys" in Cheyenne. He claimed to have met Woody Guthrie in California. "I was in Carmel, doing nothing. During the summer, Woody impressed me. Always made a point to see him again," Dylan explained to an acquaintance. His dress, his voice, his idiom, his diction, his phrasing, his posture, and his manner all were attempts at gaining authenticity in folk music circles. And he did so with apparent ingenuousness, connecting easily with audiences. In effect, Dylan made a case that artifice was the new authenticity. As the artist Harry Jackson observed after he saw Dylan perform, "He's so goddamned real, it's unbelievable."[45]

Yet, when critics chided Dylan for his invented persona, as in a *Newsweek* feature in 1963, they overlooked a key fact: his transformation occurred in New York. For the very promise of New York to immigrants and migrants alike was personal renewal. During this era, the city was the destination of African Americans fleeing Jim Crow in the South, Puerto Ricans uprooted by the declining agricultural economy in the Caribbean, and young middle-class white men and women from all over the nation escaping the stifling constraints of suburbia. They all had individual stories of struggle and hoped for a better future. In some cases, they wanted greater economic opportunities for themselves and better educational prospects for their children. In other instances, they wanted to enjoy and participate in the rich cultural and intellectual life of the city. They all faced obstacles, sometimes due to their race or ethnicity, but they also experienced personal transformation in their new neighborhoods, whether in Greenwich Village, Red Hook, Brooklyn, Ridgewood, Queens, or Mott Haven in the Bronx. In this regard, Robert Zimmerman was hardly unique. In fact, he was just one of many.

MY BACK PAGES

Recorded in the summer and fall of 1963, *The Times They Are a-Changin'* included topical songs on racism and poverty and lamentations of lovers at a crossroads. The grainy cover photograph showed a serious and intense artist, sullen and brooding. The title track described a society on the cusp of transformation. Though many commentators interpreted the ballad as a meditation on generational conflict, Dylan intended it to be a critique of the status quo and of outmoded ways of thinking. He remarked that the lyrics "separate aliveness from deadness. It had nothing to do with age." Dylan invited figures of authority, whether writers or politicians, to help advance change or get swept away by social currents. Biblical and apocalyptic, "The Times They Are a-Changin'" captured the zeitgeist and became an anthem for rebels as well as reformers. In contrast to other political songs, such as "The Lonesome Death of Hattie Carroll," "The Times They Are a-Changin'" refrained from referring to particular individuals or incidents and thereby gained universal appeal to proponents of societal change worldwide. Though the album, released by Columbia in January 1964, concluded with the personally contrite "Restless Farewell" and featured an insert of "11 Outlined Epigraphs" of poetry, signaling

below left: Concert announcement and ticket order form, Harold Leventhal Presents Bob Dylan at Carnegie Hall, Saturday, October 26, 1963. Photographed by John Halpern.

below right: Bob Dylan's Town Hall debut on April 12, 1963 was memorable. The set list consisted of 24 songs, many of them from his forthcoming *The Freewheelin' Bob Dylan*, including "Blowin' in the Wind," "A Hard Rain's A-Gonna Fall," and "Masters of War." Photographed by John Halpern.

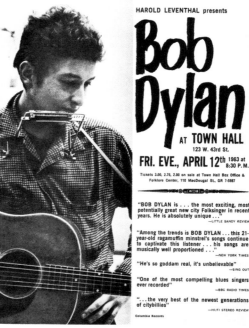

a turn to introspection, it strengthened Dylan's association with political activism.[46]

In recognition of Dylan's commitment to the fight for equality and freedom, the Emergency Civil Liberties Committee (ECLC) honored him with the annual Tom Paine Award in 1963. Formed by educators and clergymen in 1951 during the Red Scare in response to the decision of the American Civil Liberties Union not to directly defend people charged with "subversive activity" under the McCarran Act, particularly Communist Party leaders, the ECLC presented the Tom Paine Award each year on Bill of Rights Day, December 13. Previous recipients included Bertrand Russell, the eminent British philosopher, pacifist, social activist, and winner of the Nobel Prize in Literature. The award ceremony, held at the Hotel Americana in New York City, also functioned as a fund-raising dinner.[47]

Just three weeks after the assassination of President John F. Kennedy, with the nation still in mourning, Dylan's acceptance speech was an unmitigated disaster, marked by incoherent ramblings and insulting asides. It also reflected his increasing exasperation with doctrinaire politics and his refusal to accept the mantle of "Spokesman of a Generation." Unprepared, inebriated, and tense, Dylan delivered a rant at an audience whose members were shaped by the Popular Front of the 1930s. Filled with non sequiturs, his speech made references to free travel in Cuba, the March on Washington, and the House Un-American Activities Committee. The audience laughed at some of the gibes until the speaker expressed empathy with Kennedy assassin Lee Harvey Oswald. Dylan stammered, "I'll stand up and to get uncompromisable about it, which I have to be to be honest, I just got to be, as I got to admit that the man who shot President Kennedy, Lee Oswald, I don't know exactly where—what he thought he was doing, but I got to admit honestly that I, too—I saw some of myself in him." The audience booed and hissed. ECLC leader Clark Foreman, formerly a New Deal administrator and treasurer of the 1948 Henry Wallace for President Committee, was aghast. Donations fell $6,000 short of expectations, as outraged dinner attendees declined to contribute to an organization that honored such a man.[48]

Flustered, Dylan recognized his failure to articulate a coherent message and penned the group a letter, clarifying his views but not apologizing. For advice, he met with Harold Leventhal, Pete Seeger's manager and Woody Guthrie's agent. Leventhal, who was himself identified with leftist politics, informed Dylan that the people in the audience were veterans of labor struggles since the 1930s. In his note to the ECLC, Dylan acknowledged that he just should have said "thank you" but believed that the occasion called for a speech. He mentioned that he was a songwriter, not a public orator, and expressed sorrow that his speech undermined their

above: This image graced the cover of Dylan's songbook *The Times They Are a-Changin'*, published in 1963 by one of the nation's leading sheet music publishers and including material from both *The Freewheelin' Bob Dylan* (1963) and the forthcoming *The Times They Are a-Changin'* (1964) albums.

Bob Dylan is Talkin' New York

fundraising efforts, noting that he had not known the purpose of the dinner.[49]

In a subsequent interview with Nat Hentoff for a feature
in the *New Yorker*, Dylan expanded on his relationship as
an artist to political causes. He avowed, "I'm not part of no
Movement. If I was, I wouldn't be able to do anything else but
be in 'the Movement.' I just can't have people sit around and
make rules for me. I do a lot of things no Movement would
allow." On Lee Harvey Oswald, he commented that he simply
was able to identify with the anxiety of the Kennedy assassin
about the state of affairs in America and of course did not
condone the killing. Dylan declared, "I tell you, I'm never
going to have anything to do with any political organization
again in my life."[50]

Throughout 1964 Dylan distanced himself from social
causes, alienating many New York activists. In a prose-
poem letter in *Broadside* on January 20, he repudiated all
ideologues:

> away away be gone all you demons
> an just let me be me
> human me
> ruthless me
> wild me
> gentle me
> all kinds of me

He reflected on social problems, such as poverty on
the Bowery, and expounded on the futility of giving away
spare change. Dylan sardonically wondered if he was a mes-
siah, taking aim at certain depictions of him in the press. He
answered himself, "hell no I'm not." His relationship to the
media became hostile after *Newsweek* ran a fierce attack on
his character in a 1963 profile. Once accessible and clever,
Dylan became distrustful, wary, and cagey. He found refuge
in sarcasm and irony. On the burden of fame, he mused:

> I get quite paranoyd...
> an I know this isn't right

On one level, this personal change evidenced a rupture
with politics and the media. Attachment to a political cause
weakened his musical vision. But the transformation of the
artist went even deeper. Above all, Dylan valued autonomy.
His was a turn toward radical individualism. Around this
time, his relationship with Suze Rotolo ended. Dylan relied
increasingly on his own intuition and the wellspring of his
personal creativity. He maintained an entourage, including
manager Albert Grossman, that guarded him territorially,
but his bonds to New Yorkers mattered less and less starting

previous: Bob Dylan and Pete
Seeger, afternoon workshop,
Newport Folk Festival,
Newport, Rhode Island,
July 1964. Dylan's eagerly
anticipated appearances at
the festival attracted large
crowds. Oblivious to Dylan's
increasing tendency to defy
audience expectations, Ronnie
Gilbert of the Weavers told
the crowd, "And here he is . . .
take him, you know him, he's
yours." Photograph by Douglas
R. Gilbert.

in 1964. He achieved nearly complete control of the production of his albums. Dylan ruminated:

> an I've come to think that that might be the most
> important thing in the whole wide world…
> not going against your conscience
> nor your own natural sense

Bob Dylan lost faith in civic and cultural institutions and every kind of dogma. In the *Broadside* letter, he concluded:

> thru all the gossip, lies, religions, cults
> myths, gods, history books, social books,
> all books, politics, decrees, rules, laws,
> boundarie lines, bibles, legends, an bathroom
> writings, there is no guidance at all except
> from ones own natural senses
> from being born
> an it can only be exchanged
> it cant be preached
> nor sold
> nor even understood…[51]

below: Bob Dylan and Joan Baez in the closing performance of the Newport Folk Festival, Newport, Rhode Island, July 1964. Dylan played on several occasions during the festival, but many observers, such as *Sing Out!* editor Irwin Silber, criticized him for seemingly indifferent performances that featured meditative songs rather than the expected topical and political material. Photograph by Douglas R. Gilbert.

At the 1964 Newport Folk Festival, Dylan performed on three occasions, playing mostly introspective songs, sometimes in an indifferent manner. At the topical song workshop, he sang the decidedly anti-topical "It Ain't Me, Babe" and "Tambourine Man." Backstage prior to one set, Dylan remarked to blues musician Tony Glover about playing in front of 15,000 people, "I don't care. I'll just do my music. I don't care." The apathetic performance prompted Irwin Silber to chide Dylan in an "open letter" in *Sing Out!* magazine. "I saw at Newport how you had somehow lost contact with people. It seemed to me that the paraphernalia of fame were getting in your way," Silber commented. "Your new songs seem to be all inner-directed now, inner probing, self-conscious—maybe even a little maudlin or a little cruel on occasion ... in a sense we are all responsible for what's been happening to you. ... The American Success Machinery chews up geniuses one a day and still hungers for more." *Broadside* writer Paul Wolfe captured the sentiments of many in comparing Dylan with Phil Ochs, who was emerging as a dominant protest singer. The engaged Ochs and the introverted Dylan, he argued, respectively represented "sincerity vs. utter disregard for the tastes of the audience, idealistic principle vs. self-conscious egotism."[52]

Dylan had his share of defenders, among them Johnny Cash and Ochs himself. "SHUT UP! ... AND LET HIM SING!" Cash demanded in *Broadside*. Ochs remarked, "It is as if the

Dylan "goes electric" at the Newport Folk Festival, July 25, 1965. Dylan's seminal performance with ensemble members (from left) Michael Bloomfield, Sam Lay, Jerome Arnold, and Al Kooper, resulted in boos from the crowd and a maelstrom of criticism from the folk music establishment. Some claimed that the negative crowd reaction resulted from the poor sound quality, while others maintained that it was due to the shortness of the set, but all agreed that the controversial performance was symbolic of Dylan's turn away from topical songwriting and of the rise of folk rock in general. Photograph by David Gahr.

Bob Dylan
Bringing It All Back Home

Dylan's fifth studio album, *Bringing It All Back Home* (Columbia, 1965), marked a departure from his previous records, featuring electric rock 'n' roll on one side and acoustic material on the other. The performance style and lyrical content alienated some members of the folk community, who expected acoustic sounds and protest songs, but the album represented a window into the artist's psyche at the peak of his creativity and was ultimately hailed by critics as one of the greatest records in rock history.

entire folk community was a huge biology class and Bob was a rare, prize frog. Professor Silber and Student Wolfe appear to be quite annoyed that the frog keeps hopping in all different directions while they're trying to dissect him." Ochs concluded, "To cater to an audience's taste is not to respect them." In response to Ochs in private, Dylan was harsh. He characterized his friendly rival as a "journalist, not a songwriter" and told him that his topical songs were "bullshit . . . you're just wasting your time."[53]

- - -

Another Side of Bob Dylan, released by Columbia in August 1964, was an "apolitical" album, though it featured the luminous "Chimes of Freedom," a dramatic expression of solidarity with society's outcasts, in verse influenced by the symbolist poetry of Arthur Rimbaud. Dylan told journalist Nat Hentoff, "There aren't any finger-pointin' songs in here. Me, I don't want to write for people anymore—you know, be a spokesman. From now on, I want to write from inside me." Dylan's rebuttal to his critics was "My Back Pages," a rejection of political idealism characterized by simple binaries of good and bad. Dylan, then 23, looked back at his own past as a topical singer-songwriter and recognized his naiveté at espousing simplistic political solutions to complex social problems such as racial segregation. Slogans, ideologies, and jargon were no longer tenable in his world. To him, political certainty meant personal and artistic stagnancy. It was an unacceptable proposition to a musician in flux. "I'd become my enemy/In the instant that I preach," he expressed. In the refrain, Dylan reversed the traditional equation of youth with idealism, suggesting that the embrace of doctrine robbed young people of gaiety. By abandoning sanctimony, the singer-songwriter had regained his spirit and a richer view of society. "Ah, but I was so much older then/I'm younger than that now," he intoned.[54]

I'm sick of the attitude that folk music
stopped being vital after the 1960s.

Folksinger Rod MacDonald of the
Songwriter's Exchange, 1983[1]

THE
EVOLUTION
OF THE
FOLK MUSIC
REVIVAL IN
NEW YORK

(From top) Zal Yanovsky, John Sebastian, Joe Butler, and Steve Boone of the Lovin' Spoonful, 1966. Founded in New York in 1964, the Spoonful exemplified the rise of folk rock, which initially combined elements of blues and electric music. After playing shows in various Greenwich Village venues and recording tracks for Elektra Records, the group left New York City for California and became nationally successful with numerous hits such as "Summer in the City."

A myth developed in the media and popular culture that the British Invasion of 1964 and Dylan's turn to the electric guitar at Newport in 1965 spelled the end of the folk music revival. Some folksingers themselves perpetuated the narrative. "The Beatles shut us down," Ian Tyson of Ian & Sylvia remarked. "It was over. Over. We didn't know how to play with electric instruments. ... All us folkies were just standing there with egg on our faces. The only one who had the guts to challenge the rock 'n' roll guys on their own terms was Dylan."[2]

No one doubted that the arrival of the Beatles and Dylan's metamorphosis reshaped popular music. These developments contributed to the decline of the revival's commercial boom in the late 1960s. The increasing influence of rock also divided the New York folk music community, triggering a testy exchange between *Sing Out!* columnists and *New York Times* music critic Robert Shelton. Record labels in the city, such as Vanguard and Elektra, quickly embraced emerging trends in rock 'n' roll. The Greenwich Village folk music scene faded somewhat, not only in response to these developments, but also as a result of economic and cultural changes in the neighborhood. Bleecker Street music shops increasingly sold amplifiers and pickups and replaced the acoustic Gibson and Martin guitars in store windows with electric Les Pauls and Telecasters.

And yet, many New York folk music institutions, albeit in modified form, remained vibrant in the late 1960s and after. "Folk rock," a hybrid genre of folk and rock music that emerged in the middle of the 1960s, had roots in the revival. Principles of the revival concerning the value of cultural heritage endured, sparking the formation of organizations dedicated to the preservation and promotion of folk arts in the city, such as the Pinewoods Folk Music Club in 1965, the Balkan Arts Center in 1966, the World Music Institute in 1985,

above: John Sebastian in Los Angeles, ca. 1969.

and City Lore in 1986. Other outlets, including *Fast Folk Musical Magazine*, established in 1982, afforded promising singer-songwriters opportunities to circulate their work. The folk music revival in New York did not come to a halt, but rather transformed in character.

The genre of folk rock exploded in popularity in the latter part of the 1960s, fueled partly by the mellow songs of the Lovin' Spoonful, founded in New York in 1964. Led by John Sebastian, a Greenwich Village native, the Lovin' Spoonful had their origins in jug band and folk music. Sebastian, formerly of the Even Dozen Jug Band and the Mugwumps rock band, joined with Mugwumps guitarist Zal Yanovsky to form the core of the Spoonful. They recruited bassist Steve Boone through his brother Skip, guitarist in the first Village rock 'n' roll group, the Sell-Outs. Rounding out the group was drummer-vocalist Joe Butler, also from the Sell-Outs. "Our original premise was to create a hybrid between traditional bluesy style and the electric music, which was very sterile at the time," explained Sebastian, a veteran of Sunday afternoon jams in Washington Square Park and a versatile instrumentalist proficient on the guitar, harmonica, piano, and autoharp. Their first gig in the Village at the Night Owl on 118 West 3rd Street was evidently a disaster. "You guys are no fucking good," the proprietor told them and then fired them. Undeterred, the Spoonful persevered, and, after a brief stint with Elektra Records, they signed with Kama Sutra Records and left New York for California. Named after a line in the Mississippi John Hurt song "Coffee Blues," the seminal band represented an American rebuttal to the British Invasion. They enjoyed immense success on the West Coast for a couple of years, topping the charts with such hits as "Do You Believe in Magic," "Daydream," and "Summer in the City."[3]

The Mamas and the Papas, closely connected to the Lovin' Spoonful, was the other New York band rooted in the folk music revival that helped to transform folk rock into a nationally popular genre. Founded in 1965 by John Phillips, formerly of Village folk trio the Journeymen, and his wife Michelle, the Mamas and the Papas also included Cass Elliot, previously in the Big 3 and the Mugwumps, and Denny Doherty, also of the Mugwumps. The band narrated their origins in the popular hit single "Creeque Alley," making reference to the Village venue the Night Owl. Though typically associated with California, John Phillips emphasized the significance of his time with the Journeymen in New York and, in particular, at Gerde's Folk City. "One night we were playing and it was about 110 degrees, and there we were in our Kingston Trio sweaters," he recalled. "The sweat was just pouring off us. We had to suffer for style." Albert Grossman saw the Journeymen perform at a Folk City hootenanny and expressed interest in managing them, but he had second thoughts and chose Bob Dylan instead. Phillips remembered, "He said, 'Dylan will sell more records off his first album than you'll sell in your whole lifetime.' It was totally uncalled for." The Mamas and the Papas had six top-five hits in 1966 and 1967, including "California Dreamin'" and "Monday, Monday."[4]

The departure of the Lovin' Spoonful and the Mamas and the Papas from the Village signified the broader trend of musicians moving from New York to the West Coast in the middle of the 1960s. The recording industry was beginning to flower in California. Record producer Lou Adler, for example, founded Dunhill Records in 1964 and Ode Records in 1967 in Los Angeles. Elektra Records, under the direction of Jac Holzman, established a greater presence in Los Angeles and eventually relocated there. "I very quickly moved more toward rock and roll, signing the Paul Butterfield Band," Holzman explained, "and that led to frequent trips to California." In a major coup for Elektra, Holzman signed the Doors to a contract in 1966. Meanwhile, in the Bay Area, the folk scene transformed and captivated a youthful rebellious audience as the mixture of LSD and rock 'n' roll led to the birth of a psychedelic sound, embodied in the bands the Grateful Dead, Jefferson Airplane, and Big Brother and the Holding Company. *Saturday Review* rock critic Ellen Sander reflected on the shift, "The heavies evacuated the Village and split for California. Folk had become too commercial to be comfortable, tourists jamming every coffeehouse were degenerating the scene, cover charges and minimums every place we used to hang out for free were a drag, the stars of the folk world were off the streets and on the road or in secluded, exclusive enclaves."[5]

above: The Mama's and the Papa's, *If You Can Believe Your Eyes and Ears* (Dunhill, 1966).

following: John Sebastian and Bob Dylan at the Cafe Espresso, Woodstock, New York, July 1964. Photograph by Douglas R. Gilbert.

Other commentators lamented the demise of Greenwich Village in the late 1960s, especially as the East Village and SoHo emerged as edgy bohemian districts with significant populations of artists. They attributed the decline to the increase in residential and commercial rent values, the expansion of New York University, and the influx of tourists to the Washington Square area. "Around 1966 the Village was starting to die," reflected Betty Smyth, manager of several neighborhood basket houses. "We were running tourist attraction-type places." Hanging out in 1967 in the East Village's Tompkins Square Park, a haven for hippies, Rutgers University freshman Lisa Stern remarked, "You go where the action is. I used to spend weekends in Greenwich Village, but no longer." On Memorial Day, Stern relaxed by Tompkins Square Park's concrete bandstand, enjoying the rhythms of bongo drummers and other percussionists. In the nearby grassy area, members of the Society for Krishna Consciousness chanted and danced to the music of acoustic guitars.[6]

These trends exasperated many individuals in the New York folk music establishment, particularly *Sing Out!* editor Irwin Silber and columnists Josh Dunson and Izzy Young. They denounced folk rock in essays and editorials, equating it with mass culture drivel and accusing folk-rock musicians of pandering to the base instincts of audiences, especially the expanding youth market. "Its superficial electronic frenzy cannot cover up its fundamental non-involvement with life," Silber argued in a letter to the editor of *The New York Times*. Decrying the commodification of folk culture, Silber maintained his viewpoint that art should function as a weapon in the class struggle. In a similar vein, Josh Dunson remarked, "There is more protest and guts in one minute of good 'race music' than in two hours of folk rock." Izzy Young, in his "Frets and Frails" column, depicted folk rock as a "dither cooked up in a vacuum by a bunch of hip city kids" and studio musicians who "skipped from 'folk' to 'blues' to 'folk rock' as the times dictated." Folksinger Tom Paxton entered the fray with a column titled "Folk Rot," insisting that there were no genuine elements of folk music in so-called folk rock. He claimed that "it isn't folk, and if Dylan hadn't led, fed and bred it, no one would ever have dreamed of confusing it with folk music." With a circulation of 25,000 in January 1966, *Sing Out!* remained a potent force in folk music, shaping trends in the industry and framing the debates. But in electrically amplified folk rock, the magazine confronted a formidable adversary led by determined musicians and recording company executives and bolstered by college students and young adults with deep pocketbooks.[7]

Provoked by the diatribes, critic Robert Shelton "swung a two-paragraph right hook at *Sing Out!*" in an article published January 30, 1966, in *The New York Times*. Shelton characterized folk rock as a "healthy movement" that allowed for musical innovation, and declared that *Sing Out!* writers held

THERE IS MORE PROTEST AND GUTS IN ONE MINUTE OF GOOD 'RACE MUSIC' THAN IN TWO HOURS OF FOLK ROCK.

"Watching an argument in Tompkins Square Park," 1960s. The East Village emerged as a countercultural mecca in the late 1960s. This park in the heart of the neighborhood became a destination for hippies. An increasing number of individuals preferred the East Village to Greenwich Village, now dismissed as a tourist trap. Photograph by Donald Greenhaus.

elitist views and were out of touch with the values, attitudes, and beliefs of the majority of American music listeners. This was ironic, Shelton commented, given that they purported to have the interests of the "masses" in mind. It seemed, he continued, that *Sing Out!* writers had a static interpretation of folk music and wanted to impose their agenda on people, in a manner reminiscent of doctrinaire Soviet cultural organs. Shelton contended that popular folk-rock songs did not necessarily represent inferior quality or a compromise. They were part of folk music's broader process of change. "What is the function of the secular periodical if not to encourage experimentation, to help shape an avant-garde?" he asked. Shelton acknowledged that there were inept folk rock musicians, and was particularly critical of Barry McGuire and the Turtles, but concluded that it was foolish to dismiss an entire genre.[8]

Despite the hullabaloo about folk rock and reports about the death of Greenwich Village, the neighborhood continued to be the destination of talented folksingers, Eric Andersen among them. Born in Pittsburgh and raised in suburban Buffalo, Andersen played folk music clubs in Boston and San Francisco as a teenager. At the urging of Tom Paxton, he moved to New York at the age of 20, days before the Beatles landed at John F. Kennedy Airport on February 7, 1964. Excited and nervous, Andersen immersed himself in the Village scene, and his career took off. Paxton introduced him to critic Robert Shelton, who was impressed by the sensitive singer-songwriter and helped to arrange his first New York concert. Andersen opened for John Lee Hooker at Gerde's Folk City; his successful debut led to a recording contract with Vanguard and an agreement with Milt Okun at Cherry Lane Music to publish his songs. Andersen, a guitarist and harmonicist, subsequently performed at the Gaslight and captivated the audience. In a sterling review, Shelton noted the strong influence of the blues and the penetrating lyrical quality in his love songs, such as "Come to My Bedside." "His voice is a beautiful, vibrato-thick light baritone that echoes the style of Mr. Paxton and Bob Dylan and is occasionally reminiscent of the softer side of Elvis Presley," Shelton wrote. Andersen continued to distinguish himself with romantic and poetic folk songs such as "Violets of Dawn," though his topical "Thirsty Boots" about the civil rights movement Freedom Rides won him his greatest acclaim.[9]

Brooklyn native Richie Havens was another introspective folksinger who established himself in the Village amid the folk-rock craze of the late 1960s. His path to stardom was circuitous, starting with his days as a teenager singing in doo-wop groups on street corners in Bedford-Stuyvesant, Brooklyn. Havens had a lengthy history in Greenwich Village, reading poetry in coffeehouses and working as a portrait artist in the late 1950s. "There was so much talent and energy in the Village of the early 1960s that we instinctively knew that big changes in our American culture were brewing all around us," Havens recalled. He discovered folk music and started to play the guitar, performing at Folk City hootenanny nights with other hopeful artists. His rough and weathered voice, percussive guitar, and soulful expression caught the attention of crowds as well as critics. Havens signed a contract with Albert Grossman and accepted a record deal with Verve Forecast. His impassioned renditions of Dylan songs, particularly "Just Like a Woman" and "A Hard Rain's Gonna Fall," stirred audiences.[10]

Some Greenwich Village venues adjusted to the cultural and artistic developments of the late 1960s and remained dynamic performance venues. Of the top tier clubs, Gerde's Folk City maintained an unwavering commitment to folk music. Monday hootenanny nights were as popular as ever and drew young people from all over the country. Though not averse to change, Mike Porco deliberately resisted rock 'n' roll, largely as a result of his opposition to the costs of adding another microphone on stage and the association of marijuana with the music. *Village Voice* writer Linda Solomon remarked, "He felt very strongly against drugs, and in those days, all it meant was grass. He just didn't want any grass on the premises." Meanwhile, Bitter End manager Paul Colby tended to hire established acts, both musicians and comedians. The Gaslight booked many of the same musicians as Folk City and also presented numerous contemporary artists, including Bonnie Raitt, a blues singer-songwriter and slide

below: Eric Andersen performs at a *Broadside* magazine Hootenanny for Miners, New York City, May 1965. Shortly after his arrival in New York in 1964, Eric Andersen showcased his talents in the Village, earning a rave review from *The New York Times* music columnist Robert Shelton and a recording contract with Vanguard. Photograph by Diana Davies.

opposite: Eric Andersen poses as Bob Dylan, 1960s. Photograph by Diana Davies.

guitarist, and James Taylor, a singer-songwriter and guitarist. Other clubs featured a mix of styles, reflecting the diversity of movements sprouting from rock 'n' roll. Cafe au Go Go supported new rock bands and blues performers, such as the Youngbloods and the Paul Butterfield Blues Band, while the Night Owl gravitated toward psychedelic music, showcasing, among other bands, the Raghoos, later called Gandalf.[11]

As folk music decreased in popularity in the early 1970s, the Village scene diminished. In 1970 Gerde's relocated from 11 West 4th Street to 130 West 3rd Street, between Sixth Avenue and MacDougal Street, to a building formerly occupied by a jazz and strip club. Other strip clubs lined the deteriorating street, and business at Gerde's declined over the next two years. Folksinger Roger Becket recalled, "People were very upset when the club moved. It was like an anchor for the whole folk scene. Suddenly, it was changing. It was out of the way on 4th Street, yet at the same time it was such an established, known entity. ... When the new location opened, it was very much like opening a new club. There was a whole new crowd." In 1971 the Gaslight closed, and in 1973 Izzy Young locked the doors of the Folklore Center and moved to Stockholm, where he opened the Folklore Centrum and became a noted figure in Swedish folk music, in effect transplanting Village culture to Scandinavia.[12]

New York folk music revival institutions indeed exerted influence beyond the city, as evidenced not only by the birth

previous: Eric Andersen performs informally at the Philadelphia Folk Festival, Philadelphia, Pennsylvania, 1967. Photograph by Diana Davies.

above: Folksingers Odetta and Richie Havens perform at a Woody Guthrie Memorial Concert, Carnegie Hall, January 20, 1968. Photograph by David Gahr.

below: The Paul Butterfield Blues Band performs to a crowd at the Newport Folk Festival, Newport, Rhode Island, 1965. The band played on several occasions at the festival, impressing audiences and gaining the attention of Bob Dylan, who invited them to back him for his first live electric set. Photograph by Diana Davies

of the Stockholm Folklore Centrum, but also Ralph Rinzler's establishment of the Smithsonian Festival of American Folklife in 1967, a direct descendant of the Greenwich Village Friends of Old Time Music (FOTM) concert series of 1961 to 1965. President Lyndon Johnson's Great Society agenda of the mid-1960s increased the federal government's support for folk culture as the commercial boom of the folk music revival declined. The Festival of American Folklife, at first a week-long event held annually on Washington's National Mall, was immediately successful. The festival aspired to "deepen and advance public appreciation of the richness and viability of American grass-roots creativity." Rinzler and his colleagues organized educational presentations by traditional practitioners of American music, dance, art, crafts, and storytelling. The bearers of these traditions came from rural and urban ethnic communities throughout the nation, demonstrating their skills, aesthetics, and knowledge on stages and in workshops. The Smithsonian Institution initially excluded folk revivalists, such as the New Lost City Ramblers, who studied, promoted, and transmitted the music of indigenous cultures. Festival organizers particularly valued traditional and grassroots artists from ethnic communities, concerned that revivalists lacked the cultural authenticity to present native customs.[13]

At the grassroots level in New York, the folk music revival sparked the formation in 1965 of the Pinewoods Folk Music Club, an affiliate of the Country Dance and Song Society

left: Alan Jabbour (left) plays with the Highwoods String Band at the Festival of American Folklife, 1972. In 1976 Jabbour became the founding director of the American Folklife Center, at the Library of Congress, created by the United States Congress "to preserve and present American folklife." Photograph by Diana Davies.

started in 1915 by individuals inspired by the work of English folklorist Cecil Sharp. Today called the Folk Music Society of New York, the group was similar in mission to FOTM and presented traditional folk music by indigenous practitioners or by modern players respectful of tradition and history. Pinewoods co-founder Jerry Epstein, a masterful performer of the English concertina and a caller of English contra dancing, exemplified the respectful modern musician. In contrast to purists seeking to revive the essence of music in a pristine, unsullied state, Pinewoods founders embraced a fluid notion of folk art, deferential to inherited customs but open to shifts in melodic and harmonic arrangements and aware that "traditions" themselves were cultural constructs. Pinewoods was essentially a non-commercial entity, run by volunteers, communal in spirit and inclusive in orientation, though initially most members were middle-class and Jewish and had a liberal, secular outlook. The club organized concerts, weekend events, festivals, sing-alongs, and workshops in small, intimate venues and the city's parks.[14]

Another product of New York City's folk music revival was the Balkan Arts Center, one of the nation's preeminent traditional arts organizations, later renamed the Ethnic Folk Arts Center and currently called the Center for Traditional Music and Dance. Founded in 1966 by Martin Koenig, a teacher of

Balkan dance, the center sponsored festivals and tours by Greek, Serbian, and Bulgarian singers, and produced numerous LP recordings. In 1975 Ethel Raim, co-founder of the eastern European choral music group the Pennywhistlers, and longtime music editor of *Sing Out!*, joined Koenig on the staff. In the late 1970s the center collaborated with scholar Zev Feldman and two eminent Jewish musicians, clarinetist Dave Tarras and clarinetist and banjoist Andy Statman, on a research and concert project that helped to spark the international revival of klezmer music. In 1981 the center expanded its mission to include the ethnic communities of New York and has since worked with groups to research, document, and present traditional cultural expression.[15]

The prominence of the Balkan Arts Center reflected the broader ascension of ethnic cultural revivalism in New York in the 1970s, which was particularly apparent in the resurgence of Irish Celtic music. Fueled in part by the lively renditions of traditional ballads, rebel and drinking songs, and sea shanties by the Clancy Brothers and Tommy Makem during the commercial boom of the folk music revival, Irish Celtic music flourished in the city and was embraced in particular by the sons and daughters of immigrants who came to America in the 1940s and 1950s. Traditional Irish ensembles, such as the Chieftains and the Boys of the Lough, toured New York and other parts of the country, increasing the interest, and numerous Comhaltas Clubs devoted to the promotion of Irish song and dance were established in New York City, as well as in Long Island, Westchester, and New Jersey. These clubs sponsored concerts and *seisiúns*, pub sessions that offered professional and non-professional musicians opportunities to play together, typically in semi-circles. *Seisiúns* functioned as artistic and social events, marked by witty banter and commentary between tunes and a spirit of communalism. They occurred in the city's Irish neighborhoods, such as Kingsbridge and Woodlawn in the Bronx, Bayridge in Brooklyn, and Sunnyside, Woodside, and Bayside in Queens, as well as in more formal venues such as Symphony Space, founded on the Upper West Side by Isaiah Sheffer and Allen Miller in 1978. In 1985, with the support of the Center for Traditional Music and Dance, Irish musician Mick Moloney established "Cherish the Ladies," a concert tour and album series that featured women in traditional Irish music and continues to this day.[16]

Inspired by these trends, folklorist Steve Zeitlin in 1986 founded the nonprofit organization City Lore to document, preserve, and present the city's folk culture. Among other initiatives, City Lore collaborated with New York cultural and educational institutions to develop museum exhibitions, literary publications, and documentary films that related to both historical and contemporary folk culture issues. The organization, for example, raised funds to support musician and essayist Peter Siegel's project to restore and reissue tapes of

above: Ralph Rinzler performs at the Newport Folk Festival, Newport, Rhode Island, 1968. Formerly a member of the Northern bluegrass group the Greenbriar Boys and a co-founder of the Greenwich Village Friends of Old Time Music concert series, Rinzler established the Smithsonian Festival of American Folklife in 1967 to enhance the public's awareness and understanding of grassroots American cultural traditions. Photograph by Diana Davies.

FOTM's concert series. Released by Smithsonian Folkways in 2006, the recordings were released as the box set *Friends of Old Time Music*, a critical document of the peak years of the New York folk music revival. The three CDs of live concert recordings consisted of 55 tracks, including material from the first concert appearances in New York by Doc Watson, Roscoe Holcomb, and Clarence Ashley.[17]

In the Village in the late 1970s and 1980s, when punk and new wave music dominated the Lower Manhattan scene in venues such as CBGB, interest in folk music increased yet again, thanks largely to the efforts of musician Jack Hardy. A resident of the Village since 1973, Hardy was instrumental in the establishment in 1977 of the Songwriter's Exchange, an informal cooperative of musicians who performed in local cafes and met weekly in his apartment on West Houston Street to reinvigorate the neighborhood's folk music scene. Richard Mayer, an Exchange participant, recalled of Hardy, "In the middle of everybody complaining that they had no place to play, no one booking them or recording them, he'd say, 'O.K., let's build a club, let's have a weekly meeting, let's make our own album.'" During these Monday evening workshops, musicians gathered to offer constructive criticism on each other's compositions.[18]

The Songwriter's Exchange gained traction and created important local organizations. Many of the members performed at the Cornelia Street Cafe in the West Village. In 1980 several of them produced the album *Cornelia Street: The Songwriters Exchange*, positively reviewed in the nationally

above: The Pennywhistlers peform at the Newport Folk Festival, Newport, Rhode Island, 1965. The Pennywhistlers were an American singing group that specialized in eastern european choral music. Member Ethel Raim, also a music editor and singing teacher, represents a direct link between the New York folk music revival in the 1950s and 1960s and the ethnic cultural revival trends of the 1970s and beyond. Photograph by Diana Davies.

ERIC ANDERSEN

I had plenty of time on my hands in 1964 and 1965 before
my first album <u>Today Is the Highway</u> came out. I was living
in the East Village, and periodically with Gordon Friesen
and Sis Cunningham at <u>Broadside Magazine</u> in the Upper West
Side. Back then songwriters and musicians weren't ashamed
to be broke and being poor wasn't a crime. Flowing through
the streets of Greenwich Village was an astounding abundance of musical riches. I was fortunate to get to know owners of the clubs on Bleecker, MacDougal, Seventh Avenue,
West 3rd and West 4th Streets. They liked me and kindly
permitted me free entrance to their clubs to hear live
music. It was incredible because on any given night, for
six-night-a-week runs, you could hear folk, blue grass,
blues, and jazz at clubs sporting names such as Gerde's
Folk City, the Gaslight Cafe, The Village Gate, The Bitter
End, and the Village Vanguard. Here you could get to see
and meet amazing writers and performers like Ramblin' Jack
Elliott, Phil Ochs, Fred Neil, Tim Hardin, Bob Dylan, Tom
Paxton, Odetta, Richie Havens, and Dave Van Ronk. It was
like rubbing shoulders with musical monuments. Those tow-
ering Village talents could often be found on the streets,
clubs, or at the local Italian bar next to the Gaslight
Cafe, called the Kettle of Fish, where a decade before
Kerouac, Corso, and Ginsberg had hung out. Above the saw-
dust floors, we'd sit around and chat or recite lyrics to
each other while nibbling on peanuts and sipping beers.
These were the days of "Thirsty Boots," "Violets of Dawn,"
and "Dream to Rimbaud." David Blue once said it was like
Paris in the twenties. But I knew the wine in Paris was
better than what we were drinking. But where else other
than in New York could you stand next to Pete Seeger at a
Village hootenanny on a Saturday and on Sunday make a movie
with Andy Warhol?

What impressed me most and had the biggest influence were
the blues and jazz giants the likes of which we'll never
see again. On any given night, I could be found watching, listening, and sitting at their knees. These were the

blues and jazz greats of all time— true musical masters—who taught me how to hold an instrument, sing a lyric, hone my craft, and capture an audience. Week after week they would come and play. Blues colossuses like Lightnin' Hopkins and Mance Lipscomb from Texas; the great Son House, John Lee Hooker, Big Joe Williams, Skip James, Sonny Boy Williamson, and Fred McDowell from the Mississippi Delta; and others like Clarence Ashley from North Carolina, Sonny Terry and Brownie McGhee, and the Reverend Gary Davis. Though my debut shows were at Gerde's Folk City opening for phenomenal artists like John Lee Hooker and Doc Watson, these gigs weren't enough to make ends meet, so I kept scuffling along. In the jazz clubs, I would hear John Coltrane, Miles Davis, singers Betty Carter and Anita O'Day, the Modern Jazz Quartet, Bill Evans, organist Jimmy Smith, and the extraordinary Thelonious Monk and Charles Mingus.

Afterward I would be doing what my idols were doing. I began touring and would soon play my first Town Hall concert. They were lucky days.

Eric Andersen, Amsterdam © 2014

— — —

Eric Andersen is a writer who has recorded 27 albums of original material including "Bout Changes & Things", "Blue River", "Ghosts Upon The Road," and "Beat Avenue." He has written essays for the Rolling Stone Book of the Beats, National Geographic Traveler *and* Naked Lunch @ 50: The Anniversary Essays *(on William Burroughs). Andersen has recorded his music and lyrics for the "Shadow and Light of Albert Camus" and "Dance of Love & Death" and is completing his first novel.*

above top: Lucy Kaplansky, Rod MacDonald, Gerry Devine, Martha P. Hogan, David Massengill, Tom Intondi, Jack Hardy, and Bill Bachmann in front of Gerde's Folk City, early 1980s. The late 1970s and 1980s witnessed a resurgence of interest in folk music in the city. Greenwich Village musician Jack Hardy led the so-called "fast folk" movement and created the Songwriter's Exchange, a cooperative of musicians who played in area cafes and clubs. Photograph by Brian Rose.

above bottom: Suzanne Vega, 1980. Singer-songwriter Vega, a member of the Songwriter's Exchange, published many of her early songs on *Fast Folk* anthology albums and performed often at the Cornelia Street Cafe. This image derives from the photo shoot for her self-released debut album. A&M re-released it in 1985 to widespread acclaim in the United States and the United Kingdom, making her one of the first Fast Folk artists to achieve international fame. Photograph by Brian Rose.

respected *Stereo Review*. "They *are* still out there," observed critic Noel Coppage, "those troubadours with their simple acoustic backing, and Stash Records has made a beautiful little album with some of them." In 1981 Exchange members began to present folk music six nights a week in the SpeakEasy Cafe, which was housed in the back room of a Middle Eastern restaurant in the Village. Hardy founded the monthly periodical *The Coop/The Fast Folk Musical Magazine* in 1982 to support the work of new artists. Each issue of the magazine, simply called *Fast Folk*, included a record of original music by singer-songwriters. The magazine's title, conceived by Hardy, reflected his belief in the necessity of an expeditious artistic process. Too much revision, he argued, led to a diluted product. "The whole idea was to do it fast," commented Hardy, composer of hundreds of songs. "You could hear a song at an open mike or songwriters' meeting and two weeks later it was being played on the radio in Philadelphia or Chicago. It was urgent, exciting. It was in your face."[19]

From 1982 until it folded in 1997, *Fast Folk* nurtured the talent of many singer-songwriters, including Suzanne Vega, a member of the Songwriter's Exchange and the first subscription manager of the magazine. Vega gained a national following with her debut album in 1985, and her songs "Luka" and "Tom's Diner" became international hits in 1987. Steve Forbert, Shawn Colvin, Tracy Chapman, and Nanci Griffith also published some of their early work in *Fast Folk*. Other significant contributors included John Gorka, Richard Shindell, Cliff Eberhardt, and Lucy Kaplansky. The ventures by Hardy and the members of the Songwriter's Exchange illustrate the enduring appeal of folk music in New York City and indeed throughout the nation in the 1980s and 1990s.[20]

The trends after 1965 suggest that the folk music revival in New York never ended but ebbed and flowed, manifesting in different guises as performers, managers, journalists, organizers, and academics coalesced to promote the music in often ingenious ways, illuminating the potential of do-it-yourself culture even in the digital age. Currently, the folk music scene in New York is vibrant, as evidenced by the lively concerts and crowded classes and workshops at Brooklyn's Jalopy Theatre and the increasingly popular annual Brooklyn Folk Festival in the spring and Washington Square Park Folk Festival in the fall, both produced by Eli Smith, a folklorist, musician, and writer. The folk process, marked by change and continuity, remains an integral part of alternative culture in New York City.[21]

ENDNOTES

INTRODUCTION (PAGES 14-25)

1. Joe Klein, *Woody Guthrie: A Life* (New York: Ballantine Books, 1980), 153.
2. Thomas Kessner, *Fiorello H. La Guardia and the Making of Modern New York* (New York: Penguin Books, 1989), 292-341; Mason B. Williams, *City of Ambition: FDR, La Guardia, and the Making of Modern New York* (New York: W. W. Norton & Company, 2013), 175-211.
3. Nora Guthrie and the Woody Guthrie Archives, *My Name Is New York: Ramblin' Around Woody Guthrie's Town* (Brooklyn: powerHouse Books, 2012), 13-15; Klein, *Woody Guthrie*, 141-142.
4. Will Kaufman, *Woody Guthrie, American Radical* (Urbana, Chicago, and Springfield: University of Illinois Press, 2011), 28-29; Ed Cray, *Ramblin Man: The Life and Times of Woody Guthrie* (W.W. Norton & Company, 2004), 165; Robert Santelli, *This Land Is Your Land: Woody Guthrie and the Journey of an American Folksong* (Philadelphia: Running Press, 2012), 67-83, 127-135, 138-143, 160-161; Klein, *Woody Guthrie*, 283-285.
5. Marshall Berman, *All That is Solid Melts into Air: The Experience of Modernity* (New York: Penguin Books, 1988), 99; Max Page, *The Creative Destruction of Manhattan, 1900-1940* (Chicago: University of Chicago Press, 1999), 1-11.
6. Ronald D. Cohen, *Rainbow Quest: The Folk Music Revival and American Society, 1940-1970* (Amherst: University of Massachusetts Press, 2002), 8-27; John Szwed, *Alan Lomax: The Man Who Recorded the World* (New York: Viking, 2010), 140-167.
7. Grace Elizabeth Hale, *A Nation of Outsiders: How the White Middle Class Fell in Love with Rebellion in Postwar America* (New York: Oxford University Press, 2011), 1-10; Bob Dylan, *Chronicles: Volume One* (New York: Simon & Schuster, 2004), 35; Scott Barretta, ed., *The Conscience of the Folk Revival: The Writings of Israel "Izzy" Young* (Lanham: Scarecrow Press, 2013).
8. Stephen Petrus, "To Break Down the Walls: The Politics and Culture of Greenwich Village, 1955-1965" (PhD diss., CUNY Graduate Center, 2010), 141-175.
9. William G. Roy, *Reds, Whites, and Blues: Social Movements, Folk Music, and Race in the United States* (Princeton: Princeton University Press, 2010), 181-212.

CHAPTER ONE (PAGES 26-65)

1. Stephen Gammond, *This Machine Kills Fascists* (2005).
2. "Ballad Program Given," *NYT*, 4 Mar. 1940.
3. "This Young Fella, Pete, 1999," in Rob Rosenthal and Sam Rosenthal, eds., *Pete Seeger in His Own Words* (Boulder: Paradigm Publishers, 2012), 13-14; David King Dunaway, *How Can I Keep from Singing? The Ballad of Pete Seeger* (New York: Villard Books, 2008), 66-69; Kaufman, *Woody Guthrie*, 34-35; Santelli, *This Land Is Your Land*, 85-87; Morris Dickstein, *Dancing in the Dark: A Cultural History of the Great Depression* (New York: W. W. Norton & Company, 2009), 496-498.
4. Ann Douglas, *Terrible Honesty: Mongrel Manhattan in the 1920s* (New York: Farrar, Straus and Giroux, 1995), 14.
5. Peter K. Siegel, "The Friends of Old Music," 7 in *Friends of Old Time Music: The Folk Arrival 1961 – 1965* Smithsonian Folkways, SFW40160, 2006; Barbara L. Tischler, "folk music," in Kenneth T. Jackson, ed., *The Encyclopedia of New York City* (New Haven: Yale University Press, 1995), 422-423.
6. Barry Mazor, *Ralph Peer and the Making of Popular Roots Music* (Chicago: Chicago Review Press, 2014).
7. Benjamin Filene, *Romancing the Folk: Public Memory and American Roots Music* (Chapel Hill: University of North Carolina Press, 2000), 34-36.
8. Patrick Huber, "The New York Sound: Citybilly Recording Artists and the Creation of Hillbilly Music, 1924-1932," *Journal of American Folklore*, vol. 127l no. 504, Spring 2014, 140-158; Sean Wilentz, *360 Sound: The Columbia Records Story* (San Francisco: Chronicle Books, 2012); William Howland Kenny, *Recorded Music in American Life: The Phonograph and Popular Memory, 1890-1945* (New York: Oxford University Press, 1999); Andre Millard, *America On Record: A History of Recorded Sound* (New York: Cambridge University Press, 1995); Holly George-Warren, *Public Cowboy No. 1: The Life and Times of Gene Autry* (New York: Oxford University Press, 2007).
9. Paul Oliver et al., *Yonder Come the Blues: The Evolution of a Genre* (New York: Cambridge University Press, 2001); Filene, *Romancing the Folk*, 34-35.
10. Filene, *Romancing the Folk*, 39-46.

11. Siegel, "Friends of Old Time Music," 7.
12. Roy, *Reds, Whites, and Blues*, 1-27; John Patrick Diggins, *The Rise and Fall of the American Left* (New York: W.W. Norton and Company, 1992), 147-148.
13. Roy, *Reds, Whites, and Blues*, 88-93.
14. Reuss, *American Folk Music and Left-Wing Politics, 1927-1957*, 39-79.
15. Roy, *Reds, Whites, and Blues*, 92.
16. Shelly Romalis, *Pistol Packin' Mama: Aunt Molly Jackson and the Politics of Folksong* (Urbana: University of Illinois Press, 1999), 40.
17. Reuss, *American Folk Music and Left-Wing Politics*, 52-53.
18. Roy, *Reds, Whites, and Blues*, 94-97.
19. Michael Denning, *The Cultural Front: The Laboring of American Culture in the Twentieth Century* (New York: Verso, 1996), 285-295.
20. Ellen Harold and Don Fleming, "Lead Belly and the Lomaxes," http://www.culturalequity.org/currents/ce_currents_leadbelly_faqs.php
21. Filene, *Romancing the Folk*, 49-58.
22. Ibid., 54; Szwed, *Alan Lomax*, 62-64.
23. Filene, *Romancing the Folk*, 58-59.
24. Szwed, *Alan Lomax*, 65.
25. Ibid., 66-72.
26. Filene, *Romancing the Folk*, 58-60, 63-65.
27. Ibid., 58-59.
28. Szwed, *Alan Lomax*, 88-90, 152-156, 165-167; Roy, *Reds, Whites, and Blues*, 112-116; Harold and Fleming, "Lead Belly and the Lomaxes," http://www.culturalequity.org/currents/ce_currents_leadbelly_faqs.php
29. Dunstan Prial, *The Producer: John Hammond and the Soul of American Music* (New York: Farrar, Straus and Giroux, 2006), 105-122; Bob Riesman, *I Feel So Good: The Life and Times of Big Bill Broonzy* (Chicago: University of Chicago Press, 2011), 91-97; *From Spirituals to Swing*, Vanguard Records, 1999.
30. Szwed, *Alan Lomax*, 134-135; Riesman, *I Feel So Good*, 91.
31. Wilentz, *360 Sound*, 91; H. Howard Taubman, "Negro Music Given at Carnegie Hall," *NYT*, 24 Dec. 1938; Gama Gilbert, "TAC Jazz Session at Carnegie Hall," *NYT*, 25 Dec. 1939; Szwed, *Alan Lomax*, 134-135, 154.
32. We are indebted in our analysis to Denning, *The Cultural Front*, 3-50.
33. "Ballad," *NYT*, 4 Mar. 1940.
34. Dunaway, *How Can I Keep from Singing?*, 83-119.
35. Roy, *Reds, Whites, and Blues*, 127-129.
36. Dunaway, *How Can I Keep from Singing?*, 83-86.
37. Ibid., 90-93.
38. Ibid., 94-95.
39. Ibid., 99-101; David King Dunaway and Molly Beer, *Singing Out: An Oral History of America's Folk Music Revivals* (New York: Oxford University Press, 2010), 63.
40. Dunaway, *How Can I Keep from Singing?*, 101-106.
41. Ibid., 104-106.
42. Ibid., 110-116.
43. Ibid., 111-113.
44. Ibid.
45. Ibid., 116-119.
46. Cantwell, *When We Were Good*, 117-150.
47. Guthrie, *My Name Is New York*.
48. Rosenthal and Rosenthal, eds., *Pete Seeger in His Own Words*, 39; "Miss Bettis Guest With Dance Group," *NYT*, December 29, 1945; *Billboard*, December 21, 1946.
49. Peter Seeger, *How To Play The 5-String Banjo* (New York: People's Songs, August 1948), 1-2; David Bonner, *Revolutionizing Children's Records: The Young People's Records and Children's Record Guild Series, 1946-1977* (Lanham: The Scarecrow Press, 2008); Reuss, *American Folk Music and Left-Wing Politics, 1927-1957*.
50. Rosenthal and Rosenthal, eds., *Pete Seeger in His Own Words*, 40.
51. Oscar Brand, *The Ballad Mongers* (N.Y.: Funk & Wagnalls Co., 1962), 143.
52. "Sidewalk Hootenanny," People's Songs Bulletin, vol. 2, no. 1 & 2, Feb.-Mar. 1947, 6.

CHAPTER 2 (PAGES 66-103)

1. Robert Shelton, *No Direction Home: The Life and Music of Bob Dylan*, revised and updated by Elizabeth Thomson and Patrick Humphries (Milwaukee: Backbeat Books, 2011), 71.
2. Dunaway, *How Can I Keep from Singing?*, 163-164.
3. Ibid.
4. Ibid.
5. Ibid.
6. Wilentz, *360 Sound*, 122.
7. Joshua M. Zeitz, *White Ethnic New York: Jews, Catholics, and the Shaping of Postwar Politics* (Chapel Hill: University of North Carolina Press, 2007), 39-60.
8. Dunaway, *How Can I Keep from Singing?*, 164-165.
9. Ronald D. Cohen and James Capaldi, eds., *The Pete Seeger Reader* (New York: Oxford University Press, 2014), 106-108.
10. Dunaway, *How Can I Keep from Singing?*, 165.
11. Albin J. Zak, *I Don't Sound Like Nobody: Remaking Music in 1950s America* (Ann Arbor: University of Michigan Press, 2010), 60-67.
12. Dunaway, *How Can I Keep from Singing?*, 166-167.
13. Robert S. Koppelman, ed., *"Sing Out, Warning! Sing Out, Love!": The Writings of Lee Hays* (Amherst: University of Massachusetts Press, 2003), 111; Harold Leventhal with Robert Santelli, "Remembering Woody," Robert Santelli and Emily Davidson, eds., *Hard Travelin': The Life and Legacy of Woody Guthrie* (Hanover: Wesleyan University Press, 1999), 15; "Good Night, Irene," *Time*, August 14, 1950, 38; Gilbert Millstein, "Very Good Night," *New York Times Magazine*, October 15, 1950, 41.

14. Dunaway, *How Can I Keep from Singing?*, 169-172; "Music: Out of the Corner," *Time*, Sept. 25, 1950, 69.

15. Dunaway, *How Can I Keep from Singing?*, 172-189; *Counterattack*, Letter No. 164, July 14, 1950; "Folksongs at 8 at Panel Room," *Daily Worker*, 5 May 1950; Frederick Woltman, "Melody Weaves on, Along Party Line," *New York World Telegram*, 25 Aug. 1951; Dunaway and Beer, *Singing Out*, 92.

16. Brand, *The Ballad Mongers*, 121.

17. Dunaway, *How Can I Keep from Singing?*, 186-187.

18. Richard Carlin, *Worlds of Sound: The Story of Smithsonian Folkways* (Washington, D.C.: Smithsonian Books, 2008) 1-7; Gene Bluestein, "Moses Asch, Documentor," *American Music* (Autumn, 1987), 291-304.

19. Peter D. Goldsmith, *Making People's Music: Moe Asch and Folkways Records* (Washington, D.C.: Smithsonian Institution Press, 1998), 225-237.

20. Carlin, *Worlds of Sound*, 8-9.

21. Ibid., 14-16.

22. Goldsmith, *Making People's Music*, 233-234.

23. Carlin, *Worlds of Sound*, 61-69; Hale, *A Nation of Outsiders*, 90-91.

24. Cantwell, *When We Were Good*, 189-238.

25. John Hammond album notes, *Brother John Sellers Sings Blues and Folk Songs*, Vanguard Jazz Showcase, VRS 8005.

26. Jac Holzman and Gavan Daws, *Follow The Music: The Life and High Times of Elektra Records in the Great Years of American Pop Culture* (Santa Monica: FirstMedia Books, 1998), 8, 10.

27. Holzman and Daws, *Follow The Music*, 19, 20.

28. "Interview: Bob Dylan," *Playboy*, March 1966.

29. "The First Issue," *Sing Out!*, vol. 1, no. 1, May 1960, 2, 16.

30. Len Levinson, "Midnight Rally of the Folkniks: Carnegie Marathon Ethnic and Zing," undated clipping.

31. B. A. Botkin and William G. Tyrrell, "Upstate, Downstate," *New York Folklore Quarterly*, Spring 1957, 66.

32. "The Folklore Center," *Sing Out!*, vol. 7 no. 1, Spring 1957, 33; Barretta, *Conscience of the Folk Revival*, 5.

33. Clancy, *The Mountain of the Women*, 199; Dave Van Ronk with Elijah Wald, *The Mayor of MacDougal Street: A Memoir* (Cambridge: DaCapo Press, 2005), 62.

34. Van Ronk with Wald, *The Mayor of MacDougal Street*, 65.

35. Darling, *"I'd Give My Life."* 97.

36. Harry Belafonte with Michael Shnayerson, *My Song: A Memoir* (New York: Random House, 2011), 154; Judith E. Smith, *Becoming Belafonte: Black Artist, Public Radical* (Austin: University of Texas Press, 2014).

37. Irwin Silber, "Carnegie Hall Rocks As The Weavers Return," *Sing Out!*, vol. 6, no. 1, Winter 1956, 31, 32; *The Weavers at Carnegie Hall*, Vanguard VRS-9010; Rosenthal and Rosenthal, eds., *Pete Seeger In His Own Words*, 260.

38. James T. Patterson, *Grand Expectations: The United States, 1945-1971* (New York: Oxford University Press, 1996), 343-374; Cohen, *Rainbow Quest*, 129-134.

39. Hale, *A Nation of Outsiders*, 1-10.

40. David Hajdu, *Positively 4th Street: The Lives and Times of Joan Baez, Bob Dylan, Mimi Baez Farina, and Richard Farina* (New York: North Point Press, 2001), 11-12

CHAPTER THREE (PAGES 104-145)

1. Robbie Woliver, *Bringing It All Back Home* (New York: Pantheon Books, 1986), 15.

2. Michael F. Scully, *The Never-Ending Revival: Rounder Records and the Folk Alliance* (Urbana and Chicago: University of Illinois Press, 2008), 38.

3. Urban historians and anthropologists increasingly examine connections between public space and the cultural and political economy, portraying parks in particular as contested terrain with identities shaped by interest groups. Several studies have influenced this chapter, including Roy Rosenzweig and Elizabeth Blackmar, *The Park and the People: A History of Central Park* (Ithaca: Cornell University Press, 1998) Neil Smith, "'Class Struggle on Avenue B:' The Lower East Side as Wild Wild West," in his *The New Urban Frontier: Gentrification and the Revanchist City* (New York: Routledge, 1996), 3-29; and Setha Low and Neil Smith, "Introduction: The Imperative of Public Space," in their edited volume *The Politics of Public Space* (New York: Routledge, 2006), 1-16.

4. Lawrence Block, "Back in the Day," in Van Ronk, *Mayor of MacDougal Street*, xii-xiii; Cantwell, *When We Were Good*, 275-290; Dan Wakefield, *New York in the Fifties* (New York: St. Martin's Griffin, 1992), 192; Theodore Bikel, *Theo: The Autobiography of Theodore Bikel* (New York: HarperCollins, 1994), 155-156.

5. Cohen, *Rainbow Quest*, 106-107; Van Ronk, *Mayor of MacDougal Street*, 41; Cantwell, *When We Were Good*, 287.

6. Van Ronk, *Mayor of MacDougal Street*, 41-43.

7. Hilary Ballon, "Robert Moses and Urban Renewal," in Hilary Ballon and Kenneth T. Jackson, eds., *Robert Moses and the Modern City: The Transformation of New York* (New York: W.W. Norton & Company, 2007), 94-115; Joel Schwartz, *The New York Approach: Robert Moses, Urban Liberals, and the Redevelopment of the Inner City* (Columbus: Ohio State University Press, 1993), 262-266; Ballon, "Title I Developments," in *Robert Moses and the Modern City*, 244-249; "Two Housing Projects Slated South of Washington Square," *NYT*, 24 Aug. 1953, p. 1, 25; "Rebuilding the 'Village,'" *NYT*, 26 Aug. 1953, p. 26.

8. Samuel Zipp, *Manhattan Projects: The Rise and Fall of Urban Renewal in Cold War New York* (New York: Oxford University Press, 2011), 3-29; Anthony Flint, *Wrestling with Moses: How Jane Jacobs Took On New York's Master Builder and Transformed the American City* (New York:

9. Random House, 2009), 61-92.

9. Suleiman Osman, *The Invention of Brownstone Brooklyn: Gentrification and the Search for Authenticity in Postwar New York* (New York: Oxford University Press, 2011), 164-188.

10. Charles G. Bennett, "'Village' Protesters Led by De Sapio," *NYT*, 19 Sept. 1958, p. 1, 13; Daniel Wolf, "Villagers Win Major Victory," *VV*, 24 Sept. 1958, p. 1, 3; "Compromise Road Now Likely," *Villager*, 25 Sept. 1958, p. 1, 9; "Laurels, One Apiece," *Villager*, 25 Sept. 1958, p. 16.

11. Charles G. Bennett. "Washington Sq. Traffic to Halt While Road Issue Is Decided," *NYT*, 24 Oct. 1958, p. 1, 14; Mary Perot Nichols, "Villagers Win Major Victory," *VV*, 29 Oct. 1958, p. 1, 3; "Victory and Anniversary," *VV*, 29 Oct. 1958, p. 4; Nichols, "City Closed Square Saturday," *VV*, 5 Nov. 1958, p. 1, 3; "Crowd Hails Sq. Ribbon Tying," *Villager*, 6 Nov. 1958, p. 1, 7; "Villagers Call Trial Unqualified Success," *VV*, 26 Nov. 1958, p. 1-2; "One Month Later," *VV*, 26 Nov. 1958, p. 4; "Traffic Ban Asked in Washington Sq.," *NYT*, 3 Dec. 1958, p. 46; Letter from Shirley Hayes to Robert Wagner and the Board of Estimate, Dec. 1958, Box 1, Shirley Hayes Papers (hereafter SH Papers); "Close 'Square' Permanently," *VV*, 14 Jan. 1959, p. 3; "JEC To Meet With The Mayor," *Villager*, 5 Mar. 1959, p. 1, 5; Letter from Shirley Hayes to Hulan Jack, 23 Mar. 1959, Box 1, SH Papers; "The Controversial Wiley Report," *Villager*, 2 Apr. 1959, p. 16; Raymond S. Rubinow, "The JEC Rests Its Case," *Villager*, 9 Apr. 1959, p. 16; Charles G. Bennett, "City Vote Backs a Ban on Traffic in Washington Sq.," *NYT*, 10 Apr. 1959, p. 1, 19; "Washington Sq.," *VV*, 15 Apr. 1959, p. 1-2; "The Square Is Closed For Keeps," *Villager*, 16 Apr. 1959, p. 1, 7; "City Shifts to Hayes Plan," *VV*, 26 Aug. 1959, p. 1.

12. Van Ronk, *Mayor of MacDougal Street*, 146, 155-156.

13. Luther S. Harris, *Around Washington Square: An Illustrated History of Greenwich Village* (Baltimore: Johns Hopkins University Press, 2003), 267; Van Ronk, *Mayor of MacDougal Street*, 148-149; "Outbreak of Vandalism Hits S. Village Coffee Shop Area," *VV*, 16 Sept. 1959, p. 3; Robert Alden, "'Village' Tension Upsets Residents," *NYT*, 29 Sept. 1959, p. 41-42; Letter from Donald J. Pappas to Mayor Robert F. Wagner, 12 Apr. 1961, New York City Department of Parks General Files, Manhattan, Washington Square Park, (hereafter NYCDPGFWSP) 1960-61, Roll 30.

14. Interview of Art D'Lugoff by Stephen Petrus, 5 December 2005; "Outrage," *VV*, 16 Sept. 1959, p. 3.

15. Interview of Howard Moody by Stephen Petrus, 9 December 2004; "Outrage," *VV*, 16 Sept. 1959, p. 3.

16. Schwartz, *New York Approach*, 262-266; Alden, "'Village,'" *NYT*, 29 Sept. 1959, p. 42; "Moody Hits Search For Scapegoats in Village Tensions," *VV*, 11 Nov. 1959, p. 3.

17. Michael James, "Free Show in Washington Square Is a Hit," *NYT*, 25 May 1959, p. 1; Letter by Robert J. Silberstein to Parks Commissioner Newbold Morris, May 8, 1961, NYCDPGFWSP, 1960-61, Roll 30.

18. Hale, *A Nation of Outsiders*, 84-131.

19. "Newbold Morris, 64, Is Dead of Cancer," *NYT*, 1 April 1966, p. 1, 31.

20. Ibid.

21. Memorandum by Newbold Morris, Mar. 13, 1961, NYCDPGFWSP, 1960-61, Roll 30.

22. Low and Smith, "Preface," in *The Politics of Public Space*, vii; Robert A. Caro, *The Power Broker: Robert Moses and the Fall of New York* (New York: Random House, 1974), 7; Marta Gutman, "Equipping the Public Realm: Rethinking Robert Moses and Recreation," in Ballon and Jackson, *Robert Moses and the Modern City*, 72-85.

23. "City Acts to Silence Minstrels' Playing in Washington Sq.," *NYT*, 28 Mar. 1961, p. 37; Letter from Monica Killoran to Newbold Morris, 28 Mar. 1961, NYCDPGFWSP, 1960-61, Roll 30; Letter from Edward Kallop to Newbold Morris, 29 Mar. 1961, NYCDPGFWSP, 1960-61, Roll 30; Letter from Oscar Brand to Mayor Robert F. Wagner, 7 Apr. 1961, NYCDPGFWSP, 1961, Roll 31; Telegram from Howard Moody to Newbold Morris, 7 Apr. 1961, NYCDPGFWSP, 1960-61, Roll 30.

24. Letter from New York City Parks Department to Earl Reibach, 28 Mar. 1961, NYCDPGFWSP, 1960-61, Roll 30; Internal Memo, "Washington Square Park Folk Singing," New York City Parks Department, 16 Mar. 1961, NYCDPGFWSP, 1960-61, Roll 30; Israel Goodman Young, "Application for a Permit to Hold Folksinging with Stringed Instruments," Mar. 1961, NYCDPGFWSP, 1960-61, Roll 30; Letter from New York City Parks Department to Israel G. Young, 28 Mar. 1961, NYCDPGFWSP, 1960-61, Roll 30.

25. "Sunday Serenade in Square Causes Morris to Yield," *VV*, 13 Apr. 1961, p. 1, 8; Paul Hoffman, "Folk Singers in Washington Sq.," *NYT*, 10 Apr. 1961, p. 1, 25; "Folk Singers Set Protest Rallies," *New York Post* (hereafter *NYP*) , 10 Apr. 1961, p. 3; Lewis Lapham, "Police, Singers, Park Dept. Tangle in Washington Sq.," *New York Herald Tribune* (hereafter *NYHT*), 10 Apr. 1961, p. 1, 19.

26. Barretta, "Introduction," *The Conscience of the Folk Revival*, xxvi-xxvii; D'Lugoff Interview; "Sunday," *VV*, 13 Apr. 1961, p. 1, 8; Hoffman, "Folk," *NYT*, 10 Apr. 1961, p. 1, 25.

27. "Sunday," *VV*, 13 Apr. 1961, p. 1, 8; Hoffman, "Folk," *NYT*, 10 Apr. 1961, p. 1, 25; "Folk," *NYP*, 10 Apr. 1961, p. 3; Lapham, "Police," *NYHT*, 10 Apr. 1961, p. 1, 19.

28. "Sunday," *VV*, 13 Apr. 1961, p. 1, 8; Hoffman, "Folk," *NYT*, 10 Apr. 1961, p. 1, 25; "Folk," *NYP*, 10 Apr. 1961, p. 3; Lapham, "Police," *NYHT*, 10 Apr. 1961, p. 1, 19.

29. Howard Moody, *A Voice in the Village: A Journey of a Pastor and a People* (Xlibris Corporation, 2009), 205-206; Moody 2004 interview; "Sunday," *VV*, 13 Apr. 1961, p. 1, 8; Hoffman, "Folk," *NYT*, 10 Apr. 1961, p. 1, 25; Letter from Albert Roger to Howard Moody, 10 Apr. 1961, Fales Library and Special Collections, The Judson Memorial Church Archive,

New York University Libraries (hereafter Judson Church Archive); Letter from Jack McNulty to Howard Moody, 11 Apr. 1961, Judson Church Archive; Letter from Thomas F. Knapp to Howard Moody, 11 Apr. 1961, Judson Church Archive.

30. Statement by Newbold Morris, Regarding the Use of Washington Square by Itinerant Musicians, 10 Apr. 1961, NYCDPGFWSP, 1960-61, Roll 30; Philip Benjamin, "Morris Yielding on Park Singing," NYT, 11 Apr. 1961, p. 1, 42; William Federici, "Morris Lets Village Rule on Minstrels," Daily News (hereafter DN), 11 Apr. 1961, p. 2; Letter from Morris L. Ernst to Newbold Morris, 11 Apr. 1961, NYCDPGFWSP, 1960-61, Roll 30.

31. Hoffman, "Folk," NYT, 10 Apr. 1961, p. 1; Jan Kindler, "Cops, 'Beatniks,' and Facts," VV, 13 Apr. 1961, p. 7, 13; "2000 Beatniks Riot in Village," New York Mirror (hereafter NYM), 10 Apr. 1961, p. 1; Harry Israel, "2,000 Riot in Village, Fight Cops," NYM, 10 Apr. 1961, p. 2, 4; "Beatniks Riot in Washington Square," DN, 10 Apr. 1961, p. 1; Joseph Cassidy and Jack Smee, "Park Songfest In Village Boils Into a Slugfest," DN, 10 Apr. 1961, p. 3, 6; "Revolt in Washington Square," NYT, 11 Apr. 1961, p. 36; Philip Benjamin, "Mayor Backs Ban on Park Singing," NYT, 12 Apr. 1961, p. 43.

32. Ronald Maiorana, "Folk Singers Sue on Park Ban," NYT, 14 Apr. 1961, p. 23; Letter from New York City Parks Department to Israel G. Young, 12 Apr. 1961, NYCDPGFWSP, 1960-1961, Roll 30.

33. Statement by the Committee to Preserve the Dignity and Beauty of Washington Square Park, 13 Apr. 1961, NYCDPGFWSP, 1961, Roll 31; Maiorana, "Folk," NYT, 14 Apr. 1961, p. 23.

34. Letter by Sydney F. Spero to Newbold Morris, Apr. 13, 1961, NYCDPGFWSP, 1961, Roll 31; Letter by Daniel A. Shirk to Newbold Morris, May 24, 1961, NYCDPGFWSP, 1960-61, Roll 30; Letter by John W. Frost to Newbold Morris, Apr. 17, 1961, NYCDPGFWSP, 1961, Roll 31; Letter by E. Camoin de Bonilla to Newbold Morris, Apr. 15, 1961, NYCDPGFWSP, 1961, Roll 31; Letter by Mrs. Abraham Starr to Mayor Robert Wagner, May 6, 1961, NYCDPGFWSP, 1961, Roll 31; for other examples, see Telegram by Ruth G. and Morton Minsky of 1 Fifth Avenue to Newbold Morris, Apr. 10, 1961, NYCDPGFWSP, 1961, Roll 31 and Letter from Edward W. Wood Jr. of 25 Fifth Avenue to Newbold Morris, Apr. 11, 1961, NYCDPGFWSP, 1961, Roll 31.

35. Emily Kies Folpe, It Happened on Washington Square (Baltimore: Johns Hopkins University Press, 2002), 310-311; Letter from Mrs. Marie Di Giorgio to Police Commissioner M. Murphy, carbon copy to Newbold Morris, Mar. 21, 1961, NYCDPGFWSP, 1960-1961, Roll 30; Letter by Alma Maravelo to Newbold Morris, Apr. 22, 1961, NYCDPGFWSP, 1961, Roll 31; Letter by Eugenia O'Connor to Newbold Morris, Apr. 27, 1961, NYCDPGFWSP, 1961, Roll 31; Mary Perot Nichols, "Morris Ban on Singers In Sq. Divides Villagers," VV, 27 Apr. 1961, p. 16.

36. Letter by Professor F. Thrasher to Mayor Robert F. Wagner, May 1, 1961, NYCDPGFWSP, 1961, Roll 31; Letter by Charles Rao to Newbold Morris, Apr. 13, 1961, NYCDPGFWSP, 1961, Roll 31; for examples of anti-beatnik commentary, see Letter by Robert Salter to Newbold Morris, Apr. 11, 1961, NYCDPGFWSP, 1961, Roll 31; Letter by Roy Pascal to Newbold Morris, NYCDPGFWSP, 1961, Roll 31; Letter by Louis H. Solomon, President of the Greenwich Village Chamber of Commerce to Newbold Morris, Apr. 20, 1961, NYCDPGFWSP, 1961, Roll 31.

37. Stephen Petrus, "Rumblings of Discontent: American Popular Culture and Its Response to the Beat Generation," Studies in Popular Culture 20 (October 1997): 1-17; Ned Polsky, "The Village Beat Scene: Summer 1960," Dissent, Vol. 8, No. 3 (Summer, 1961): 339-59.

38. Letter to Newbold Morris, Apr. 21, 1961, NYCDPGFWSP, 1961, Roll 31; Van Ronk quoted in Cohen, 108; Letter from Carroll V. Newsom, President of New York University to Newbold Morris, June 26, 1961, NYCDPGFWSP, 1961, Roll 31.

39. Martin Duberman, Stonewall (New York: Dutton, 1993), 82-83; David Carter, Stonewall: The Riots That Sparked the Gay Revolution (New York: St. Martin's Press, 2004), 31; Alden, "'Village,'" NYT, 29 Sept. 1959, p. 42; J. Owen Grundy, "Village 'Sing' Opposed," NYT, 13 June 1961, p. 34.

40. Howard R. Moody, "Folk-Singers, Factions, and Our Faith," VV, 11 May 1961, p. 16; Letter from Harwood Gilder to Newbold Morris, Apr. 13, 1961, NYCDPGFWSP, 1961, Roll 31; Letter from Mrs. Forrest Rutherford to Howard Moody, Apr. 12, 1961, Judson Church Archive.

41. Hale, Nation of Outsiders, 13-48; Caro, The Power Broker, 850-894; Zipp, Manhattan Projects, 197-249.

42. Letter from Elias S. Wilentz to Newbold Morris, Apr. 13, 1961, NYCDPGFWSP, 1961, Roll 31; Letter from Amos Vogel to Newbold Morris, Apr. 17, 1961, NYCDPGFWSP, 1960-61, Roll 30; Letter from Ed Gold to Newbold Morris, May 8, 1961, NYCDPGFWSP, 1960-61, Roll 30; "Keep It Safe for Buses!," VV, 13 Apr. 1961, p. 4.

43. "De Sapio Backs Sq. Singing; Village Divides," VV, 20 Apr. 1961, p. 1.

44. Letter from Lawrence C. Goldsmith to Newbold Morris, Apr. 10, 1961, NYCDPGFWSP, 1960-61, Roll 30; Telegram from Theodore Bikel to Newbold Morris, Apr. 11, 1961, NYCDPGFWSP, 1960-61, Roll 30; Letter from Mrs. Jeanette Kellman to Mayor Robert F. Wagner, Apr. 13, 1961, NYCDPGFWSP, 1960-61, Roll 30; Letter from Mrs. Ethel L. Elkind and Mr. and Mrs. Edward G. Echeverria to Newbold Morris, Apr. 13, 1961, NYCDPGFWSP, 1961, Roll 31; Letter from Donald P. Lazere to Newbold Morris, Apr. 16, 1961, NYCDPGFWSP, 1960-61, Roll 30; Nichols, "Morris," VV, 27 Apr. 1961, p. 16; Phone interview of David Rosner by Stephen Petrus, Feb. 7, 2006.

45. Jane Jacobs, The Death and Life of Great American Cities (New York: Random House, 1961), 89-111; Nichols, "Morris," VV, 27 Apr. 1961, p. 16.

46. James, "Free," NYT, 25 May 1959, p. 34; J. R. Goddard, " 'Right to Sing Rally' Scores Ban by Morris; Ready to Fight," VV, 20 Apr. 1961, p. 1; Verna and Leonard Small, "The Park," VV, 27 Apr. 1961, p. 4, 8; Letter from Mrs. Doris Diether to Newbold Morris, 11 Apr. 1961, NYCDPGFWSP, 1961, Roll 31; Letter from Mr. and Mrs. Robert G. Benson to Mayor Robert F.

Wagner and Newbold Morris, 12 Apr. 1961, NYCDPGFWSP, 1960-61, Roll 30; Letter from Joan Goodwin to Newbold Morris, 12 Apr. 1961, NYCDPGFWSP, 1960-61, Roll 30.

47. Moody, A Voice in the Village, 207; "right to sing rally" flyer, Judson Church Archive; Telegram by Greenwich Village Sponsors Association to Mayor Robert F. Wagner, 14 Apr. 1961, Judson Church Archive; Telegram by Congressman John Lindsay to Howard Moody, 14 Apr. 1961, Judson Church Archive; Letter by City Councilman Stanley M. Isaacs to Howard Moody, 13 Apr. 1961, Judson Church Archive; Goddard, " 'Right,'" VV, 20 Apr. 1961, p. 1, 13; Philip Benjamin, " 'Village' Singers Rally in Church," NYT, 17 Apr. 1961, p. 24; "Pastor Will Fight For 'Open Park,'" NYP, 17 Apr. 1961, p. 5; Lewis Lapham, "They Sing in Village of Cruel Kings," NYHT, 17 Apr. 1961, p. 21; Daniel O'Malley, "Singers Stay Under Roof – Don't Raise It," DN, 17 Apr. 1961, p. 3; "Singers Rally Indoors, Raise Defense Fund," NYM, 17 Apr. 1961, p. 9.

48. Right to Sing Committee Meeting Minutes, 21 Apr. 1961, Judson Church Archive; Right to Sing Committee flyer calling for non-violent protest, 23 Apr. 1961, Judson Church Archive; Right to Sing Committee Statement on Non-violence, 23 Apr. 1961, Judson Church Archive; Nan Robertson, "Folk-Song Rally Mocks Park Ban," NYT, 24 Apr. 1961, p. 20; "1,500 (Off Square) Sing 'Morris Is A Grizzly Bear,'" NYHT, 24 Apr. 1961, p. 14; " 'Morris and the Minstrels' Goes Into Act III," DN, 24 Apr. 1961, p. 5.

49. Robert Conley, "Folk-Singing Arrest Stirs 2,000," NYT, 1 May 1961, p. 1, 25; David Gelman, "Echoes of Forbidden Songs Haunt Washington Sq.," NYP, 1 May 1961, p. 7; "Folk Songs Gain Seats In Square," NYHT, 1 May 1961, p. 21; "Allow Protest So Police Get Village Cheer," DN, 1 May 1961, p. 5; "2,000 in Village Park; Only Anthem Is Sung," NYM, 1 May 1961, p. 4.

50. Nan Robertson, "Court Backs Folk-Singing Ban By City in Washington Square," NYT, 5 May 1961, p. 1, 19.

51. Moody, A Voice in the Village, 207-211; Moody, "Folk-Singers," VV, 11 May 1961, p. 1, 16-17.

52. Nan Robertson, "600 Sing in Square But Without Guitars," NYT, 8 May 1961, p. 1, 41; "Law's Instrumental, Park Minstrels Find," NYP, 8 May 1961, p. 6; "In Park: Sing Yes, Play No," DN, 8 May 1961, p. 7.

53. David Anderson, "Folk Singers Get Another Chance," NYT, 13 May 1961, p. 1, 11; "Folk Singers Hail Mayor's Decision," NYT, 14 May 1961, p. 53; Edward Kosner, "The Village Minstrels Invite Morris to Lead the Singing," NYP, 14 May 1961, p. 5.

54. Paul Hofmann, "Singers Return to Park in Peace," NYT, 15 May 1961, p. 27; J. R. Goddard, "Mayor Relents, Opens Square to Folk-Singers," VV, 18 May 1961, p. 1, 6; "Village Singers Face a New Foe," NYP, 15 May 1961, p. 4; Lewis Lapham, "Folk Singers Rally At Washington Sq. in Thanks to the Mayor," NYHT, 15 May 1961, p. 17; Joseph Cassidy, "Park Songs Back, but Zing Isn't," DN, 15 May 1961, p. 3; "Truce Plan Works A Second Sunday In Washington Sq.," NYT, 22 May 1961, p. 33.

55. "Meeting in 'Village' Scores Park Singing," NYT, 16 May 1961, p. 21; " 'Villagers' Score Park Folk Singing," NYT, 19 May 1961, p. 25; "Square Peaceful, Anti's Still Angry," VV, 25 May 1961, p. 3.

56. "Folk-Singing Ban Upset on Appeal," NYT, 7 July 1961, p. 52.

57. "5 Park Folk Singers in Protest Cleared," NYT, 11 May 1961, p. 41; "Cleared in Folk-Music Fight," NYT, 6 June 1961, p. 22; "Humes Is Convicted of Illegal Speech," NYT, 23 May 1961, p. 80; Letter from Howard Moody to Mike Marmelstein, 24 May 1961, Judson Church Archive; Letter from Deborah Lockeretz to Howard Moody, 8 May 1961, Judson Church Archive; Letter from A. David Roberts to Howard Moody, 9 May 1961, Judson Church Archive.

CHAPTER FOUR (PAGES 146-195)

1. Woliver, Bringing It All Back Home, 104.

2. Ibid., 119.

3. Dan Wakefield, New York in the 50s (New York: St. Martin's Griffin, 1992), 116; David Boroff, "An Introduction to Greenwich Village," in Fred McDarrah, Greenwich Village (New York: Corinth Books, 1963), 4-14.

4. Ed Glaeser, Triumph of the City: How Our Greatest Invention Makes Us Richer, Smarter, Greener, Healthier, and Happier (New York: Penguin Press, 2011), 1-15; Wakefield, New York in the 50s, 7.

5. Van Ronk, Mayor of MacDougal Street, 149-150; Dylan, Chronicles, 16-18.

6. Bernard Scott, Field Work Report, March 3, 1956, Judson Church Archive.

7. Kevin Michael McAuliffe, The Great American Newspaper: The Rise and Fall of the Village Voice (New York: Charles Scribner's Sons, 1978), 11.

8. Anatole Broyard, Kafka Was the Rage: A Greenwich Village Memoir (New York: Vintage Books, 1993), vii; Thomas Bender, New York Intellect: A History of Intellectual Life in New York City, from 1750 to the Beginnings of Our Time (Baltimore: Johns Hopkins University Press, 1987), 333-336.

9. Judith Malina, The Diaries of Judith Malina, 1947-1957 (New York: Grove Press, 1984), 159, 234, 239, 256-258; Wakefield, New York in the 50s, 129-130; Harris, Washington Square.

10. Ross Wetzsteon, Republic of Dreams Greenwich Village: The American Bohemia, 1910-1960 (New York: Simon & Schuster, 2002), 471-74, 479-81, 484-86, 506-7; Wakefield, New York in the 50s, 126-134; Jacobs, Death and Life, 40-41.

11. Wetzsteon, Republic of Dreams, 520, 538, 551-55, 560-64; Harris, Washington Square, 208-209, 236, 240.

12. Ren Grevatt, "Folkniks on March: Hill Sound Upsurge," Billboard, June 8, 1959, 1, 11.

13. "New York Scene," *Caravan*, No. 10, May 1958, 29.

14. Wakefield, *New York in the Fifties*, 313; Van Ronk, *Mayor of MacDougal Street*, 87-88.

15. Paul Colby with Martin Fitzpatrick, *The Bitter End: Hanging Out at America's Nightclub* (New York: Cooper Square Press, 2002), 21; John Strausbaugh, *The Village: A History of Greenwich Village* (New York: HarperCollins Publishers, 2013), 289-317; Van Ronk, *Mayor of MacDougal Street*, 127.

16. Laurel Klinger-Vartabedian and Robert A. Vartabedian, "Media and Discourses in the Twentieth-Century Coffeehouse Movement," *Journal of Popular Culture* (Winter 1992): 211-18; "The Alluring Cupful," *Newsweek*, Oct. 8, 1956, p. 86-88; Stanley Meisler, "Letter from Washington," *Nation*, Aug. 29. 1959, p. 99-100; Jim Morad, "The Coffee Houses of America," *Playboy*, July 1959, p. 43; "Bach Beats Police Rap," *VV*, 28 Oct. 1959, p. 1; "Coffee Houses Get 1-2 Punch from Equity, Fire Department," *VV*, 3 Nov. 1960, p. 17; J. R. Goddard, "Coffee Houses," *VV*, 30 Nov. 1961, p. 1, 14.

17. Dylan, *Chronicles*, 15; Van Ronk, *Mayor of MacDougal Street*, 127, 141-56.

18. Woliver, *Bringing It All Back Home*, 119.

19. Van Ronk, *Mayor of MacDougal Street*, 129.

20. Woliver, *Bringing It All Back Home*, 4-7.

21. Schwartz, *New York Approach*, 262-266; Joshua B. Freeman, *Working-Class New York: Life and Labor Since World War II* (New York: The New Press, 2000), 114; Ballon, "Title I Developments," 244-249; "Two Housing Projects Slated South of Washington Square," *NYT*, 24 Aug. 1953, p. 1, 25; "Rebuilding the 'Village,'" *NYT*, 26 Aug. 1953, p. 26.

22. Woliver, *Bringing It All Back Home*, 7.

23. Ibid., 18-19.

24. Ibid., 18; Barretta, *The Conscience of the Folk Revival*, 188.

25. Woliver, *Bringing It All Back Home*, 19-21; Barretta, *The Conscience of the Folk Revival*, 188.

26. Woliver, *Bringing It All Back Home*, 21.

27. Barretta, *The Conscience of the Folk Revival*, 188-190; Woliver, *Bringing It All Back Home*, 21-22.

28. Woliver, *Bringing It All Back Home*, 24-31.

29. Ibid., 32.

30. Ibid., 32-33.

31. Robert Shelton, "Folk Music Makes Mark on City's Night Life," *NYT*, November 17, 1960.

32. Colby with Fitzpatrick, *The Bitter End*, 27, 37.

33. Ibid., 26-27.

34. Fred Weintraub with David Fields, *Bruce Lee, Woodstock and Me: From the Man Behind a Half-Century of Music, Movies and Martial Arts* (Los Angeles: Brooktree Canyon Press, 2011), 141-142, 145-146; Colby with Fitzpatrick, *The Bitter End*, 37-39.

35. Woliver, *Bringing It All Back Home*, 38, 55-58; Colby with Fitzpatrick, *The Bitter End*, 41-43; Barretta, *The Conscience of the Folk Revival*, 64.

36. Colby with Fitzpatrick, *The Bitter End*, 42-45.

37. Colby with Fitzpatrick, *The Bitter End*, 45-46; Weintraub with Fields, *Bruce Lee, Woodstock and Me*, 167-168.

38. Joan Barthel, "From The Bitter End," *NYT*, May 20, 1962, 17; Weintraub with Fields, *Bruce Lee, Woodstock and Me*, 206; Bikel, *Theo*, 179.

39. Colby with Fitzpatrick, *The Bitter End*, 55-60.

40. Siegel, "Friends of Old Time Music," 5-6; John Cohen, "Finding F.O.T.M.," 22-23 in *Friends of Old Time Music: The Folk Arrival 1961 – 1965* Smithsonian Folkways, SFW40160, 2006; Allen, *Gone to the Country*, 89.

41. Siegel, "Friends of Old Time Music," 5-6; Cohen, "Finding F.O.T.M.," 24; Allen, *Gone to the Country*, 89.

42. Siegel, "Friends of Old Time Music," 9-10; Cohen, "Finding F.O.T.M.," 23-24.

43. Siegel, "Friends of Old Time Music," 10-11.

44. Robert Shelton, "Folk Group Gives 'Village' Concert," *NYT*, 27 Mar. 1961.

45. Siegel, "Friends of Old Time Music," 7, 15-17.

46. Robert Shelton, "Students Import Folk Art to Chicago," *NYT*, 12 Feb. 1961; Allen, *Gone to the Country*, 89-90; Siegel, "Friends of Old Time Music," 21.

47. Woliver, *Bringing It All Back Home*, 116.

48. Howard Moody, "Christianity and Real Obscenity," *VV*, 18 Mar. 1965, p. 5-6, 13-14.

49. Woliver, *Bringing It All Back Home*, 134-135.

50. Nicholas Breckenridge, "Village '63," *Dude*, January 1963, 41, 44; Art D'Lugoff, "Greenwich Village at Night," *Cavalier*, March 1963, 31.

51. "De Sapio," *NYT*, 2 Sept. 1963, p. 12; Susan Goodman, "South," *VV*, 11 Apr. 1963, p. 1; "Politics Rears Its Head Over M'Dougal St. Scene," *VV*, 13 June 1963, p. 1, 6; Edith Evans Asbury, "Greenwich Village Argues New Way of Life," *NYT*, 4 Aug. 1963, p. 1, 62; "Debate," *VV*, 15 Aug. 1963, p. 3; Raymond S. Rubinow, "De Sapio's 'Village' Record," *NYT*, 20 Aug. 1963, p. 32.

52. J. R. Goddard, "Modern Version of a Bosch Painting," *VV*, 20 June 1963, p. 1, 6, 7; Asbury, "Greenwich," p. 62.

53. Zeitz, *White Ethnic New York*, 61-62, 72, 80, 84; J. R. Goddard, "Summer Turns Up Heat Under Pressure Cooker," *VV*, 23 May 1963, p. 1, 6; Goddard, "Modern," 6.

54. Ed Koch Statement to Planning Board No. 2, Aug. 5, 1963, VID Archives; Susan Goodman, "SRO Audience Views MacDougal St. 'Mess,'" *VV*, 8 Aug. 1963, p. 1, 10.

55. Edward I. Koch Oral History, Columbia University Oral History Archives (hereafter CUOHA); Interview of Ed Koch by Stephen Petrus, 13 December 2002; "Primary Scoreboard," *VV*, 11 June 1964, p. 1; Stephanie Harrington, "Koch Enlists City Aid On M'Dougal St. 'Mess,'" *VV*, 2 July 1964, p. 1, 6, 7; Arnold Lubasch, " 'Villagers' Hold a Town Meeting," *NYT*, 29 July 1964, p. 35; Susan Goodman, "South Villagers Cheer Koch Move

56. Koch interview; Koch Oral History, CUOHA; "Nocturnal Parkers Can Park No More On MacDougal St.," *VV*, 22 Aug. 1963, p. 3; "Koch to Confer with City Official on MacDougal St.," *VV*, 10 Dec. 1964, p. 3; Thomas P. Ronan, "Traffic Is Limited On MacDougal St.," *NYT*, 20 May 1965, p. 45; "City Cools the Crowds On MacDougal Street," *VV*, 27 May 1965, p. 1.

CHAPTER FIVE (PAGES 196-245)

1. Irwin Silber, "Politics and Folk Music," *Caravan* 10 (May 1958): 10-11.

2. Robert Shelton, "Folk Music Rings Out Vividly In Hootenanny at Carnegie Hall," *NYT*, 23 Sept. 1963, p. 34.

3. Allen, *Gone to the Country*, 3-8.

4. Roy, *Reds, Whites, and Blues*, 1-4.

5. Michael Smith, "Peace Strike Set to Go," *VV*, 25 Jan. 1962, p. 2, 7; "March for Peace Held on 5th Ave.," *NYT*, 30 Jan. 1962, p. 3; Smith, "Peace," *VV*, 1 Feb. 1962, p. 1; Joseph Wershba, "A Theatrical Couple Leads 'General Strike for Peace,'" *NYP*, 30 Jan. 1962, p. 32; John Tytell, *The Living Theatre: Art, Exile and Outrage* (New York: Grove Press, 1995), 173.

6. Martha Biondi, *To Stand and Fight: The Struggle for Civil Rights in Postwar New York City* (Cambridge: Harvard University Press, 2003), 1-16.

7. Wald, *Josh White*, 60-65; Roy, *Reds, Whites, and Blues*, 4-7.

8. Goldsmith, *Making People's Music*, 345-352.

9. Ronald D. Cohen, *Folk Music: The Basics* (New York: Routledge, 2006), 149, 151-152.

10. Goldsmith, *Making People's Music*, 354-355.

11. Aldon D. Morris, *The Origins of the Civil Rights Movement: Black Communities Organizing for Change* (New York: The Free Press, 1984), 141-157; Roy, *Reds, Whites, and Blues*, 155-180.

12. Guy Carawan, *Songs with Guy Carawan*, Folkways, 3544, 1958; Alan Lomax, Liner Notes Introduction, in Guy Carawan, *Guy Carawan Sings Something Old, New, Borrowed and Blue*, Folkways, 3548, 1959.

13. Goldsmith, *Making People's Music*, 359.

14. Cohen, *Rainbow Quest*, 183-185.

15. Roy, *Reds, Whites, and Blues*, 166-169; Cohen, *Rainbow Quest*, 184.

16. Goldsmith, *Making People's Music*, 360.

17. Some researchers contend that the original source of the song was the gospel hymn "If My Jesus Wills," written in the 1930s and published in 1942, and copyrighted by African-American Baptist choir director Louise Shropshire in 1954. Ron Eyerman and Andrew Jamison, *Music and Social Movements: Mobilizing Traditions in the Twentieth Century* (Cambridge: Cambridge University Press, 1998), 2-4; David King Dunaway, *How Can I Keep from Singing? The Ballad of Pete Seeger* (New York: Villard Books, 2008), 275-276; Roy, *Reds, Whites, and Blues*, 192-193; Robert Shelton, "Rights Song Has Own History of Integration," *NYT*, 23 July 1963, p. 21.

18. Goldsmith, *Making People's Music*, 360-362; "Tennessee Seeks to Close School," *NYT*, 13 Aug. 1959.

19. Carlin, *Worlds of Sound*, 20-23, 214-217.

20. Goldsmith, *Making People's Music*, 364-366.

21. Guy Carawan, "How This Record Came About," *The Nashville Sit-in Story: Songs and Scenes of Nashville Lunch Counter Desegregation (by the Sit-In Participants)*, Folkways, 5590, 1960.

22. Goldsmith, *Making People's Music*, 366-368.

23. Cohen, *Rainbow Quest*, 184-185.

24. Guy Carawan Liner Notes Introduction, *We Shall Overcome: Songs of the "Freedom Riders" and the "Sit-Ins"*, Folkways, 5591, 1962.

25. Robert Shelton, "Folk Crusade on Disks," *NYT*, 2 Dec. 1962, p. 203.

26. Belafonte, *My Song*, 3-16, 250, 440-441, 444-451, 460-485; Smith, *Becoming Belafonte*, 110-175.

27. Robert Shelton, "Songs a Weapon in Rights Battle," *NYT*, 20 Aug. 1962, p. 1, 14; Robert Shelton, *The Face of Folk Music* (New York: The Citadel Press, 1968), 168-197.

28. Reuss, *American Folk Music and Left-Wing Politics, 1927-1957*, 239; Goldsmith, *Making People's Music*, 282-287; William Grimes, "Irwin Silber, Champion of the Folk Music Revival, Dies at 84," *NYT*, 11 Sept. 2010, D8.

29. *The Collected Reprints Vols. 1-6: From Sing Out! The Folk Song Magazine* (Bethlehem, PA: Sing Out Corporation, 1990), 14, 51, 79, 106, 115, 145, 160, 223.

30. Cohen, *Rainbow Quest*, 179-180.

31. Ronald D. Cohen, "Broadside Magazine and Records, 1962-1988" in Jeff Place and Ronald D. Cohen, *The Best of Broadside, 1962-1988: Anthems of the American Underground from the Pages of Broadside Magazine* (Washington, D.C.: Smithsonian Folkways, 2000), 11-16.

32. Place and Cohen, *The Best of Broadside, 1962-1988*, 74-83.

33. Goldsmith, *Making People's Music*, 370-373.

34. Szwed, *Alan Lomax*, 322-323.

35. Goldsmith, *Making People's Music*, 373-375; Dunaway, *How Can I Keep from Singing?*, 277; Robert Shelton, "Negro Songs Here Aid Rights Drive," *NYT*, 22 June 1963.

36. "Northern Folk Singers Help Out At Negro Festival in Mississippi," *NYT*, 7 July 1963; Goldsmith, *Making People's Music*, 376; Cohen, *Rainbow Quest*, 204-205.

37. Goldsmith, *Making People's Music*, 377-378; *The Story of Greenwood, Mississippi*, Folkways, 5593, 1965.

38. Cohen, *Rainbow Quest*, 207-208.

39. Dunaway, *How Can I Keep from Singing?*, 271-277.

40. Roy, *Reds, Whites, and Blues*, Dunaway, *How Can I Keep from Singing?*, 298-299.

41. Alexander Bloom and Wini Breines, eds., *"Takin' it to the Streets: A*

Sixties Reader (New York: Oxford University Press, 2011), 107-109.

42. Cohen, *Rainbow Quest*, 230.
43. Bikel, *Theo*, 252-262; Dunaway, *How Can I Keep from Singing?*, 299-300.
44. James Tracy, *Direct Action: Radical Pacifism from the Union Eight to the Chicago Seven* (Chicago: University of Chicago Press, 1996), xiii-xv, 85-86, 101-104; Maurice Isserman, *If I Had a Hammer . . . : The Death of the Old Left and the Birth of the New Left*, (New York: Basic Books, 1987), 145-6; "Hold Nuclear Weapons Rally," *Villager*, 12 Dec. 1957, p. 1; " 'Sane' in National Drive To Stop Bomb Testing," *VV*, 7 Oct. 1959, p. 16; "Sane Nuclear Committee Asks Villagers to Give Support to Disarmament," *VV*, 9 Mar. 1960, p. 3; " 'Sane' Campaign," *VV*, 23 Mar. 1960, p. 3; "Kennedy 'Peace Race' Wins Cheers of 'Sane,'" *VV*, 5 Oct. 1961, p. 3; Greenwich Village Women Strike for Peace, "Issue, Not Candidate," *VV*, 25 Oct. 1962, p. 4, 8; Timothy W. Hubbard, "Packed Peace Center Opens To Battle Man's Main Vice," *VV*, 16 Nov. 1961, p. 1-2; John W. Darr Jr., "Peace Center: I," *VV*, 23 Nov. 1961, p. 4, 16; Ted Wilentz, "Peace Center: II," *VV*, 23 Nov. 1961, p. 16.
45. Dunaway, *How Can I Keep from Singing?*, 234-248.
46. Ibid., 250-252; Alfred E. Clark, "3,500 Picket U.N.; Seek A-Bomb Ban," *NYT*, 2 Apr. 1961.
47. Dunaway, *How Can I Keep from Singing?*, 252-260.
48. Michael Smith, "Peace Strike Set to Go," *VV*, 25 Jan. 1962, p. 2, 7; "March for Peace Held on 5th Ave.," *NYT*, 30 Jan. 1962, p. 3; Smith, "Peace," *VV*, 1 Feb. 1962, p. 1; Joseph Wershba, "A Theatrical Couple Leads 'General Strike for Peace,'" *NYP*, 30 Jan. 1962, p. 32; Tytell, *Living Theatre*, 173; Dunaway, *How Can I Keep from Singing?*, 258-260.
49. Cohen, *Rainbow Quest*, 194-196; Dunaway, *How Can I Keep from Singing?*, 263-266.
50. Cohen, *Rainbow Quest*, 196-197; Dunaway, *How Can I Keep from Singing?*, 266-269.
51. Cohen, *Rainbow Quest*, 197-199; Dunaway, *How Can I Keep from Singing?*, 269-270.
52. *Collected Reprints*, 272, 295, 302, 333, 352.
53. *Best of Broadside*, 33-40, 42-43, 52-55.
54. Ibid., 28-29; *Collected Reprints*, 353.
55. *Best of Broadside*, 36; Glasgow Song Guild, *Ding Dong Dollar: Anti-Polaris and Scottish Republican Songs*, Folkways, 05444, 1962.
56. Goldsmith, *Making People's Music*, 307-310; *Broadside Ballads, Vol. I*, Folkways, 05301, 1963; *Broadside Ballads, Vol. II*, Folkways, 05302, 1963; *Broadside Ballads, Vol. III: The Broadside Singers*, Folkways, 05303, 1964.
57. Michael Schumacher, *There But for Fortune: The Life of Phil Ochs* (New York: Hyperion, 1996), 53-5, 62-63, 68-69, 73, 77, 82-92.
58. Cohen, *Rainbow Quest*, 244-247.
59. Izzy Young, "Bob Dylan Taunt," in Barretta, *Conscience of the Folk Revival*, 196-198.

CHAPTER SIX (PAGES 246-289)

1. Clinton Heylin, *Bob Dylan: Behind the Shades: The Biography— Take Two* (London: Viking, 2000), 73.
2. Dylan, *Chronicles*, 51.
3. Ibid. 61-62
4. Ibid, 64-68.
5. Ibid, 64-65.
6. Allen, *Gone to the Country*, 56-58.
7. Dylan, *Chronicles*, 69-72.
8. Ibid, 71.
9. Remarks of Mayor Robert F. Wagner, Aug. 28, 1961, Village Independent Democrats Archives.
10. Sally Banes, *Greenwich Village 1963: Avant-Garde Performance and the Effervescent Body* (Durham: Duke University Press, 1993), 1-11.
11. Dylan, *Chronicles*, 9; Anthony Scaduto, *Bob Dylan* (New York: Signet, 1971), 36-38, 42-43.
12. Klein, *Woody Guthrie*, 237-258; Scaduto, *Bob Dylan*, 50.
13. Hajdu, *Positively 4th Street*, 70.
14. Shelton, *No Direction Home*, 62-65; Hajdu, *Positively 4th Street*, 68-70; Todd Harvey, *The Formative Dylan: Transmission and Stylistic Influences, 1961-1963* (Lanham, Maryland: Scarecrow Press, 2001), xx.
15. Shelton, *No Direction Home*, 79-80; Harvey, *The Formative Dylan*, 98-101; Scaduto, *Bob Dylan*, 60.
16. Sean Wilentz, *Bob Dylan in America* (New York: Anchor Books, 2010), 1-14; Dylan, *Chronicles*, 9; Scaduto, *Bob Dylan*, 58.
17. Dylan, *Chronicles*, 9-15.
18. Van Ronk, *Mayor of MacDougal Street*, 13-25, 41-59, 141-156; Dylan, *Chronicles*, 15-16, 258-263.
19. Kaufman, *Woody Guthrie*, 183-196; Shelton, *No Direction Home*, 81-82.
20. Bob Spitz, *Dylan: A Biography* (New York: McGraw-Hill, 1989), 143-145; Woliver, *Bringing It All Back Home*, 67-71; Shelton, *No Direction Home*, 76-77; Dylan, *Chronicles*, 64.
21. Goldsmith, *Making People's Music*, 311-312; Shelton, *No Direction Home*, 23, 77; Dylan, *Chronicles*, 15.
22. Shelton, *No Direction Home*, 82-83; Hajdu, *Positively 4th Street*, 75; Eric Von Schmidt and Jim Rooney, *Baby, Let Me Follow You Down* (Amherst: University of Massachusetts Press, 1994), 75.
23. Shelton, *No Direction Home*, 83.
24. Dylan, *Chronicles*, 278; Shelton, *No Direction Home*, 84-85; Woliver, *Bringing It All Back Home*, 78-80; Harvey, *The Formative Dylan*, 109-110.
25. Shelton, *No Direction Home*, 85-86.
26. Robert Shelton, "Bob Dylan: A Distinctive Folk-Song Stylist," *NYT*, 29 Sept. 1961, p. 31.
27. Shelton, *No Direction Home*, 86-87.

28. Dylan, *Chronicles*, 18-21; Barretta, *Conscience of the Folk Revival*, 193-195, 223-225; http://soundcheck.wnyc.org/story/ wnyc-90-bob-dylans-first-radio-interview/
29. Dylan, *Chronicles*, 278-279; Wilentz, *360 Sound*, 182.
30. Dylan, *Chronicles*, 5-6, 279-287.
31. Shelton, *No Direction Home*, 87-95, 103, 115.
32. Cunningham and Friesen, *Red Dust and Broadsides*, 273-301; Shelton, *No Direction Home*, 103-108; *Broadside #1*, February 1962; *Broadside #6*, Late May 1962.
33. *Broadside #20*, February 1963; "The Port Huron Statement" in Alexander Bloom and Wini Breines, eds., *"Takin' It to the Streets": A Sixties Reader* (New York: Oxford University Press, 2011), 50-61; Harvey, *The Formative Dylan*, 69-71; Edna Gundersen, "Dylan is positively on top of his game," *USA Today*, 10 Sept. 2001.
34. Dylan, *Chronicles*, 97-98; Shelton, *No Direction Home*, 108-111.
35. Dylan, *Chronicles*, 289-290; Wilentz, *360 Sound*, 187.
36. Shelton, *No Direction Home*, 115-118.
37. Harvey, *The Formative Dylan*, 3-6; Mike Marqusee, *Wicked Messenger: Bob Dylan and the 1960s* (New York: Seven Stories Press, 2005), 64-66; Shelton, *No Direction Home*, 117, 122, 126; Christopher Ricks, *Dylan's Vision of Sin* (New York: Ecco, 2004), 329-344.
38. Marqusee, *Wicked Messenger*, 7-15, 78-91.
39. Shelton, *No Direction Home*, 132-137; Dylan, *Chronicles*, 254-256.
40. Harvey, *The Formative Dylan*, 24-26; Shelton, *No Direction Home*, 117, 124-125; Spitz, *Dylan*, 199-201.
41. Shelton, *No Direction Home*, 124-125.
42. Harvey, *The Formative Dylan*, 48-50; Martin Scorsese, *No Direction Home: Bob Dylan*, 2005; Spitz, *Dylan*, 175.
43. Harvey, *The Formative Dylan*, xxiv; Shelton, *No Direction Home*, 124-125.
44. Allen, *Gone to the Country*, 41-66; Cantwell, *When We Were Good*, 1-10, 117-150; Marqusee, *Wicked Messenger*, 40-42.
45. Hajdu, *Positively 4th Street*, 72-75; Filene, *Romancing the Folk*, 204-207.
46. Shelton, *No Direction Home*, 152-157.
47. Ibid., 142; Marqusee, *Wicked Messenger*, 93.
48. Shelton, *No Direction Home*, 143-144; Marqusee, *Wicked Messenger*, 93-95; Spitz, *Dylan*, 239-246.
49. Shelton, *No Direction Home*, 143-144; Marqusee, *Wicked Messenger*, 96.
50. Shelton, *No Direction Home*, 144-145.
51. Bob Dylan, "A Letter from Bob Dylan," *Broadside #38*, January 20, 1964.
52. Shelton, *No Direction Home*, 181-183; Marqusee, *Wicked Messenger*, 109.
53. Ibid.
54. Marqusee, *Wicked Messenger*, 103, 111-113.

CONCLUSION (PAGES 290-310)

1. Scully, *The Never-Ending Revival*, 54.
2. Cohen, *Rainbow Quest*, 262.
3. Woliver, *Bringing It All Back Home*, 15, 115-118.
4. Cohen, *Rainbow Quest*, 255; Woliver, *Bringing It All Back Home*, 60-61.
5. Cohen, *Rainbow Quest*, 242-244, 253-256.
6. Paul Hofmann, "Hippies' Hangout Draws Tourists," *NYT*, 5 June 1967, p. 63; Woliver, *Bringing It All Back Home*, 137.
7. Barretta, *The Conscience of the Folk Revival*, xxxvi-xxxviii; Cohen, *Rainbow Quest*, 250-252; Shelton, *No Direction Home*, 218-220.
8. Robert Shelton, "On Records: The Folk-Rock Rage," *NYT*, 30 Jan. 1966; "A Symposium: Is Folk Rock Really 'White Rock?'," *NYT*, 20 Feb. 1966; Shelton, *No Direction Home*, 218-220.
9. Robert Shelton, "This Long-Haired Singer Is No Beatle," *NYT*, 21 Feb. 1964; Woliver, *Bringing It All Back Home*, 113-114.
10. Cohen, *Rainbow Quest*, 162; Douglas Martin, "Richie Havens, Folk Singer Who Riveted Woodstock, Dies at 72," *NYT*, 22 April 2013; Woliver, *Bringing It All Back Home*, 9-11, 33, 47.
11. Woliver, *Bringing It All Back Home*, 134-146.
12. Barretta, *The Conscience of the Folk Revival*, xvii, xxxix-xli; Woliver, *Bringing It All Back Home*, 154.
13. Allen, *Gone to the Country*, 192-220.
14. Daniel J. Walkowitz, *City Folk: English Country Dance and the Politics of the Folk in Modern America* (New York: New York University Press, 2010), xix-xxxviii; E-mail from Rosalie Friend to Stephen Petrus, September 19, 2014.
15. Mark Slobin, *Fiddler on the Move: Exploring the Klezmer World* (New York: Oxford University Press, 2000), 93-132; http://www. ctmd.org/ about.htm; Ellen Harold, "Ethel Raim," http://www. culturalequity.org/ alanlomax/ce_alanlomax_profile_raim.php.
16. Rebecca S. Miller, "'Our Own Little Isle': Irish Traditional Music in New York," *New York Folklore Quarterly* 14 (Summer/Fall, 1988): 101-116.
17. http://citylore.org/; Ben Ratliff, "Rounding Up the Best of the Boxed; Friends of Old Time Music—The Folk Arrival, 1961-1965," *NYT*, 24 Nov. 2006.
18. Scully, *The Never-Ending Revival*, 52-54.
19. Ibid.; Bruce Weber, "Jack Hardy, Folk Singer and Keeper of the Tradition, Dies at 63," *NYT*, 12 Mar. 2011.
20. Scully, *The Never-Ending Revival*, 52-54.
21. Sara Beck, "Jubilation amid Banjos and Harmonies," *NYT*, 8 Mar. 2012.

INDEX